'THE transformational book of our time.'

Uri Geller

'You will not want to put this book down, as you journey to meet brilliant minds of today's scientific community ... sharing profound insights, life-transforming experiences, and mind-boggling research that will expand your perception in ways you hardly thought possible.'

Gundi Heinemann, educator, healing arts practitioner and co-author of *Orbs: Their Mission and Messages of Hope*

'An extraordinary contribution to mending the rift between science and spirituality .... This book is in a league of its own! You will be compelled to pick it up again and again until you have read it cover to cover.'

Klaus Heinemann, Ph.D., physicist and co-author of *The Orb Project* and *Orbs: Their Mission and Messages of Hope*

Terry Fischer
318 Fairview Rd, Grantsville, MD 21536

Hazel Courteney has been a health and metaphysical columnist and author since 1993. She has contributed to numerous magazines and national newspapers and authored several health books as well as two books on spiritual science. In 1997 she was voted Health Journalist of the Year for her column in the London *Sunday Times*. She lives in Henley-on-Thames in the UK, and you can find further details of her work at www.hazelcourteney.com.

By the same author

Divine Intervention

The Evidence for the Sixth Sense

500 of the Most Important Health Tips You'll Ever Need

500 of the Most Important Ways to Stay Younger Longer

COUNTDOWN
to COHERENCE

A Spiritual Journey Toward a
Scientific Theory of Everything

Hazel Courteney

WATKINS PUBLISHING
LONDON

Designed by Jerry Goldie

Printed in the U.S.A.

ISBN: 978-1-906787-83-7

Distributed in the USA and Canada by Sterling Publishing Co., Inc.
387 Park Avenue South, New York, NY 10016-8810

Contents

For all the dedicated scientists who are now raising
their heads above the parapet.

One day mankind will realize just how brave you are.

For my grandson, James, and the children of the world
– may we not let you down.

For Nicole Hambro, Carole Nayach and all true
light workers.

Above all, for Stuart – my rock.

Acknowledgements

I owe a huge debt of gratitude to all the scientists and experts who have patiently spent dozens of hours either face to face or on the phone with me, sharing their scientific results, evidence and theories. Their wisdom, patience and sheer breadth of knowledge have at times left me speechless. They include Gary Renard, Professor Emeritus William A Tiller, Professor Gary E Schwartz, Professor Frederick Travis, Professor Alberto Villoldo, Dr Klaus Heinemann, Dr Miceal Ledwith, Professor Bernard J Carr and Robert Schwartz. Big hugs of thanks for Dr Serena Roney-Dougal and Dr Jude Currivan, who remained calm even when I e-mailed them several times a day during the seemingly endless final checking processes.

Thanks also to Chris Robinson, aka Premonition Man, and also to astrologer Linda Joyce in New York for your valuable contributions.

My trip to Damanhur in Italy was made even more special by the kindness extended to Lindsay and myself by our interpreter, Esperide Ananas, and by Falco. Thank you both.

My gratitude also to Veritas Publishing and Dr David R Hawkins's biographer, Scott Jeffrey, for allowing me to quote extensively from Dr Hawkins's book *Power vs. Force*.

To Lindsay Jarrett, my friend and ex-PA, who spent hundreds of hours typing up all those tapes – my very grateful thanks, Lins.

This section would not be complete without also thanking Claire – who triggered the journey that has become this book – and Nicole Hambro, a dear spiritual friend, who introduced me to soul researcher Robert Schwartz and scientist Dr Jude Currivan.

Thanks also to computer scientist David Gordon and Rita Leek for their technical advice on a cold Sunday evening.

Finally, my thanks and appreciation to my editor, Anne Barthel, in New York, who did not cut as much copy as I feared she might. To my publishers, Watkins and Michael Mann, thanks for believing in this book and the information it contains.

A heartfelt thank you, one and all.

Chapter One

Divine Intervention – Again

What lies behind us and what lies
before us are tiny matters compared
to what lies within us.

– Ralph Waldo Emerson

24 April 2008 – Park Lane, London

I NEEDED SOME INSPIRATION. It wasn't that my life was going badly per se; as an alternative-health and spiritual journalist, I was busy writing features, and I had a home to run and a husband and a life to take care of – yet something was missing. After the extraordinary experiences I had been through in 1998 and beyond – events I thought would change my life for good – somehow life had become mundane again. For several months I had had the distinct feeling of being in limbo. It was time to shake myself up.

A change, it is said, is as good as a rest, so I booked myself into a fashionable hotel spa for a much-needed massage. Better by far than sitting at my computer for several hours a day, which can play havoc with my chronic back problem. Little did I realize how my seemingly innocuous spur-of-the-moment decision was about to catapult me into inspirational overdrive.

While a young woman called Melanie silently massaged the dehydrated skin on my face, a stranger entered the softly lit room and began practising reflexology on my feet. Even Cleopatra would have been envious.

The urge to let go overwhelmed me and my mind began drifting. Maybe, I speculated, the young therapists perceived me as a boring 'lady who lunches', a woman of a certain age with time on her hands. Or maybe they weren't thinking any such thing. I wondered how differently they might feel if they knew more about me. Perhaps they would consider me crazy. Lazily, I recalled my happy years during the '90s as a columnist in the British national press and how all that was snatched away after a fateful event in early April '98 . . .

My decision to pop into Harrods, the world-famous store in the heart of London's West End, to buy Easter eggs for the family who were coming to share that Easter weekend with us at our home in Birmingham had also seemed innocuous. Yet it had almost cost me my life and my sanity.

As I had walked through the turnstile, then situated at the entrance to the bread hall, it stuck fast. And during those few seconds, I felt as though a volcano had erupted within my body. Electrical-type tremors shot up my spine, causing intense pain in my heart and head. Within three or four seconds the turnstile inexplicably moved forward. As I turned, with panic rising in my throat, to make my way out of the store and back to the safety of my car, a voice that I knew had not emanated from my mind 'shouted' in my head, 'Find a doctor – *now!*'

Within 15 minutes I was lying on my doctor's couch. Take my word for it, if you truly believe that you have only minutes to live, it *really* focuses your mind. While I tearfully blurted out loving farewell messages for my husband and daughter, our doctor urgently attached heart monitors to my chest, believing that I had suffered a heart attack. Then things started to get seriously interesting.

As the doctor played my heart readout over the phone to a cardiologist, a feeling of total calm washed over me. To my utter astonishment, I realized that I could 'feel' the doctor's thoughts in my head and inherently I knew that my heart was fine. Moments passed before the cardiologist told my doctor that my heart readings were in fact normal, at which point I shared with him what he was thinking. I am not sure who was more shocked, him or me.

The memory of that moment made me smile and shudder simultaneously, and the therapist thoughtfully placed another blanket over me. It was amazing, I reflected, how I could now recall with an almost total sense of detachment events that had almost killed me.

Within hours of seeing my doctor – who advised that I should go home and rest – my eyes began changing colour. Surprisingly, considering what I had gone through, I looked younger – much younger. I could barely look into my own eyes in a mirror, as the reflection caused me intense pain. And every time a question came to my mind in the silence of our London home, instantly I 'felt' numerous answers in my head, but had no idea which answer was correct, if any. I began asking my increasingly alarmed husband to 'look into my eyes and he would know who I was' – yet I had no idea how to identify the seemingly all-powerful 'I' that was inside my head and spoke though me.

As a person who loves to eat, I was amazed to find that I could not face physical food. At midnight on that first dreadful night, I called a friend, Bob Jacobs, a naturopath, who suggested that some kind of intense spiritual event was unfolding and advised me to eat something sugary to 'ground' myself. At that time I had no idea what was happening to me, but I knew that sugar was not a healthy food – yet at that moment I would have swallowed almost anything to stop the burning feeling in my brain. Months later Bob told me that the brain utilizes pure glucose as its fuel source, and at that moment my brain was so overworked that it was calling for fuel to keep functioning.

The next day I managed the journey back to Birmingham, feeling as though I had been injected with some kind of 'rocket fuel' that had triggered myriad symptoms including a high fever alternating with bouts of intense shivering. At times the feeling of cold was beyond anything I could have ever imagined. Everything became a paradox. And the voice in my head simply would not go away. With such confusing symptoms, I had little choice but to take to my bed. On Good Friday, two days after the event in Harrods, I levitated while an amazing and unseasonal blizzard raged outside.

When another spiritual friend, Dr Richard Lawrence, suggested on the phone from London that I might be 'possessed' by the spirit of someone who had died, I thought he must be joking ... and called another doctor friend in London. Dr John Briffa, a nutritional physician, was a fellow columnist and a good friend, and after listening to my ever-increasing and alarming symptoms he offered to get on a train from London and come and see me. Intuitively I knew that I should not involve our local orthodox medical doctor.

By the time John arrived, I stank of death. I could see and feel negative energies being emanated by people's thoughts, I was losing weight fast, and the fever and cold, along with the persistent voice, had drained my energy and emotions to the core. I knew that my body and mind could not take much more and realized I was slipping away.

With John quietly holding my hand on a bitterly cold, snow-covered, silent Saturday afternoon, the day before Easter, I underwent a near-death experience – caused mainly by shock – in which I, my consciousness, left my physical shell behind. At the moment of what felt like 'death', my only regret was that I would not be able to say farewell to my darling daughter, who at that time lived in Australia. Otherwise, being free from 'my' physical body was bliss ....

Obviously I returned, or you would not be reading these words! As the days turned to weeks I began working consciously with the powerful energy that pulsed through and around me and eventually I learned to direct the energy from my eyes into other people's eyes, which I knew in some way would help them. As the experience unfolded, hearing the spirit world became more like child's play; I was also intensely psychic and telepathic, which brought some interesting revelations about what people really think compared to what they say! I was also affecting and being affected by electrical equipment, whilst ash began manifesting near me.

Today, I know that what I went through is known as a Spiritual Emergency, a term coined by the brilliant professor of psychiatry Stanislav Grof, who has spent 60 years studying altered states. A Spiritual Emergency is when a spiritual awakening becomes a physical crisis, and mine most definitely became a crisis. All in all, a story I don't generally rush to share – not with beauty therapists I have just met, anyway.

Melanie brought me back into the moment by applying a cold astringent to my face, telling me she was leaving me in the capable hands of the stranger who was still working on my feet. Her name was Claire, and she was also booked to massage my poor back. Bliss indeed.

When I finally sat up to turn over for my massage, I saw the stranger for the first time. Her eyes radiated light and knowledge, and I knew instantly that before me stood a spiritually aware soul.

The moment passed and she continued her work. As her hands soothed my aching back muscles, I cast my mind back to how my own eyes had looked back in '98 – like huge dark pools through which an ultimate energy containing all knowledge had pulsed when I had felt and known that *anything* was possible.

As a journalist, obviously I had been keen to discover what on earth had happened to me – so in 1999 I began researching the work of numerous highly accredited scientists in the hope that they could explain the myriad phenomena that had happened to and around me the year before. They willingly shared their cutting-edge research, explaining how many of the so-called miracles widely associated with fully enlightened men and women now have logical explanations in 'new science'. Until that moment I had had no idea that such authoritative work on the science of miracles and enlightenment existed. Having read several spiritual books over the years, I was aware of a few revered 'enlightened' spiritual teachers, such as Sai Baba in India and Mother Meera in Germany, and had heard tales of the many healing 'miracles' they were said to effect. Yet in my wildest dreams I had never conceived that ordinary people like myself could become even a fraction like such highly regarded beings.

Over time I met or interviewed dozens of people who were undergoing experiences similar to mine. Each story was unique, yet there were distinct similarities as well, and you will read more on this subject as the book unfolds. Today, I know that – although achieving such states of being can be a baptism of fire – we are all potentially capable of miracles.

Meanwhile, by May of 1998 the continuing phenomena occurring within and around me forced me to resign from my high-profile position as a columnist for *The Sunday Times,* Britain's foremost broadsheet. I had almost lost my life, and now I had lost my job – and if I had not had such wonderful friends and an amazing husband, my marriage too would have failed.

During that Easter weekend, I had made a pact with the spirit world that if I survived I would truthfully relate the story of what happened to me, and in December 1999 my book *Divine Intervention* appeared. It was, for a time, to destroy my credibility as a serious health journalist – yet I inherently felt my experience was something that I had agreed to go through before I was born into this lifetime, and that I should share what I had learned in the hope of helping others.

My continuing journey and the scientific knowledge I was gaining became my second spiritual book, *The Evidence for the Sixth Sense,* which was published in 2005. A health book followed in March 2006. Now – as I lay on the massage table enjoying the therapist's treatment – for over a year I had been sensing that it was time to start my third book on spiritual science. I wanted to somehow bring my experiences full circle, and in that respect felt it needed to be related to 'going home'. Because during 1998 I had felt at times totally 'at home' – in a state of total oneness, totally connected, with what people term God. Since those heady days I had often grieved for the loss of that intense connection. Yet, when I shared my vision for this new book, friends politely suggested that the phrase 'going home' was an overworked cliché in spiritual writing – and I had to agree. After all 'going home' means many things to many people.

The inspiration simply wasn't forthcoming, so I returned to writing health and spiritual features in the hope that when the time was right, something special would happen. That moment was now upon me.

When my treatment finally ended, as I sat up to thank the stranger, Claire, I looked deeply into her eyes – and found myself asking, 'Who are you?'

We both knew I wasn't talking about her everyday name. She looked intently back at me before answering in a gentle but firm voice, 'I'm known as Divine Intervention.'

I was stunned. Was this her idea of a joke? No – we had never met before, and my appointment had been made in my married name, not my pen name. She could not have known, she just couldn't.

Before me stood a virtual stranger, using the same two words that a deceased spirit had used when communicating with me during my incredible near-death experience ten years earlier – words that had become the title of the book in which I wrote about my experience.

Attempting to sound casual, I asked, 'What do you mean by using those words? Have you read my books?'

'What books would those be?' she enquired without a trace of guile.

I was nonplussed, to say the least.

'When I was young,' Claire continued, 'an angel appeared to me and told me that my spirit name is "Divine Intervention" and that sometimes, when a person is going in the wrong direction or needs help, I intuitively know what to tell them.'

She certainly had my full attention now. I had not visited that hotel spa for several years and had only ended up there that day because my usual therapist elsewhere was not free. An accident, surely – and yet, when I found that my usual salon was booked, why had the name of this spa suddenly popped into my mind? I had thought it was my decision alone to come . . .

The higher realms, it seemed, were back on my case.

My mind flooded with questions for Claire. Unfortunately, our time together was over and she had another client waiting, but she agreed we could meet another time. I found myself counting the hours.

As my taxi home was bathed by early spring sunshine, I had no idea just how interesting my life was yet again to become.

Chapter Two

The Journey Begins

A human being ... experiences
himself, his thoughts and feelings, as
something separated from the rest –
a kind of optical delusion of his
consciousness.

– Albert Einstein

28 May 2008 – Heathrow Airport, London

As THE AIRCRAFT BANKED STEEPLY out of London's Heathrow and turned northeast, heading towards the unforgiving North Sea and Stockholm, I pinched myself. Events had unfolded so quickly, it was hard to believe that this was happening at all.

The stranger, Claire, had helped set a sequence of events in motion that began over a casual supper at the end of April. After my surprising experience with her at the spa – when she had introduced herself to me using the same words a departed spirit had spoken ten years earlier – I felt certain that another meeting was important.

Our conversation would have sounded quite surreal to the average person. Claire told me that her mother had tried to strangle her when she was young; her earliest memory was of 'standing over' her lifeless body at the age of three, watching two 'big men' pump her chest whilst she screamed at them, 'I'm over here' – and when she awoke again, she was back in her physical body in hospital. She also claimed, as many people do, to have travelled to other dimensions and met several discarnate spiritual beings.

Most intriguing of all, Claire was completely dismissive of anything associated with this physical reality. 'It's all a dream,' she stated categorically with the look of someone who is 100 per cent sure she is right and everyone else is wrong. 'We are living in a movie that's already been played. We, the universe and everything in it, is a hologram – it's all one big cosmic joke.'

'And what or who,' I enquired, with raised eyebrows, 'might be projecting such an enormous and mind-bogglingly huge hologram?'

'Oh, it's being projected by a mind that thinks it has split away from God,' she replied with complete and utter conviction. 'And,' she continued, mesmerizing me with her huge soulful eyes, 'God is perfect, so he or she couldn't have made us, as we are a long way off perfect.'

I knew that the concept of a holographic universe was not new – it had been mooted by several scientists including the late, great theoretical physicist David Bohm, who once said, 'The universe may be nothing more than a giant hologram created by the mind.' But I was keen to know how Claire had come to the same conclusion. 'Where did you get such ideas?' I enquired.

'It's all in this incredible book called *The Disappearance of the Universe* by a chap called Gary Renard. That's why we were brought together. You have to read this book and something special will happen.'

Oh, really? I was hoping for something a little more exciting than simply being told to read a book – more, perhaps, that Claire could 'zap' me with her energies and catapult me back into the super-heightened state I had experienced in '98.

But no such luck. In the ten years since my 'Divine Intervention' experience I had sought out a number of enlightened men and women in the hope they could 'switch me back on', but they had pretty unanimously recommended that I return to regular spiritual practices such as meditating. Infuriating, but highly sensible. After all, I didn't really want to 'die another death' in order to understand that we are all spiritual beings having a physical experience.

Claire had ordered pasta. Of course, a vegetarian – no meat or mercury-riddled fish that might contaminate her physical body and energy field. As I tucked into my chicken, I remembered how ten years earlier I had recoiled in horror when a piece of meat was served in my presence, as I could 'feel' the energetic imprint of fear held within the meat's energy field from when the animal had died. But those super-heightened senses had dissipated over time and now I was truly 'grounded' again. And at times, as

Claire talked on, I was seriously tempted to laugh – or to offer her the name of a good psychiatrist. Since going through my own near-death experience I had met or spoken to dozens of men and women going through their own intense spiritual awakenings – and I could understand why many people in varying states of confusion and disruption that intense spiritual awakenings can trigger are eventually committed to psychiatric wards. Believe me, it's not a state I would wish on anyone.

Yet Claire's eyes, as she sat with me on that rainy April evening, were earnest and full of light. And who was I to judge her anyway? How many times had people – even spiritual people – looked at me with complete incredulity when I shared my own story? For once I simply listened without judging. In any event, I could choose whether to read Gary Renard's book or not. We all have some degree of free will – don't we?

As we parted, Claire repeated, 'You are being called again. Please read the book and everything will unfold in its own good time.'

———— ∞ ————

I had nothing to lose. The book was duly ordered – and before I even opened it, more 'coincidences' began to happen.

For starters, my part-time assistant, Lindsay, received an unsolicited e-mail from an old friend telling her about a workshop taking place in London on 19 May – with best-selling American author Gary Renard! Someone 'out there' was definitely sending me a message. Intrigued to find out more, Lindsay and I booked to attend. Meanwhile, I started reading his book.

Gary claims that in 1992, two enlightened beings called Arten and Pursah appeared to him in physical form in order to share huge amounts of knowledge. These appearances were spread over years and continue to this day. As Claire had informed me four weeks earlier, Arten and Pursah have indeed told Gary that the entire universe is nothing more than a hologram, being projected by a collective ego mind which appears as many (meaning us and our world), and that we are living in a movie that's already been played. Like many spiritual teachers, Gary is also heavily into forgiveness, stating that if we can all forgive anything, everything and everyone unconditionally – as enlightened men and women do – then the 'ego mind' that he believes we all emanate from can be totally healed and thus return from whence it came, merging back into its mother/father God.

During the lecture, Gary focused on this topic of forgiveness by inviting us to visualize someone for whom we felt an intense dislike – and instantly a picture of Robert Mugabe, the Zimbabwean president, came into my mind.

'Now,' Gary instructed in his happy-go-lucky American accent, 'I want you to open your hearts and completely and unconditionally forgive this person.'

As I visualized Mugabe and attempted forgiveness, no matter how hard I tried, my heart centre remained firmly closed. Suddenly I began to more fully appreciate the scope and enormity of what Gary and others promote. Reading the newspapers in any one day, just how many judgements do you make?

I wanted to hear more from Gary – but he had to leave immediately after the lecture for his next workshop. His assistant told me that if I really wanted to conduct a one-on-one interview with him for the book that was beginning to take shape in my mind, I would have to be willing to travel ...

A stewardess interrupted my thoughts, requesting that I unfold my tray table for the lunch service. As I ate, I looked around at my fellow passengers and wondered how many, apart from Lindsay, had even heard of spiritual enlightenment or had the faintest inkling of what it truly meant. Smiling to myself, I speculated that if I asked everyone on board what they desired most in their lives, not one would say, 'Well, I want to be enlightened.' More likely it would be 'I want a Ferrari' or 'I'd love to win the lottery.' Or those who were sick would wish for better health. We all have our wish list, and few people, rich or poor, would say they have 'enough' of whatever it is they believe they need in their lives, whether that is money, time, peace of mind or health – or, in my case, the chance to relive even a fraction of the heightened states I had experienced during '98 and '99, but knowing what I know now!

To some degree, I was starting to get my wish. After reading the first chapter of Gary's book prior to his lecture, I had noticed that my intuition was becoming sharper. When I met certain strangers, I instantly knew a great deal about them, just as I had in '98. Physically, I felt much stronger, and on a couple of occasions I had found myself once again pulsing divine energy through my eyes into others', until I intuitively knew that they had received sufficient to aid their spiritual growth and their individual capacity to hold the energy, which contains information.

Certain phrases and words in Gary's book had obviously triggered memories of how I had felt during that heady time.

As I prepared my questions for Gary, I became ever more intrigued by his story and excited at the prospect of meeting him that afternoon. Some of what Arten and Pursah related to Gary totally resonated with me, especially the advice to forgive people unconditionally and let go of guilt. But his statements about us being nothing more than a hologram and existing inside a movie that's already ended simply felt wrong. Also, his book is heavily linked to Jesus' teachings and the ideas found in *A Course in*

Miracles, which I found somewhat irritating, as over the millennia there have been numerous great spiritual teachers.

As I read on, Arten and Pursah shared with Gary that once we all realign our whole minds with the Holy 'wholly' Spirit and work on forgiving others with our whole heart, we can cumulatively help to heal the 'ego mind' that thinks it has separated from its source. Once mankind can achieve this, they explain, *our consciousness* will once again merge back with the Whole Mind of God – and *our universe will disappear.*

I realize that such statements sound completely 'flaky' to most people – yet, if my memory served me correctly, I had heard a similar theory from a renowned scientist a year earlier, which until reading Gary's words I had all but forgotten.

In 2007 I had travelled to Arizona to attend the world's first-ever conference on the phenomenon of Orbs, which you will read more of in chapter 7. During a light-hearted discussion with one of the scientists I had met while investigating my 1998 experience – material physicist Professor William A Tiller, who has spent over 40 years studying matter and consciousness, most of it at Stanford University – I somewhat irreverently asked him to draw in the simplest terms his representation of God.

Tiller, a highly regarded physicist who usually writes in lengthy mathematical equations that go way beyond 99 per cent of people's ability to understand – including mine – had proceeded to draw a straight line across a sheet of paper.

'What's that?' I had asked.

'It's *total coherence,*' came Bill's reply. He smiled with a knowing twinkle in his eyes. 'This is what God, or pure Isness, is.'

Coherence. Over the years I had heard this word used many times by scientists and spiritual teachers alike and knew it had several connotations depending on the context. The adjective *coherent* is often used to describe something that is presented in a logical, meaningful, orderly, organized or systematic way. I would love to think that by the end of this book you might consider the ideas it offers as being 'coherent'! The noun *coherence* denotes 'everything coming together as one', a union, a unity of consciousness. In mathematical terms everything that we describe as physical reality can be expressed in the form of waves – and all that we call reality is essentially the interaction of those waves at all scales of existence. Leading-edge scientists now describe our universe as a unified entity, *coherently* linked beyond space and time, matter and energy, by a primordial cosmic field of information and intelligence.

And when I asked Bill, 'In your straight-line coherence scenario, where did *we* come from?' he told me that there had to have been some kind of 'decohering' to bring the world as we know it into being. And as he said this, he drew a line down from the horizontal 'coherent' line towards the bottom of the page.

As the word *decoherence,* in my humble opinion, simply means no longer coherent – no longer what scientists term 'in phase', no longer in complete harmony as one – I asked, 'Might this decohering in some way have been linked to the Big Bang, which emanated from this ultimate "coherent core" that you term "God"? And might it have seemed like a mere hiccup of energy being released?'

'Maybe,' he mused, smiling somewhat nervously at my incredible presumption, which would have had most scientists laughing in my face. 'But for the sake of my extremely simple drawing,' he continued, 'let's say there was a birthing from a metaphorical womb that already existed ... ' and as he said this, his downward line reached the bottom of the page and he turned it back on itself so it was heading back up towards the 'Isness' horizontal line of pure coherence.

'Why have you done that?' I asked.

'Well, my theory is that the universe and everything in it has decohered about as far as it can get, but now the tide is starting to turn towards another epoch. We are returning back whence we came, back towards coherence. To God.'

Then I asked Bill, 'What would happen to the world as we know it now if this total recohering occurred?'

And if my memory of our discussion was correct, I thought he said something like, 'Well, you would no longer be able to see anything of this physical world, as it would be operating on a higher frequency, which would mean it would no longer be visible to physical eyes.'

Our universe will disappear. Crikey! And *if* my recollections of that conversation with Bill were indeed accurate, it made what Arten and Pursah had supposedly related to Gary Renard considerably more interesting. I made a note to call Professor Tiller as soon as I returned from Stockholm to check this out.

As the seat-belt sign illuminated, announcing that we were starting our descent to Stockholm, I began to consider that God might indeed be like some kind of ancient ultimate supercomputer counting itself back down – and wondered if we are indeed being drawn 'home'.

Tiller had always preferred the analogy that God breathed out (the Big Bang/decohered) and was now breathing back in (recohering back towards a perfect 'oneness and Isness').

After all, enlightened beings have long been known to disappear from physical view, and when you consider that most humans can only see a minuscule fraction of the electromagnetic spectrum, this makes more sense. Our universe contains far more than what we see with our physical eyes. In fact, if you imagined that the Empire State Building was the whole universe – how much of that building do you think you could see with your physical eyes?

Only one speck the size of a grain of sand ... Just because we cannot 'see' something, it doesn't mean it's not there! Enlightened beings have reportedly 'disappeared' from physical view, but it does not mean they have ceased to exist – they are simply operating on a different frequency.

This had made sense to me – as in 2003 when I set out to discover how I was able to effect what some people might term 'miracles' back in '98, Professor Frederick Travis, head of the Center for Brain, Consciousness, and Cognition at the Maharishi University in Iowa, had patiently explained that their validated research and that of other scientists has revealed that the fundamental difference between an enlightened person and the rest of us is that their brains are totally 'coherent', totally synchronized, in that activity in their brain waves rises and falls together until their whole brain functions at a coherent level all the time. They and their mother/father God become as one – there is no longer any separation from the All That Is.

Most of us, when awake and active, produce beta brain waves, as you do while reading this book. When we relax we produce alpha waves, then theta waves when very drowsy, during deep meditation or hypnosis, and eventually delta waves during deep sleep or coma. But fully enlightened men and women can produce a full spectrum of totally coherent broadband waves including 'alpha, beta, gamma (produced when we are highly focused) and theta all at the same time. And coherent brain functioning is the basis for many external phenomena that are often termed 'miracles'.

To retain such abilities, these people have undergone years of spiritual training and have learned to integrate their capabilities into their lives – usually in a way that serves the Whole, rather than themselves. We all have access to these capabilities; if you meditate regularly and tune in to the space between your thoughts, similar effects will eventually be produced within you – and if you believe something with your whole heart and mind, your brain may become sufficiently coherent that your wishes can materialize. The crucial point here is that truly enlightened men and women's brains remain in a coherent state *all the time,* whilst also allowing them to function on an everyday level. And in that coherent state, they can experience an unbounded bliss no matter what their circumstances. In reading Gary's words, my brain had evidently begun to synchronize a little more, but not all the time … There's the rub!! To maintain brain coherence, one would need not only years of spiritual training but also maturity and infinite wisdom.

As we began our final approach, upon seeing the runway, I thought again about the straight line that Bill Tiller had drawn for me and the fate that Gary Renard had predicted for the universe. An ultimate process of 'going home' …

Holding such thoughts, we landed safely to a beautiful, sunny spring afternoon at Stockholm airport. It was 3pm and our meeting with Gary was scheduled for 4pm. I had trusted that our flight would be on time, and the universe had not let us down. As Lindsay and I dashed through the terminal to find a cab, it felt like an auspicious beginning to yet another journey which might help me discover the truth.

Chapter Three

Men in Black

Seek not to change the world, but choose to change your mind about the world.

– **A Course in Miracles**

28 May 2008 – Stockholm – 4pm

As our taxi sped towards the outskirts of Stockholm and Gary Renard's hotel, my mind was working overtime. I had been allotted two hours with Gary and wanted to make the most of every minute. Our timing was tight and the traffic dreadful, because several thousand United Nations delegates were also arriving in the Swedish capital, along with the President of Iraq and US Secretary of State Condoleezza Rice, for peace talks on the future of Iraq. To cap the chaos, Ms Rice was staying at our hotel, and we were warned that gaining access later that evening might prove difficult.

Never mind – for now, I just wanted to live in the moment and get on with interviewing Gary.

Until reading Arten and Pursah's controversial statement that God did not make us or our world, I had imagined that God was like some kind of 'ultimate computer' that had created this universe and everything in it so that he/she/it could become self-aware through us. Ten years earlier I had certainly felt like an awesomely powerful, superhuman being, connected to the Ultimate I, the Whole Mind, that emanated from the beginning of time. It was indeed like being plugged into a supercomputer, or a mind that 'knows' everything and yet at its core simply is.

Gary believes as I do that God, the Holy Spirit, which is totally coherent, is within each and every one of us, but he also says there is another mind, an ego mind which projects an ongoing holographic projection that is our world, and it is this ego mind that controls our thoughts on an everyday level. And the secret to 'going home', he believes, is to realign with the God mind by switching channels, away from our seemingly separate existence and individual ego mind over to the channel of coherence, Isness, pure love.

No wonder that while reading his book I had become more psychic, as his words were truly reminding me of just how much I had 'decohered' in recent years.

How I had grieved the loss of my intense connection to the All That Is, which I enjoyed for several weeks in '98. There had been magical moments when I experienced no fear, none at all, and I was full to bursting of unconditional love for everyone and everything. There was no judgement – instead I 'saw' people and situations through different eyes, from a different level of being. Looking back, I felt certain that I had been aligned with pure Isness – that I and my mother/father God became for a time as one.

Yet now, after reading Gary's words, I was no longer certain which mind I had been connected to! Surely, I thought, he must have mixed up certain of his concepts – and I decided to make it my mission to discover the truth. In my case, there had been at times a total lack of ego, and I realized that if everyone could feel as I did in those moments, then the world really could become a 'heaven on earth'. But there were also episodes of extreme ego, when it would have been incredibly easy to sway the way others thought. The 'fight' between the 'right' mind and the ego had at times become quite a battle!

As we arrived at Gary's hotel with five minutes to spare until our meeting, I smiled to myself at the irony of Condoleezza Rice being in the same city on the same day to talk of peace. If only politicians could all connect to the All That Is, there would never have been a war in the first place.

The problem is that 99 per cent or more of the people on this planet think of everything as separate entities, and so we have 'right' religions and 'wrong' religions, light and dark, good and evil – everything is duality. We are indeed 'separate' at a physical level – but not necessarily at other levels, *especially at certain levels of the mind.* Unfortunately, if you were to suggest to a religious fanatic that *we are all part of God and all parts make the Whole* – that we all have God within us, even as we see the world from the individual perspective of our ego mind – you might find yourself on the receiving end of considerable abuse. Most people have no idea who or what they truly are!

For instance, virtually every atom (which everything in our universe, including us, is ultimately made of) was 'birthed' at the time of the Big Bang, 14 billion years ago. Physically, we are little more than recycled atoms – which are *energy and information.* We may appear solid in this dimension, but in scientific terms we and everything around us are 99.999 per cent empty space.

If the universe is counting itself back towards coherence, as Professor Tiller and others who share his beliefs think – whether we like it or not – this process of being truly home, and at one with God, could be made far easier and less traumatic if we all practised having sustained, focused intentions and thoughts, plus an understanding that *we are good enough to align with pure coherence,* the Infinite Mind, rather than constantly feeling guilty and concentrating on our own everyday ego-type thoughts.

The ultimate question for all of us is: How badly do you want to go home?

It's a big question.

For instance, if you want to lose weight, you need to be focused and disciplined – eat less, think thin, exercise. And if you truly want to move toward coherence, you need to be disciplined and focused on your spiritual goals. At a certain level you are already 'home' and always have been – you just need to know it and experience it.

This earthly reality offers myriad temptations that seem extremely real to most people, including me. For starters, I was looking forward to a cup of tea at Gary's hotel. Gary is, of course, entitled to his beliefs, including the belief that our whole universe is an illusion, but in my humble opinion it would be impossible for me to eat or drink a holographic image of a cup of tea and a piece of freshly baked carrot cake, as my hand would pass straight through them!

As I joked with Lindsay about the holographic tea while ordering the real thing, Gary appeared. He is a humble, shy, private individual with kind, smiling eyes. Yet his shyness quickly dissipates when he begins sharing his passionate beliefs.

I began by asking why Arten and Pursah appear to him and no-one else.

'Everyone asks me that,' he sighed, still smiling. 'I always respond, why not me? It's like a person who's just had an accident saying "Why did this happen to me?" Some people might say it's karma, or it could be that the soul chose a specific incident to happen at that time for a life lesson or purpose. In the case of Arten and Pursah, we have various past-life links, and they told me they have chosen only to appear to me in this specific lifetime as I have recorded and reported their words verbatim. If you consider how Jesus' and other great teachings have at times been misreported, misunderstood or even made up, Arten and Pursah's decision to speak to only one person makes sense. Because they physically appeared to me and I was able to record their every word, this prevented my beliefs and thoughts from corrupting their words and meanings, as so often happens when people channel information.'

Seemed fair enough; after all, if any major celebrity utters a statement, multiple versions tend to appear around the world – but which one is correct, if any?

'Some people are annoyed that Arten and Pursah appear to me,' he continued, 'yet no-one need be envious. After all, in previous incarnations we have all been many things – beggars, rich men or women, psychics, powerful people, princes, thieves, famous or infamous.'

Before we moved on, I related to Gary some of what had happened to me in '98. I was keen to have him clarify his terms about the ego mind and the God mind and ask him which he thought I had been 'on line' to.

'That's a good question. I would say that for a brief time you were at home, at one, with God. Remember that bliss? It could be like that all the time, but to remain in that state takes time and work.'

Every time, I mused, it comes back to the same question: How badly do you want to go home?

'There are three parts to mind,' Gary continued. 'Firstly you have the part that is doing the observing, and then you have two possible interpretations of what you are observing. One would be the Holy (whole) Spirit and the other would be the ego.'

I was obviously looking somewhat confused, as he added, 'I have come to believe that the ego is the part of the mind that believes in separation and the Holy Spirit is the part of the mind that remembers the truth and wants to lead you home.

'But what is *really* important,' he emphasized, 'is which teacher you choose to listen to. It is almost like you watch a movie and you have the Holy Spirit sitting on one side of you and the ego sitting on the other side and they are both whispering in your ear. Which one gets your attention?'

And what, I wondered, about his concept of our entire universe being nothing more than a projection of our collective ego mind – a shared illusion?

'The whole ego mind is outside of space, time and form, whilst spirit is immortal,' Gary explained. 'As immortality is a constant state, God is constant, whereas our world is always changing, not constant, which is why Jesus said in *A Course in Miracles*, "Whatever is true is eternal and cannot change." Therefore anything other than God I consider to be an illusion.'

His statement seemed a tad extreme. 'So where,' I asked, 'does consciousness enter this illusion?'

'In order to have consciousness, you need separation – you need more than one thing. You need some *thing* to be conscious *of*.' Holding out his left hand, Gary asked us to imagine that in his palm he was holding an ego mind, of which we are all a part, that projects what we think of as our reality onto a screen – and his right hand became the screen. 'What this ultimately means is that we all emanate from one source, we just think we are separate, and thus everything that we do we are doing to ourselves.'

I would have to think over Gary's analogy of ego minds and screens, but I believe that ultimately we do emanate from one source and that what goes around comes around – but I also firmly believe that we can get caught up in events or situations that overwhelm us, which we as separate individuals did not individually create. I knew that Einstein had compared our experience of our individual reality to 'an optical delusion of consciousness'. I also knew how persuasive a hologram could be. My son-in-law, who once designed equipment for the military, has acknowledged (as have several scientific publications) that the armed forces use holographic 'inserts' in war zones. The technology exists to project an image of, say, a warship – one that looks 100 per cent real to anyone nearby. Of course, when it doesn't fire any real weapons, the illusion is quickly dispelled.

Thinking of advanced technology, I reflected that anatomically 'modern' humans have been on the planet for only around 200,000 years. I asked Gary, 'If we are nothing more than a holographic projection of mind, who was doing the "thinking" and "projecting" as the planets were cooling, as they were here long before we came on the scene?'

'You are equating the word *mind* with something that's human,' he replied. 'The mind is the projector, and you cannot confuse the projector with the screen. The projector was always there, otherwise there would have been nothing on the screen. Mind is mind and it doesn't matter what the container appears to be, so our bodies are no more important than this table; it's only *the Ultimate Mind* that people call God, not the ego mind, that's important – and real. Eons ago the ego mind projected the conditions that eventually led to planets, dinosaurs and all that has evolved since, which all have or had levels of consciousness, of mind.

'It's like we are in a huge movie theatre and the projector is hidden, so your attention is drawn out onto the screen. The projection, you could say, is coming from this one mind that thinks it has separated itself from its source, and then that one appears as many. Basically, we are living a dream that is not real. Every night you dream, and events do appear to happen in that dream, but what happens when you wake up?'

'The dream which seemed very real to me disappears,' I responded, somewhat lamely.

'Exactly, and that's what we are living in – a dream.'

'So what happens when we die?' I asked.

'You move from one dream to the next. And if you are not fully enlightened, then you merge back into this separate ego mind and are recycled back here again. To stop this cycle of living in an illusion, people need to understand that they are all part of God and all parts make the Whole, and by realigning with God they can truly go home – which means they no longer need to reincarnate into this reality again.'

I remembered that Arten and Pursah had told Gary that if people knew how wonderful 'life' is after our illusory physical death, then the people left behind wouldn't mourn those they had lost quite so much – they'd be envious instead. Finally a statement I could fully resonate with, as, for reasons you'll read more of later, I totally and completely believe that our consciousness survives physical death.

Listening to Gary Renard in Stockholm, though, I didn't feel like a hologram. I did feel somewhat confused. 'Where *do* you consider God fits into all this?'

Gary smiled 'The Holy Spirit, God, is not *in* the physical world. How can he/she be in a world that does not exist? He/she is in your mind – *at the mental level, not the physical*. This is crucial. You just need to switch thought systems; when your mind returns to wholeness, there is no longer any separation *at any level* and therefore no movie being projected. Your body would then disappear, and time as you know it would also collapse.'

I realize this may sound quite preposterous to some people – if not downright alarming. As I sat listening, I couldn't help thinking that in some respects Renard had mixed up his levels of reality. I would begin researching as soon as I returned home.

Meanwhile, there was more I wanted to discuss. Gary was also told by Arten and Pursah, who he says appear as solid to him as we do to each other, that we are living in a movie that has already played and everything that happens to us is predestined. But all the scientists I had interviewed in the past few years had categorically stated that though certain major events in our own lives and at a planetary level may well have been set in place eons ago, the rest is all in potential. 'By changing our minds and our actions,' I asked Gary, 'can't we change some of our potential futures?'

'Arten and Pursah once told me that most humans are like robots,' he replied. 'If you are only linked to the ego mind, then you are living out a predetermined script and nothing can be changed. Even our day of death is predetermined. I believe, and *A Course in Miracles* teaches, that the end of time has already happened, and our return home to oneness is already guaranteed.'

Thank goodness for that, I thought.

'But, and it's a big but, once you choose to align with the God mind, then you can switch to a different dimension or reality. There are multiple alternate endings happening in multiple dimensions, the way moviemakers often film alternate endings and the studio picks which one they like best. Multiple scenarios are going on right now, and we are all in all of them. So, if you want your life to be different and happier, then switch to the God channel and switch realities. All the God script is – is a *reinterpretation* of the ego script.'

It's difficult for most of us to conceive that every 'script' imaginable has already been written and is playing out in various dimensions. I thought of the film *Sliding Doors*, in which Gwyneth Paltrow's character kept slipping between realities, finding herself in a different storyline with a different ending each time.

Gary had told me that we choose most of the incidents in our predetermined lives before we come into them. 'But this is the ego's script, not the Holy Spirit's.' He sighed. 'We are not always going to have a choice as to what we experience, but we always have a choice as to *how* we experience it.' Arten and Pursah, he claims, once took him physically into the future to view a scene and the people in it – and six months later, when he arrived at that same scene, the only thing he could change was his *attitude* towards it. 'As Jesus said via *A Course in Miracles,* "Seek not to change the world, but choose to change your mind about the world."'

He went on, 'What we need to do is to find a way that we can be happy and peaceful regardless of what appears to be happening in the world. You can do this by aligning with God, the Ultimate Mind. This is why enlightened men and women are always at peace within themselves, no matter what their circumstances.'

His words rekindled memories of '98, when I was in such a state of bliss that if someone had put a gun to my head and threatened to kill me physically, I would have simply smiled. I knew that the ultimate *I* is not a physical body but a huge and infinite mind of pure Isness and pure love. I no longer had much interest in my physical form.

That had sure changed today. Gary could see, by my constant wriggling in the special seat I carry everywhere, that I suffer with chronic, at times intense, back pain. I joked that I would love to switch to a reality in which my back was perfect.

With great kindness Gary placed his hands on my back and told me that if I could follow Arten and Pursah's advice of practising true and heartfelt forgiveness, then I could hasten my realignment with God – and then with His/Her help, I would be able to switch realities once again.

During his lecture two weeks earlier when he had asked us to visualize someone we loathed – then to open our hearts and totally forgive him or her – I had tried to forgive Mr Mugabe in Zimbabwe. As I sat listening to Gary now, I still couldn't do it. Over the years I had read of people who had, for instance, publicly forgiven the IRA for murdering a child, a mother, a father. Could you do that?

'You can talk about degrees of oneness and enlightenment till you are blue in the face,' Gary said, as if reading my thoughts. 'But to *feel* it and *live* it and *experience* it is virtually beyond physical words.'

There was so much to discuss, and my time with Gary was drawing to a close. As he stood to leave, he reminded me of the fact that, 'The Course teaches that the last two obstacles to peace are fear of death and fear of God. Millions of people still live in fear of God.'

I might not agree with all his theories, but these words I knew to be true. How many religions continue to instil fear, the fear of hell, damnation and retribution? Only man tells you what he thinks God says is 'good ' or 'bad'; it's a great way to exert power over others, and it's still going strong. I believe that what God, which is pure love, really wants is for you and all of us to return home.

Before dashing off to his next lecture, Gary added, 'If we can all learn to forgive everything completely, we will eventually heal the *whole* ego mind, and when this happens, there will no longer be any projection, as we will have all "gone home". This world will disappear. Time will no longer exist, *only eternity.*'

A controversial man indeed. He had certainly given *me* food for thought. After we hugged him goodbye, Lindsay and I found another taxi, and as we made our way into the centre of Stockholm we discussed some of Gary's concepts. It's hard enough, we concluded, to forgive everything and everyone. In just one day's papers, how often do we judge people and situations without knowing the whole story? But we felt especially guilty about his additional advice, which was never to gossip in negative terms or slander anyone – ever! Well, there's 75 per cent of the world's conversations gone, for starters. Even I enjoy a bit of a gossip now and again.

We were jolted back to reality when our taxi driver was suddenly stopped by the police on the four-lane overpass near our hotel.

Much discussion in Swedish followed.

Eventually, in faltering English, our driver said, 'You must get out here and walk, as your hotel is surrounded by security.'

Surely he was joking. 'What about our luggage?' I wailed.

'Sorry, you must go.'

All thoughts of forgiveness vanished as Lindsay and I picked up our bags, computers and my special back seat to hump them across the freeway, though an underpass and on to our hotel. We joined dozens of people doing the same. Large, black, ominous police helicopters circled like massive vultures above us. Talk about Big Brother is watching you.

The cordon of armed police around the hotel was solid. But I wanted a shower and my supper. As I tried to get through the cordon, a very officious man said to me, 'You need to wait. Ms Rice is about to arrive.'

'Well,' I stammered, 'I'm just as good as her and this is my hotel.' And with that I pushed my way through the line and walked towards the entrance. Rather stupid, I know, yet thankfully I lived to tell the tale!

The lobby was buzzing with grim-faced men in black, and when we were finally allowed in a lift, it was filled with staffers working for the Secretary of State. They tried big, cheesy, unconvincing smiles while apologizing for the inconvenience that we had suffered.

'You're not sorry at all,' I snapped through thoroughly gritted teeth.

Oh dear, I thought as I stomped out of the lift when we reached our assigned floor, *I obviously need to work on my forgiveness skills.*

That night the helicopter hovering about our hotel kept me awake much of the time. As dawn finally broke, I opened Gary's book at random and read: *The ego mind asks many questions, such as how did the impossible occur? But the impossible to Jesus was the idea that we can somehow be separated from our source and have a personal identity and existence.*

As my tired eyes stared back at me from my bathroom mirror, I sure felt separate. Yet deep within me, I knew those words to be true.

Chapter Four

The Secret

In the middle of every difficulty
lies opportunity.

– Albert Einstein

June 2008 – London

Almost 20 years ago, I read a channelled spiritual book entitled *The Guide Book* by Tony Neate, published in 1986, which foretold a time when banks, insurance companies and whole countries' economies would collapse.

As Lindsay and I passed the newsstand on the Heathrow concourse on our way back from Stockholm, the newspapers were full of the news of how banks in the UK and the US were facing meltdown. Finally, I thought, it's dawning on even the greater majority that we *are* all linked. Most people have no conception that we are all one, let alone that we emanate from one mind, but when the money in anyone's pockets is threatened, along with their jobs, security and way of life – *then* they start looking for alternative answers. The countdown towards a new epoch has indeed begun. This birth can be painful or it can be made easier – the choice is ours to make.

———— ∞ ————

I was longing to chat with Professor Tiller to find out if my memory of our conversation in Arizona the previous spring about our return to coherence was indeed correct. I had myriad questions for him, such as: Are we seriously being controlled by some kind of ancient supercomputer? Are we ourselves biological computers? Could the world as we know it be holographic – and how is something holographic in nature different from an actual hologram of light, which is produced by splitting a beam of *coherent* light in two and creating interference between them? And is God truly counting Himself/Herself back down to coherence, though scientists tell us that our physical universe is still expanding?

During my years on the spiritual path I had read theories stating that our world was going to split in two and that those who became enlightened would move to another reality, which would *seem* as real as this one, but would not be 'seen' by people who remain in this dimension. I presumed this was what Gary Renard meant when he said that our universe would disappear. Back in '98 such concepts had seemed so simple – and yet as I pondered all that Gary had shared in Stockholm, suddenly many things seemed more complex again. For example, I knew many people believed, as he did, that pretty much everything in our lives – every incident, accident, death, birth and so on – was predestined, yet something had happened to me a year or so earlier to convince me this was not necessarily so.

I had so many questions – but when I telephoned Professor Tiller, I discovered that he was going to be away until August. My questions would have to wait. No matter, it gave me time to think – and remember ...

January 2007 – Dubai

As midnight struck, I celebrated the New Year in Dubai with my husband, overflowing with thanks for my life, my family and my good health.

Within four days, my silent thank you's were forgotten as I lay bedridden screaming in pain after three discs in my back herniated. How our lives can change in a microsecond – as mine had during that fateful moment in Harrods in April 1998.

The previous October, a bad fall onto my coccyx while alighting in a rush from an airport bus had caused considerable damage to my spine. Doctors had warned me that the fall would trigger ongoing problems in my lower back. Now, as I floated in and out of reality thanks to the painkillers, terrified to move, I figured my situation definitely constituted a 'problem'.

My thoughts had returned to 1998, when it would never have occurred to me to worry about the possibility of missing a flight, or even to feel impatient – and therefore, I presumed, I would not have fallen. What had changed since then?

Several enlightened men and women had told me that once you resonate and connect with the ultimate universal energy that flows through and around them – which eventually awakens the ultimate energy within and around you – then you are less likely to become ill or have accidents. And even if you do, any resulting injuries are less serious than they might have been. One devotee of such a guru had told me that he was knocked off his bike by a bus and then dragged along the road underneath the bus. Yet to the astonishment of the firemen who cut him from the wreckage, he was virtually unscathed. This lucky individual said he was saved by his guru, with whom he connected daily through meditation. Was he right? I cannot answer for him, but I do know that miracles can and do happen when you become connected to the All That Is, just as Gary Renard says – when you align with the Ultimate mind rather than your ego mind. You switch to a different movie!

As I lay in bed hardly able to move, such notions seemed very remote, especially when my husband carried me to and from the toilet. Then the calls started.

'You are a health writer,' pontificated one friend, as if that meant I could heal anything at will. 'How this could possibly have happened to you? Can't you take something? Surely you'll be fine in a week or so?'

Other well-meaning spiritual friends suggested that my back condition had been triggered by my not standing up for myself, or that perhaps I did not feel supported in some area of my life.

Oh, please! At some level, maybe – yet on a physical level, I argued, it had happened simply because my haste led to my missing my step and falling off the bus. Cause and effect.

At a down-to-earth level I still adhere to that so-called 'law'. If, for instance, I were to eat copious amounts of chocolate cake every day for the next couple of months, then I would not be surprised to find my cholesterol levels somewhat raised. On a grander scale, mankind's actions over the long term have triggered an ominous cascade of global changes. In this case, the effect of my being in a hurry, wearing heels and missing the top step was that I had fallen badly.

My self-berating thoughts – 'If only I had been calmer, if only I had worn flatter shoes' – were further compounded when another well-meaning friend sent me a DVD of *The Secret*. For anyone who has not seen this highly successful quasi-spiritual film – or read the best-selling book that followed – allow me to give you a brief overview. Rhonda Byrne, an Australian television producer, came up with the idea of amalgamating a host of self-improvement and self-empowering advice delivered by spiritually orientated psychologists and teachers into a two-hour documentary film, and later a book, cleverly entitled *The Secret*.

Why? Because we are told over and over again that we can all have everything that our hearts desire by thinking more positively and taking more actions to bring our desires into reality. So far, so good.

As I lay on my side, hardly daring to move, metaphysician Dr Joe Vitale appeared on screen to tell me:

'Everything that surrounds you now in your life, including the things that you are complaining about, you've attracted. I know this is something you won't want to hear and I'll bet you're saying, for instance, "I did not attract the car accident or this client," or whatever is that you are moaning about, and I'm saying YES YOU DID.'

His statements rather infuriated me. It's like saying there is only one shade of red, pink or green – when there are hundreds. Black-and-white statements such as these have caused many people much guilt and grief. I recalled any number of dinner parties when the talk turned to the situations in Darfur or Zimbabwe – and inevitably some bright spark would pipe up, 'Well, this is the life they chose. It's their karma.'

And I would sigh in frustration while noticing the pleading look on my husband's face begging me not to take the bait.

We may have learned considerable amounts about spirituality in the last few years – yet these types of statements make me realize how far we still have to go. The need to think on multiple levels is definitely expanding. People still search for answers to all their ultimate questions: why are we here, where do we come from, do we live on after physical death, are we all capable of miracles and so on. But we tend to be more comfortable with neat boxes in which to file our answers.

Many times I have written and reminded people that everything is a paradox and that we all need to think on multiple levels – and most definitely 'outside the box'.

The film played on ... On came a lovely man, Morris Goodman, who told how in March 1981 he had crashed an airplane and suffered appalling injuries, including a crushed spinal cord and broken vertebrae. His swallowing reflex was destroyed and he could not breathe. All he could do while lying paralysed on a respirator was blink his eyes. So he decided to tap the incredible power of his mind and use visualizations to become well. Nine months later, with assistance, he walked out of the hospital. Today he gives inspirational talks all over the world. His closing words were very apt: 'Man becomes what he thinks about.'

Meanwhile, fear of pain was overwhelming me and I knew that somehow I had to take control of the fear within my mind. After all, myriad scientists have told me again and again that whatever the majority of our thoughts contain is what we eventually magnetize into our lives. Literally. Therefore we urgently need to pay more attention to what we want more of – and less attention to what we don't want. The science behind this is now in place thanks to investigators such as Marilyn Schlitz PhD, a director of research at the Institute of Noetic Sciences in California, and physicist Bill Tiller in Arizona, who has definitively shown through his scientific experiments – which you will read about shortly – that our thoughts can affect physical matter and thus physical outcomes. This is what Morris Goodman achieved – by using *sustained, focused intention* he healed his physical body.

The Secret ended. It was very inspiring and reminded me that we are all indeed capable of miracles. Hoping to experience one as quickly as possible, I closed my eyes for 30 minutes and visualized myself being able to sit and move without feeling any pain. I also invited my spirit guides to assist in the healing process. And for a brief second I thought something special had happened, but when I tried to move, the pain seared once again through my spine.

Tears of frustration welled in my eyes. I told myself these things can take time; after all, it can take years of training and discipline for spiritual masters to attain fully sustainable enlightenment and thus have the ability to heal themselves instantly (if they choose to). Professor Frederick Travis at the Center for Brain, Consciousness, and Cognition in Fairfield, Iowa, had explained that the EEG of an enlightened person shows his or her *whole* brain (at a physical level) working as one, functioning in a totally synchronized, totally coherent way. And as such people *think*, so it is they can literally create their reality instantly, just as I had done on occasion years earlier.

If only I could do that now.

In '98 I knew that if you believe something with your whole heart and mind, it's possible to trigger a state of total brain functioning – for a split second or longer, or, in the case of a totally enlightened person, all the time – that can create objects seemingly from nowhere, change the weather, alter one's appearance or initiate a spontaneous healing. After all, as scientist Professor Gary Schwartz from the University of Arizona had told me in 2003, 'Matter is nothing more than organized energy, and what *organizes* that energy is *mind and intention*. Your thoughts create patterns, which create matter.'

You really need to get this: *mind is ultimately everything*.

Gary had also explained that all physical 'matter' – including you, me, my computer, my mug, the flowers, the planets, the whole universe – is fundamentally made from atoms, zillions of them, which formed after the Big Bang. A million carbon atoms in a row would fit behind a human hair. Yet if I were to remove all the empty space from every atom that makes up your body right now, you would shrink to the size of a grain of sand – and if I did this to every living person on the planet, we would all fit inside an apple!

The secret to grasping this surprising truth is to comprehend that the Whole Mind is both outside us and inside us. As Gary Schwartz puts it, 'The All is in the small and the small is in the All.'

In 1998, whenever I had asked questions of this Whole Mind, to which I seemed to have instant access, I would 'hear' within my head dozens of potential answers. But which one was right? And who or what was judging right and wrong? I also had a fantastic glimpse of what our minds are truly capable of: we all have the *potential* ability to manifest our dreams, perfect health, a new job or even a brand-new pain-free back. But do we have the training to do such things? There's the rub.

To cheer myself up, I rang my old friend Dr Serena Roney-Dougal, a highly regarded scientist and parapsychologist, who had spent the previous seven years working with and studying yogis and Tibetan Buddhists in India.

Serena listened patiently as I told her about Joe Vitale's words in *The Secret* and shared my frustration about not being able to heal my back problem, which in '98 would have seemed like child's play. Even Jesus is reported as having said, in Mark 11:24, 'When you pray for something, believe it is already yours and then it will be so.'

Easy to say, not always so easy to do.

After listening to my diatribe of moans and groans, Serena asked, 'Hazel, how often do miracles happen?'

'Not often enough,' I whined.

'Exactly,' she said. 'That's why they are called miracles – they happen now and again and remain rare. All the monks and gurus I have studied continually reiterate that if you want miracles to happen all the time, you need to be a very highly trained lama or someone like Jesus or Buddha. Yes, quite a few people who have gone through intense spiritual awakenings as you did are able to effect the occasional miracle, but usually only for a short time, and the ability rarely lasts unless they have had the training – and you haven't.'

I sighed. 'So, do you believe that Joe Vitale is right and I caused my back problems, or that sometimes things go wrong based upon our actions – as in cause and effect?'

'Let's deal with cause and effect first. The modern scientific understanding of cause and effect introduced about 300 years ago was a deterministic Newtonian philosophy. In simple terms, let's say you hit a billiard ball and it goes in a straight line, or planets circle around the sun because of gravity. Every effect has its preceding cause. All very clear.

'But,' she added, 'with the emerging science of quantum entanglement, when two things have been part of one other thing, whatever happens to one automatically affects the other.'

Her comments reminded of an experiment published in the magazine *Advances: The Journal of Mind-Body Health* in 1993, designed by Cleve Backster, who has spent 36 years researching consciousness and communication between various organisms. In one such experiment, a sample of DNA was taken from army volunteers, then each soldier's DNA was isolated in a container in another building. Later, the soldiers were shown disturbing pictures to trigger an emotional response. The scientists found that as the soldiers' emotions peaked while they looked at the pictures, their samples of DNA *in the other building* showed a powerful electrical response *in the very same instant*. Most orthodox scientists state that such a phenomenon is impossible. Perhaps they could do with having a Spiritual Emergency, as I did – then they might think differently.

'There have been many experiments which demonstrate the effect of consciousness on quantum events,' Serena continued. 'Some of the best were done by Professor Robert Jahn at Princeton University, in the Princeton Engineering Anomalies Research (PEAR) lab. And these types of experiments show us that when quantum entanglement occurs, cause and effect as it is commonly understood goes out the window. In such cases, *events* can be affected purely by *meaning* – there is no physical cause, only an information cause. So when I talk about "quantum" in this context, I am talking about a reality in which mind and matter are interacting.'

I needed another example here – or a pot of tea. Science has never been my strongest subject. Yet even I know that it will be through science that we will truly begin to comprehend who we are.

Serena sighed. 'Okay, let's say, for example, someone is very ill and his doctor, whom he really admires and trusts one hundred per cent, offers him some "new" medication, which the doctor categorically states will cure his ailment. In fact, it's only a sugar pill – but it does cure him. We know this placebo effect can be more effective than conventional drugs, because the person really, fully *believes* this treatment will work. Just as Jesus said, if you can believe completely that what you desire has already happened, then anything is possible.'

Fine, but I still wasn't sure whether I had caused my own back problem. Thinking of those dinner-party conversations about the peoples of Zimbabwe and Darfur, I decided to ask Serena about karma.

'There is great confusion on the subjects of cause and effect and karma,' she agreed. 'What a lot of people are doing is Westernizing complex and profound Eastern teachings on these types of philosophical subjects. So you need to be really clear.'

'What kind of confusion?'

'To answer that, I need to go back to the Big Bang,' Serena replied. 'That's when the *physical* aspect of our universe began with an explosion of *light* – so everything in our physical universe emerged from a oneness at the quantum entanglement level. In the beginning of our physical world there were electrons and photons of electromagnetic light, which work at the quantum level, but not at our everyday "see/touch" level, and at this quantum entanglement level where mind and matter are inter-connected, all is one. You could also call this the holographic universe level, as David Bohm did. At this level the Whole *is in* every part – the whole universe is inside you, Hazel, from the perspective of Hazel. And at this holographic universe oneness level, I am the whole universe from the perspective of Serena – so everything we do and think affects the Whole, and thereby what I do and think comes back to affect me too. This is the deeper, more profound understanding of karma. The confusion arises *when we mix the levels*.

'About three hundred and eighty thousand years after the Big Bang,' she went on, 'as the temperature within the primordial soup began to cool, protons came together with electrons to form atoms. As Gary Schwartz has told you, your body, your bed and the whole *physical* universe are ultimately made from atoms. But my point is that once you get to the material bit – that is, this physical world – most people are not aware of the holographic oneness level of reality, only of our see/touch level of reality, the one we all know.'

'In other words,' I interjected, 'if I want to experience effective healing at an entangled level of reality for my back right now, my mind needs to be sufficiently trained to "turn it on" one hundred per cent.'

'Yes,' agreed Serena. 'Obviously there is a part of us which is always working at this entangled level. This is why you hear stories of people who heal themselves through regular visualization. But it's usually only the trained yogis and spiritual masters who can bring the unmanifest into the manifest one hundred per cent of the time. For the rest of us it could be twenty-five or thirty per cent; it just depends on how evolved you are.

'This is why it's really crucial that people understand that our see/touch physical level does not work the same way as the holographic universe oneness level. If one of your friends states that starving people chose their lives, this is a gross misunderstanding of the laws of karma. The quantum level is only events *in possibility.* They are not necessarily set until consciousness becomes involved – when mind and matter interact.

'The child is starving because of social causes,' she went on, 'political conflicts, lack of water or seeds – not *necessarily* because the child chose it, not on a *physical* level, anyway. The child is part of the Whole and is presenting that aspect of the Whole, which is a dreadful reality. We are all at a holistic level part of the Whole, and in some sense that suffering child is in us too, but we just don't notice it, because we tend to notice only our own perspective.'

'So when people say you are the cause of everything in your life –'

'They're mixing up the levels,' she finished.

Okay, I was really beginning to get this.

Serena's voice softened. 'You might have been able to effect what others term a miracle ten years ago, but for now, you need to start from the beginning again. Do all the physical stuff that you know can help your back, and meditate when you are able, to help the nonphysical manifest into the physical. In this way, you help bring potential into reality. Most importantly, think positively as much as you possibly can, or higher-dimensional healing at your current level of consciousness is going to take a long time.'

Just what I needed to hear. Yet I felt somewhat better because Serena had confirmed what I have long believed, that not absolutely everything in my life is my fault at this physical level, what Serena terms our 'see/touch' reality, the Newtonian level of cause and effect. Bad luck happens the same as good luck happens. Sometimes you can be in the wrong place at the wrong time.

Before saying goodbye, Serena added, 'If you want more things to happen at the entanglement level, then I say again, you need to do the work necessary to make it happen. These two levels can and do work together, but they only combine consistently in the hands of highly trained spiritual people.'

So, on this level, I was right! I had worn the wrong shoes and run late and so I fell. Things happen! In the meantime, I resolved to do what I could at every level – the physical, emotional, mental and the higher-dimensional – to become well.

Out came large doses of the amino sugar glucosamine, which helps to replace the gelatinous fluid between the joints and discs. To this I added Celedrin, a fatty-acid-like substance proven to help reduce inflammation and lubricate cell membranes, and omega-3 fish oils, again to reduce the painful inflammation. I also began taking more digestive enzymes with meals to increase the absorption of nutrients from my food. And on a mental level, every time I managed a simple task, such as cleaning my teeth, over a basin, I congratulated myself that this indeed was a great leap forward.

A week later, with the help of a chiropractor and a physiotherapist, I learned how to gingerly get down the stairs. I was painfully slow and rather fearful – but as I placed my foot carefully on the first step, I kept in mind the phrase 'All great journeys begin with but one step.' I had just taken mine.

And if you would like to know more about Serena's research, log on to www.psi-researchcentre.co.uk or read her wonderful book *Where Science and Magic Meet*.

Chapter Five

Another Piece of the Jigsaw

We are all spirits having a physical experience. Our spiritual parents dressed us in these bio-bodysuits and put us in a playpen that we call a universe, in order to grow in coherence, in order to develop our gifts of intentionality, and in order to become what we were intended to become – co-creators with our spiritual parents.

– Emeritus Professor William A Tiller

April 2009 – Phoenix, Arizona

Wɪᴛʜ ɪɴᴛᴇʀᴍɪɴᴀʙʟᴇ ᴅᴇʟᴀʏs, the journey from London to Phoenix had been long. Even though two years had passed since my back injury, chronic pain was my constant companion, hence why my husband thought I had lost the plot – flying over 5,000 miles to talk to a scientist for two days.

Yet I felt compelled to make the journey. Once you become aware that we are all part of something far greater than most of us can even begin to conceive, and you consciously align yourself with humanity's awakening process, you often find yourself at a loss to explain your actions, let alone justify them to others – even those you love.

The previous autumn, when I had finally spoken with Professor William Tiller to ask if our universe would one day truly 'disappear' as Gary Renard predicted, I had listened intently as this brilliant physicist shared just a fraction of his conclusions – some of which you will discover in a moment. Yet my lack of any formal grounding in science prevented me from understanding the incredible picture that Tiller was painting with his words.

Sensing my frustration, he gently told me that in his experience the spirit world will – if your motives are honourable – help you on your journey. But they won't do everything for you; you too need to do your part. I thought of the saying 'God helps those who help themselves.'

I had to find a way to transform Tiller's technical, mathematics-based science into something that the public could understand. I made the decision to get on a plane and speak with him face to face, figuring it might be the only way I could grasp the enormity of his theories and his evidence.

Believe me, it was well worth the effort. Several large pieces of my personal jigsaw were about to fall into place.

Now, if like me, you are rather intimidated by science, please keep going with this chapter. Even better, read it twice. Please don't allow my simplification of Tiller's work and words, edited with his permission, to in any way diminish the importance of his achievements.

At 80, Bill Tiller has spent a lifetime researching consciousness and matter, and for 35 years he was a full professor at Stanford University. More than 350 of his scientific papers have been published and he has authored seven books. An 'ordinary' scientist he is not! For one thing, he and his wonderful wife, Jean, have been meditating for over 40 years. Like millions of us, they know that every one of us has the potential to effect 'miracles' that many people still dismiss as nonsense.

From our previous meetings and interviews, I knew that Tiller and his colleagues had demonstrated and verified over the course of a decade, through orthodox, scientific experiments on intention documented in Tiller's book *Conscious Acts of Creation*, that there are two distinct levels of physical reality. The first is the 'dense' electric atom/molecule physical world we see around us. The second is a normally invisible level termed the magnetic information wave level – previously known as the etheric level – which travels faster than the speed of light and is outside of space-time but can be influenced via consciousness.

Tiller states that both these levels are part of the physical world, but the magnetic information wave level, which cannot be measured by current orthodox means, is the template upon which the electric atom/molecule physical level is built. Quantum physics can only measure within space-time, but Tiller and his team are developing equipment that *can* measure the second level – and the implications are awesome.

Bill has demonstrated that these two distinct levels remain 'uncoupled' most of the time, but has found that via human consciousness, utilizing sustained, focused intentions, we can facilitate the two levels to 'couple', thus triggering physical events manifested solely by human intention. This 'coupling' also offers good evidence to explain phenomena such as telepathy, distance healing, and seeing into the future or the past. Many enlightened men and women can manifest physical effects and objects instantaneously with their minds; for the rest of us, it takes somewhat longer. And it's this increased 'coupling' between the two levels of reality that Tiller believes holds the key to our conversion from ordinary human beings to extraordinary human beings, then to adepts, masters and finally avatars.

What Tiller and his team have discovered amounts to a new type of mentally/emotionally imprinted 'software', linked to consciousness, which triggers precise and measurable physical effects in this normal reality. According to current orthodox science, which has been in place for almost 400 years, this is impossible, and therefore it's a miracle from that perspective.

Tiller has witnessed, practised and/or scientifically studied numerous phenomena that most people would term paranormal, such as pictures taken with an everyday non-digital camera that 'see' straight through people (*see* plate 1B). And he has now formulated the mathematics and science to back up some of his theories. Along the way, he has made some important discoveries: for example, that our acupuncture meridian channels are linked via our chakras to the magnetic information wave level – *all the time,* whether we are consciously aware of it or not – and that practices such as homeopathy, qi gong and kinesiology work at a 'coupled' higher-dimensional level (known in scientific terms as a higher electromagnetic gauge symmetry state) all the time as well. That's surely why some sectors of the orthodox medical establishment dismiss such practices as 'snake oil' – they simply cannot measure the effects with their current instruments.

Which brings me back to my feeling rather jet-lagged, with reams of questions for an extremely clever man! Never mind, we can only do our best in the moment. To give my brain a boost, I enjoyed an all-American breakfast: oatmeal and blueberries, followed by poached eggs. Such a feast, I knew, would balance my blood sugar while the protein in the eggs plus the blueberries nourished my tired brain. There can be no better way to start a day, I mused, as I walked in the Arizona spring sunshine, awaiting my guest.

Bill and I greeted each other as old friends and made our way to a quiet corner in my hotel. There was much to discuss and little time for chitchat, so I plunged in by asking Bill if our universe was in fact going to disappear.

'Yes and no,' came Bill's paradoxical response. 'Before I expand on this, it's vital that your readers really get their heads around what constitutes our physical universe.'

Bill used an analogy I had heard from other scientists, inviting me to imagine a reel of movie film approximately 2,500 miles in length. If that were our universe, the portion that most people (unless they are highly sensitive) can see within our visible light spectrum would be about two frames of film measuring about 2 inches . . . .

Bill let this fact sink in before continuing. 'Just because we cannot see the vast majority of our physical universe doesn't mean it's not there. You cannot see consciousness – yet we are conscious, sentient beings. You cannot see frequencies, or magnetic information waves, which travel faster than the speed of light – 186,000 miles a second – yet we know they are real.

'There are numerous levels of reality, as you know. First comes the electric atom/molecule level, our everyday reality, which is inside the reference frame of space-time. Next is the magnetic information wave level, which I term reciprocal space or

R-space; then the emotion domain level, followed by the mind domain level and then the spirit domain level. All of these are *outside* our space-time.

'Most people think our touchy-feely world is the only reality, and this is a huge mistake. In fact, the visible matter we see around us, including this world, other planets and other galaxies, makes up around four per cent of the energy and matter content of the physical universe. But we now know, thanks to the Wilkinson Microwave Anisotropy Probe launched by NASA in 2001, that approximately seventy-three per cent of our universe is made of something called dark energy and twenty-three per cent is dark matter. So ninety-six per cent of our universe is invisible matter and energy hidden within the physical vacuum of space. And this is where the magnetic information wave level functions. If a person learns how to connect, or "couple", with this vacuum level of physical reality, which we can access in the spaces between our thoughts through spiritual practices such as meditation, then what many people think of as miracles could become child's play.'

Listening to Bill, I was fascinated, but wondered whether I should include so much science in the book. Yet within a week of my conversation with Bill, out of the blue a friend gave me an esoteric book entitled *The Hathor Material: Messages from an Ascended Civilization* by Tom Kenyon and Virginia Essene, and as I flicked through it, a sentence jumped out at me: 'The balancing of electrical and magnetic forces within one's own being is one of the goals of Egyptian Alchemy ... ' That an intelligence supposedly channelling information from ancient cultures linked to Egypt knew what we are only now discovering was, to me, amazing.

Meanwhile, Bill's words came as no surprise. Anyone on a spiritual path is aware of realities other than the one we see around us; it's just that until now we've had a hard time proving their existence. And for years I have reminded people that we are far more than our physical bodies, which are collections of atoms, held together by form-shaping fields, held in place by gravity, electromagnetism and nuclear forces, that emit and receive energy, which is information. Science has shown that 99.999 per cent of every atom in our bodies is empty space, and this empty space is the vacuum level of reality.

'So,' I prompted, 'can you expand on whether our world is really going to disappear?'

'I can,' Bill said, 'but we'll need to deal with the issues of coherence and the Big Bang first, and then you will understand how our story is evolving. Be patient.'

That's my weakness, a need for instant answers. Patience has never been my strong point! We were in for a lengthy chat, so I ordered a pot of green tea to help keep my brain sharp. Bill continued: 'Although some people question the Big Bang, there is a huge body of definitive evidence to show that a significant release of energy happened around thirteen-point-seven billion years ago. But in fact there would have been no "bang", as there is no air in outer space to conduct sound waves, and it was not "big" at all, as this birthing of our physical universe originated from a tiny singularity much smaller than an atom – keeping in mind that a million atoms would fit behind a human hair. That's the first issue. The second issue is, what happened before the Big Bang? And that's where we can now talk about coherence.'

I smiled with anticipation.

'My view is that there is stability only in a dynamic state of change – this includes what you call God, the Core, the zero point and so on. You have often mentioned that when you were in that super-heightened, 'coupled' state in 1998, you felt like you were standing on the top of a pinnacle on Mount Everest looking down. You felt super-coherent, at a level of coherence that was outside space and time. Your physical brain probably was functioning at a coherent, or coupled, level – but for total coherence, true discernment and integration, one first needs to master *all* aspects of the physical self, followed by the magnetic information wave etheric level, then the level of emotion and eventually the Whole Mind core level. Avatars and some enlightened men and women have learned to maintain and control pretty high degrees of coherence, but even some of them are not completely coherent.

'As you experienced, it's like balancing on a pinhead, virtually impossible to maintain all the time. So the state of coherence started to unravel for you, and over time you felt as though you were back at base camp looking up and wondering how you could have fallen so low again. You were back at the electric atom/molecule level in an "uncoupled" state.

'Now, apply this analogy to our physical universe, keeping in mind that you can only see a minuscule fraction of it from this dense see/touch level.'

I was trying to figure out what this had to do with our universe disappearing. Bill noted my quizzical look. 'Your book is entitled *Countdown to Coherence*,' he went on, 'so allow me to share with you a speculative myth, which I believe one day will be proven to be much more than a myth, that will answer your question.'

I was listening.

'It's my interpretation of a metaphor that's commonly used in Eastern philosophy: "the out-breathing and in-breathing of the All".'

'And what is the All, God, to you?' I interrupted.

Bill smiled. 'In our current state of being we are nowhere near sufficiently conscious to even speculate as to what God really is. But for now, think of God as total coherent intelligence, total Isness, which is primarily outside of space and time. In the "beginning", everything was totally coherent, which in physics is termed "in phase". All things, all levels of energy, all levels of consciousness were one.'

Bill picked up a pen and paper.

'My working hypothesis, which I believe one day will be demonstrated through science, is that in order to grow in capability, this pure coherence decoheres and recoheres periodically over and over again – though not in any time scale that we could comprehend. My point is that we were birthed out of something that was already there. The Big Bang was simply an ongoing process.'

He began by drawing a dot. 'This represents the Core, God, total coherence. Now I'll expand out of this core in a small spiral, which represents the beginning of the cosmic out-breathing, or decohering, phase. The unravelling continued in the first half of this first spiral turn, and a separation of consciousness began at the finest levels of substance. This eventually nucleated into a nonphysical society at the level of mind, which in mythology, I believe, was called something like Mu – it would have been a highly coherent society. This was the first epoch in a "new" out-breathing cycle. On every full turn of each expanding spiral there would be seven epochs, three and a half on each out-breath (the decohering phase) and three and a half on each in-breath (the recohering phase).'

Bill could see I was struggling to understand his theory. 'Can you give me an idea,' I asked, 'as to how long each out-breath and in-breath might represent in our time scale?'

He considered. 'Well, even though I am describing a nonphysical event, I estimate that every out-breath could represent several millions of years in our time and the same for each in-breath.'

'Does this mean,' I stammered, appalled, 'that it's going to take us millions of years to go home?'

'Not at all,' he laughed. 'Just hang on a minute!'

'So, what happened next in your metaphorical scenario?'

'Well, I believe that the process of decohering, or separation, continued and another society known as Lemuria evolved at the level of the emotion domain – again prephysical – which became the second epoch. The third epoch in this first out-breath cycle could have been something like Atlantis, whose outer envelope of cognition was at the coarse vacuum level of physical reality.'

I interrupted yet again, asking him to clarify what he meant by 'the coarse vacuum level'.

'The deeper you go into the vacuum, the finer the level of substance and the faster it travels – and the magnetic information wave level is what I would term the coarsest, slowest-speed level of the vacuum substances. It's basically a variation in density. And the electric atom/molecule level – our reality – is very coarse indeed and slower than electromagnetic light.'

Though I tried to follow what Bill was saying, I was also beginning to think about chocolate cake. How I struggle with science! I focused my attention as Bill continued. 'These societies, like Mu, Lemuria and Atlantis, over time formed what we presently term the physical vacuum. And, in very simple terms – although there is currently no serious evidence – I hypothesize that they then "intended" our physical epoch into being, which triggered the Big Bang, and our electric atom/molecule physical universe was born. This was the beginning of the space-time "classroom" as spirit entered into dense matter through consciousness. My working hypothesis is that consciousness is a by-product of spirit entering dense matter. For spirit to attach to dense matter, it needed a suitable interface with space-time, and this is why our physical form evolved. We are all spirits having a physical experience. Basically, our spiritual parents dressed us in these "bio-bodysuits" and put us in a playpen that we call a universe in order to grow in coherence.'

For those of you who, like me, wonder how it's possible for any being to simply 'intend' and then birth a whole universe, you may want to consider that at the time of the Big Bang our universe was microscopically small. As theoretical physicist Michio Kaku of the City University of New York states in his fascinating book *Parallel Worlds*, 'To create a universe like ours may require a ridiculously small net amount of matter, perhaps as little as an ounce.'

It's mind-boggling – and I found myself asking, 'If these prophetical beings were so evolved, why bother creating us in the first place?'

'Well,' Bill said, smiling patiently, 'it's so that the All can experience itself at every level of reality – so that the All can experience reality as a separate soul, thus affording it a further opportunity to learn and grow. This is how the process that we term God grows in capability.'

'We sure have taken our time about "growing",' I muttered – history definitely keeps repeating itself, going round in circles, making the same old mistakes. Surely now is the time for us to grow up and graduate.

As Bill went on with his drawing, he said, 'Notice how the spiral grows and expands, the further we are from the total coherence at our "source". In my opinion, this current physical reality is a point of minimal coherence, so from here on in, we are heading back towards maximal coherence – we are on our way home.'

I sat back smiling from ear to ear. Oh, how my heart had ached for years after my experience, when I used to weep and weep with a deep longing, saying over and over again, 'I want to go home ... ' It still makes me sigh even now.

Bringing myself back into the moment, I asked, 'You mean back to being nonphysical beings?'

'Absolutely – eventually. Our physical universe as we know it, unless we destroy it, will go on expanding for billions of years. It's not our physical universe that's "going home", but our consciousness. We are talking at a level of mind here, going home and merging our consciousness back with its source. I believe that over time we will evolve into "light" beings. Our soul self will evolve beyond this space-time reality. Those left behind will think we have died, as we will have transcended to another level of reality, just as Jesus and others like him did and still do.'

His words were music to my ears. Remembering how I had 'seen' people who had 'died' and beings from other worlds back in '98, I wanted to clarify this. 'When we reach the next level of coherence and beyond, will we still "see" and be "seen"?'

'Of course you will,' Bill replied. 'The other dimensions/realities/frequencies will seem as real to you as this one does. Over time, we will recreate societies similar to Atlantis, then evolve back through each level until we reach home. But we and our surroundings will be different, as some of us will be living in a different universe. Some beings will still be able to interact with this reality as they do now, but for the most part, transcended souls will no longer be seen in this space-time dimension. This is what Gary Renard means when he talks about the disappearance of the universe.'

Needless to say, I wondered when this split might occur. Bill suggested it would be gradual, saying, 'Over the next one hundred to two hundred years we will begin, through sustained and regular spiritual practices such as meditation, which afford us access to the vacuum level of reality, plus regular acupuncture treatments and so on, to increase our "coupling" capability with the substance of reciprocal space.'

'Which will,' I interjected, 'hugely develop our potential psychic capabilities; improve our ability to manifest, heal ourselves and others and communicate telepathically; and increase access to more knowledge and more realities.'

Bill nodded. 'Absolutely all of the above and more. The Akashic records, which contain all knowledge, are believed to be in reciprocal space. A few people have had psychic abilities since mankind evolved – this will now increase exponentially. You will see more "thought-based" computers and technology, and as our ability to maintain and integrate coherence increases, we will become much kinder to ourselves and others. We could reverse global warming through intention, and one day we will understand how to birth universes just as the ancients did. They are only "ancients" to our way of thinking because we are inside a space-time classroom in a bio-body suit, which is needed to interact with this reality. The higher realms and other universes are outside physical time and space, so "time" as we know it has no meaning.'

Bill's words finally helped me to more fully comprehend how other societies such as Atlantis might still be in existence outside our space-time. A few months earlier I had travelled to Turin to meet an enlightened man, Falco, who has formed an incredible community called Damanhur. They have built awesome underground temples that are being hailed by many as the Eighth Wonder of the World. Most importantly, some of those in the community of over a thousand people, from many countries and walks of life, claim to time-travel and connect to the energy of Atlantis. And indeed, the technology they use within the temples is incredible. As I sat with Bill, I considered for the first time that mythical societies such as Lemuria and Atlantis might have been nonphysical, at least in part. I made a note to return to Italy later in the year (and you can read my adventures with the time travellers in chapter 13).

Bill brought me back into the moment, adding, 'On every out-breathing cycle you have these type of societies, like Atlantis or Lemuria, forming and on every in-breath cycle they/we return to coherence. All of this happens over and over again. God is constantly birthing itself, there are a host of realities coexisting alongside us, but for now, most people cannot see them. Within two hundred years many of us will have "moved on" in every sense of the word to the next level, the magnetic information wave level – but getting all the way home could take a few epochs!'

Amazing – but by now my brain was on overload and the eight-hour time change was beginning to take its toll. Bill and I agreed to reconvene the next day. There was still so much to discuss. I wanted to hear Bill's comments on the holographic concept, how the ego mind can help us, how the word *quantum* is being misused and misunderstood – and, most importantly, to understand how each and every one of us can accelerate our progress towards coherence.

Yet if you find Bill's theories 'far out', you may be interested to learn that several scientific centres, including the US government–funded Fermilab in Illinois, are conducting research into multiple universes and dimensions that they believe exist alongside this reality – and how to travel between them. Bernard Carr, professor of mathematics and astronomy at Queen Mary University of London, told me that any mechanism that can produce one universe is likely to generate other universes, and there are several theories in mainstream science on multiverses. Carr's book *Universe or Multiverse?* is well worth a read.

Science and metaphysics are finally coming to similar conclusions. Even the great theoretical physicist Stephen Hawking acknowledges eleven dimensions in nature. Theoretical physicist Michio Kaku, who was featured in the popular documentary TV series *The Universe*, believes, like Professor Tiller, that in the not-too-distant future, countless other realities that coexist alongside our own will be scientifically proven, and that travel between them will become commonplace. Kaku's theories and science are discussed in *Parallel Worlds*.

Professor Tiller's theories may not resonate with everyone; in the field of science he has plenty of detractors. At times in the past ten or more years I too have been termed 'flaky', even by other spiritual writers! Yet his concept of the spiral struck a chord with me. At the height of my experience I had felt myself 'spinning' out of control. An intense circling of energy seemed to come in through the top of my head and go out between my legs, around and around and around. At times this 'circle' was huge beyond words, and at other times I felt that 'I' was smaller than a pinhead. I finally realized that thinking of myself as an individual 'I' was stupid, as little me had for a brief moment in time merged with the Ultimate I. There was no longer any separation; all was one. My words do not accurately describe how this felt – yet they are all that little, seemingly separate 'me' has.

A few weeks after my meeting with Bill Tiller, a friend suggested I should look at the website of a healer based in California – one Mellen-Thomas Benedict. On the site, Mellen tells how he 'died' from cancer – but instructed his caregivers at the hospice to leave his body untouched for several hours after his physical death. He then relates a story of moving beyond physical death, through the galaxies, back to the beginning of time and on into total silence – a total nothingness. He reports, 'I saw during my life-after-death experience that the Big Bang is only one of an infinite number of Big Bangs creating universes endlessly and simultaneously.'

Some of Mellen's descriptions made me cry. Read them for yourself on www.mellen-thomas.com. His words are not correct in scientific terms, and, yes, they are anecdotal and 'unproven', yet here is the story of a man who has experienced what scientists now believe could be an ultimate truth. Science and supposition, too, are beginning to find common ground.

That first night in Phoenix, after sleeping blissfully through a beautiful sunny afternoon, I sat and watched the stars appear. Arizona laws prohibit excess artificial-light emissions, so the heavens in all their glory shone around me. Back in 2004, a stunning picture taken by the Hubble space telescope showed a jumble of faint galaxies, over 13 billion light years from earth, that were formed only half a billion years after the Big Bang. Scientists can now 'see' way back into our past and are within a stone's throw of seeing the Big Bang itself. Perhaps then we will finally figure out what came before.

Chapter Six

Beyond 'The Secret'

A man is but the product
of his thoughts. What he thinks,
he becomes.

— Mahatma Gandhi

April 2009 – Phoenix, Arizona

My SECOND DAY IN PHOENIX dawned with clear blue skies. As I was flying back to London the very next day, I needed to make today count. Thankfully, after a good night's sleep, my brain felt altogether sharper, and Professor Tiller arrived in one of his more determined moods. He was keen to begin by setting the record straight about the misunderstandings and misuse surrounding the word *quantum,* which has become such a buzzword in recent years. As we shared the breakfast buffet, I knew better than to interrupt.

'How often,' Bill asked, 'do you hear the phrase "a quantum leap"? It has become synonymous with some kind of huge leap forward – yet it's anything but. And the word *quantum* is often used as if it describes something that is *outside* physical reality – for example, "quantum healing". This is New Age crapola.'

Sheepishly, I confessed that I had always associated the word *quantum* with something 'otherworldly' myself. I was aware that quantum physics is the science of the very, *very* small, but I had not delved a whole lot further. Bill set about broadening my education.

'Words such as *quantum* are being bandied about by people with little or no grounding in science, and this incorrect usage is causing the science establishment to dismiss important emerging science which demonstrates the varying levels of what we term "reality" and beyond. If numerous groundbreaking studies and equations are eventually to be taken seriously, it's important that we at least get our facts straight.'

As I nodded in agreement, Bill's impromptu lecture continued: 'Quantum is indeed the science of the very, *very* small, and it was discovered by Max Planck in the 1890s. It refers to a minuscule – we term it "discrete"-sized – "bit" of electromagnetic energy involved in energetic reactions between atoms and molecules. Although we cannot see such interactions with our physical eyes, nevertheless they *are physical interactions within our space-time universe.* Out of Planck's work physicists developed quantum mechanics, using space-time mathematical formalism. The reason I am sharing this with you is that orthodox science, unlike emerging science and data like that of the Global Consciousness Project out of Princeton' – more on this in chapter 16 – 'still has no accurate method of measuring levels of reality associated with human consciousness, human intention, human emotions, mind or spirit that are outside our space-time domain. Therefore, to associate the word *quantum* with huge leaps forward or as being outside our space-time domain is, from the perspective of physics, incorrect.'

I had learned something important – always a good way to start a day – and asked Bill if there was anything else he wanted to mention before we continued.

'Only that once you move beyond our space-time to higher-dimensional levels of reality, the coordinate reference frame shifts from space and time to *frequencies,* which are everywhere. At our core level we are made up of different frequencies. And there are many types of frequencies – sound, light and so on.'

I smiled. For almost 12 years I have written about frequencies; most of us cannot see them, but they are everywhere. I distinctly recall being able to see and *smell* negative frequencies that emanated from newspaper stories and from people's thoughts. As long as I live I'll never forget a scientist who had gone through a spiritual awakening similar to mine asking, 'And how does the world smell to you?' Taken aback, I laughingly told him that for the most part this world *stinks!*

Everything in our physical world – rocks, plants, foods, medicines, animals, humans – emits a range of signature frequencies as unique as a DNA profile. Most people cannot see these frequencies, yet they are there. Biophysicist Harry Oldfield in the UK has developed a specialized PIP (Polycontrast Interference Photography) scanner, designed to produce images of a person's energy field, which clearly show that we emit, receive and interact with some of these frequencies. And this is how he can diagnose many potential illnesses before they manifest in the physical body. It's also how he 'sees' esoteric energies such as the kundalini and chakras (*see* plates 6 and 7). The metaphysical kundalini – which in Sanskrit means 'coiled' – is often depicted as a snake that 'resides' at the base of our spines and rises up like a fine channel or pipe through to the tops of our heads. And along this 'pipe' are the seven chakras: energy vortices that act as coupling devices between this reality and others.

At NASA, cosmologists can ascertain what other planets are made up of by measuring spectral frequencies emitted from them; in this way they can determine the presence of iron, sulphur, basalt and so on. And researchers at the Breakspear Hospital in Hertfordshire in the UK, which specializes in environmental medicine, have long recognized why someone suffering from, for instance, a severe peanut allergy can react even when the peanuts are across the room: it's because the person is sensitive to the *frequencies* that are being emitted by the peanuts! Hence why some of the vaccines they produce are frequency-based.

Sound is also made up of frequencies, so is colour, and, crucially, so are our *thoughts*. We need to grasp this: our thoughts count. Thoughts are palpable things that create real effects, and sustained, focused, heartfelt thoughts are the most potent of all. You have 40,000 thoughts a day. What is the content of most of them? Think about it before you read on.

After breakfast, Bill and I took a walk in the sunshine. Looking around us at all the trees and flowers, I asked, 'Are we real, Bill, or are we just holograms being projected from some huge mind?'

Sensing my heartfelt desire to understand, Bill looked reflective. 'There is so much we don't yet know. Our story is unfolding and much of that story remains a paradox. But are we real? It depends on the context of what you perceive to be real. At our coarse physical electric atom/molecule level in our bio-bodysuits existing in this simulator/classroom – yes, we are separate, the physics makes us separate. But at the "coupled" level, beginning with the acupuncture meridian and chakra system (which operate at the magnetic information wave level, in reciprocal space), and on into the domains of mind, spirit and beyond, which are *outside* our space-time – at *that* level we are all interconnected.'

'But,' I interjected, 'what about this notion of us being nothing more than a hologram?'

'Are you carrying any credit cards?' Bill asked. Luckily, several. Imprinted on one was a holographic image of a very real-looking three-dimensional eagle in flight. 'At present,' Bill explained, 'we can make holograms from light like this one – but *not* of physical substance that we can touch and feel. Yes, we can create objects or images that *appear* real, but if you touched them, you would quickly realize they are nothing more than beams of light. We do not yet have the technology to make holograms of *substance*. People often ask me if extraterrestrials could have projected us and our world using advanced physics in which holograms made of physical matter might be possible, but we don't know. Maybe, maybe not.

'I can only tell you what we know now. We can say that our physical universe is holographic in nature in that we and everything, including consciousness, are an evolving extension from a core mind, and as extensions of that core mind, we "see" our world from our individual earthly perspectives. In this way the intelligence that we term God is expanding its awareness through us and our world. But, as far as current thinking throughout all levels of science goes, we are not holograms per se. We and our universe *are* real.'

Thank goodness for that!

For those of you who may not be aware of how a hologram is formed, they are produced when a single beam of *coherent* light, such as that of a laser, is split into two. One beam is bounced off an object and the second beam is aligned to 'interfere' with the reflected light of the first. The resulting wave pattern is then recorded on film and when light is subsequently shone through the two-dimensional film, a three-dimensional image of the object – or hologram – is projected. The holograms on credit cards and banknotes are etched on two-dimensional plastic films. And when light bounces off them, it recreates a 3D image.

I had first contacted Bill back in 2004 after reading his book *Science and Human Transformation,* which featured pictures of dual-camera experiments he had carried out with psychic researcher Stanislav O'Jack. These were similar to the pictures I mentioned in chapter 5, which 'saw' straight through people, whilst in some of the pictures taken by the Scole Group of psychic researchers in Norfolk in the UK, anomalous objects, faces and old pictures appeared *within* pictures taken with the lens cap left on in a totally darkened cellar.

A thorough investigation by the Society for Psychical Research in the UK later concluded that the Scole pictures were genuine. Still, when I first saw such pictures I wondered if they were holographic images created by the photographers. As Bill and I meandered back to the hotel, I asked him to explain how such phenomena are possible.

'In the picture taken with Stan's camera (*see* plate 1B) you see Uri Geller as being semi-transparent, as the camera traditionally uses photons of electromagnetic energy. But there are a host of other energies that go faster than such light, which can pass right through "solid" objects – radio waves, for instance. You have known for years that we and our world, apart from minuscule amounts of matter that we can see, mainly consist of "empty space", but this vacuum level of physical reality is not "empty" at all. The energy stored in all the physical mass of our universe is minuscule in comparison to the energy stored within the "stuff" of the vacuum. It is highly intelligent latent potential that underlies all of life, and what we need to do is to "couple" with it through intention, which activates or wakes up this infinite intelligence into this physical reality. Think of gasoline, for example – it has great latent potential, which is only released when it's utilized or converted as the car engine is running.

'This is what Stanislav O'Jack did. Firstly he created a "conditioned space" – most people would call this a sacred space – which facilitates a coupling between our space-time and reciprocal space, which is outside space-time. In Stan's case, he became so used to creating this conditioned space that he was able to do it almost unconsciously. His intention awoke the indwelling latent consciousness that is everywhere and in everything. In science, this is known as raising one's consciousness to a higher-gauge symmetry state.

'Then, by bringing the camera into his conditioned energy field for a day or so, Stan changed the way the camera functioned. *Conditioned space is intelligent space that becomes part of the process.* The camera itself began working at a "coupled" level, in which the electric atom/molecule slower-than-electromagnetic-light reality coupled with the faster-than-light magnetic information wave reality. This is when seeming "miracles" become possible. And this is why, when you remain in an enlightened person's energy field for a while, you often begin to exhibit signs of growing coherence yourself. Coherence is catching!'

Bill's words reminded me of a study carried out in Lebanon over two and a half years during the 1980s, in which several groups of meditators, more than 200 people, were asked to meditate with nothing more than an intention of 'waking up' the underlying field of 'wholeness' or pure intelligence in a specific area. Once all the data was examined – using strict scientific protocols that took into account variables such as holiday periods, temperature, stress levels, weekends and other variations – there was a 66 per cent increase in cooperation and a 48 per cent reduction in conflict among the people living in the areas on which the meditators concentrated. The 'awakening' of the underlying intelligence triggered a raising of coherence in these areas – and clearly it was catching.

Coming back into the moment, I asked Bill, 'If we were being threatened by the asteroid that some people think could be heading our way soon, could we redirect it?'

'Of course we could – as long as we were all thinking and believing coherently with our hearts and minds as one. And as we evolve back towards coherence *at all levels* and learn how to integrate and maintain the coherence – *and* learn true discernment – our potential will become virtually limitless.'

Bill's point about discernment was important, I knew. As psychiatry professor Gary Schwartz at the University of Arizona had mooted last time we chatted, if we were all to become fully coherent in a short space of time, it could spell disaster. Imagine a world where millions upon millions of people experienced a mass spiritual awakening – experiencing almost instant access to other levels of reality, overwhelming their brains' ability to cope, and not having the framework to discern what was real from what was not. A nightmare indeed – especially as the results can be devastating. Since 1998, I have read and heard firsthand of numerous cases in which people who I believe were going through intense spiritual awakenings ended up in mental institutions or even, in some cases, killed themselves or others.

When I mentioned this to Bill, he agreed that the symptoms of awakening can be problematic. He was keen to explain that in his opinion, when people throughout history, such as Joan of Arc, believe they are communicating directly with God or what they perceive to be the Devil, it's more likely to be a discarnate spirit, either someone who has 'died' on this plane or a higher- or lower-dimensional being. And from my experience I would say he is correct.

'This is why,' he cautioned, 'the process of "going home to coherence" is more beneficial if it unfolds gradually. Those who are living and maintaining an existence at a "coupled" level all the time, free from many of the constraints associated with personal ego, are the masters and avatars.'

Talking of ego, I asked Bill's opinion on Gary Renard's concept that we are nothing more than a construct emanating from a collective ego mind that 'thinks' it has separated from God.

He turned the tables on me by asking, 'What do you think?'

As I looked up at the beautiful blue sky, trying to compose a suitably intelligent response, my own ego thoughts whispered, 'Wouldn't it be easier to put on your bikini and go sunbathe?'

Discipline and patience are definitely my weak points. I shifted my attention away from my personal ego. A healer friend, Philippe Coffin, once told me that our mental body is concerned with survival, so in order to survive – to protect our physical separate identity – over time we developed our individual ego. And for many people our ego identity – 'who we are' – is equated with what we look like, the colour of our skin, how we feel about ourselves, what we do for a living, what we own or whom we know. Without this ego, we might be said not to exist as separate beings at all. All the enlightened men and women I have met tell me that when they say 'I', they are speaking as the Ultimate I, as God; there is no longer any separation at any level. No duality. They speak of the *death* of the ego.

Therefore, in answer to Bill's question, I replied, 'On an individual physical level, yes, we sometimes allow our ego to take over too much. And at times groups of people show signs of "collective ego" – a country rooting for its team at the Olympics, for instance. Yet you have told me that in this physical reality we are separate physical bodies. The great majority still believe that God is "out there" somewhere, rather than within them. In that sense I believe that the majority are still being "run" by their individual ego minds, as that's all they know.' At this point, I lost my thread somewhat. But Bill smiled.

'Not bad,' he said. 'Yet ego is necessary, and of course it's also a very personal thing. Some people are humble whilst others have huge egos. We need our egos; however, if an individual is not very evolved, his or her ego tends to be self-orientated, whereas if you do the inner work, through meditation, qi gong or whatever, it gradually increases levels of coherence within your bio-bodysuit and you start to put your ego into service for the good of the Whole – and then you can make a *huge* difference, as you will receive assistance from higher realms.'

Well, thinking only of *me* – my stomach was rumbling yet again. Over lunch, Bill explained the science of homeopathy and told me more about his team's findings that our acupuncture meridians and our chakra systems already work at a 'coupled' level of reality. Good to know that part of us is already coherent! Bill spoke of magnetic monopoles, dipoles, deltrons, duplex spaces and a host of technical science that was beyond my capacity to understand. Afterwards, while he stepped out for more fresh air, I considered my options. I needed to become more focused, as our time together was slipping away. My list of questions could have lasted us a week. It was time to prioritize.

I scanned my notes and my attention turned to Bill's thought experiments, which I had explored in detail when I first sought him out while researching my book *The Evidence for the Sixth Sense*. Here was a fruitful direction for our conversation – the science that explains how our thoughts can create reality.

Back in the mid-'90s, Professor Tiller devised a thought experiment involving a small black box fitted with a simple electrical circuit. Four highly experienced meditators gathered round a table in the centre of which stood the black box, plugged into an electrical wall socket. After mentally creating a sacred space, Bill read a specific intention aloud to the group and towards the black box, and they all held his specific intention throughout their meditation. The intention was that the device should increase the pH of purified water by one full unit with no chemical additions. Keep in mind that the human body (our blood) has an average pH of between 7.35 and 7.45; if you move it half a unit in one direction, you will probably die, and if you move it half a unit the other way, you'll also probably be dead. So if Bill's team could achieve a change of one full pH unit, this would be a significant result indeed.

The box with the 'intention' in it was shipped 1,500 miles away to a laboratory and placed near some purified water in a pH measurement vessel. After a month or so, slowly but surely the pH within the water began changing in the direction of the requested intention until it had increased by *exactly* one full unit. The experiment was then repeated, this time setting an intention for the water to go down one full pH unit – and again it worked. This experiment was repeated in several independent laboratories in America and Europe with the same results. The probabilities of this happening again and again by chance were infinitely small.

Further, when the black box containing the intention 'imprint' had achieved its 'intention' of raising the pH in the water one full unit and the water had remained at that level for a month or so, the device was then moved out of the room where the experiments had taken place and placed in a copper Faraday cage, which prevented any further electromagnetic energy from going into or out of the black box. And the pH levels in the water *stayed at the level of the original intention, in some cases for as long as two years.* However, if the box was removed while the pH level was slowly climbing or falling, depending on the set intention, then gradually the water returned to its original state. It was only when the water reached the plateau of one full unit up or down that the result lasted for any significant length of time.

Bill returned and took up the story. 'The crucial point is, if you want something to manifest, you have to get past a threshold so that the conditioned state/space stabilizes.'

According to Bill's scientific model, our intentions flow via our chakras and begin to form a specific pattern in what he calls the mind lattice grid of space, which can 'hold' any sustained intention. To help me further understand the lattice, Bill asked me to imagine a group of like-minded people congregating in a church or building every day and visualizing or praying for a specific intention. By the time they leave, their specific intention has begun to 'condition' that space – they have left their energy there – but overnight the energy will dissipate or decay somewhat. 'But if they return daily and keep raising the conditioning, the coherence,' Bill continued, 'then it eventually creates an invisible structure in their environment – something akin to builders erecting a fine scaffold – that can "hold" the intention. This is how shamans create "sacred spaces".

'And once the plateau, the critical point, is reached, the intention becomes "set" in geometrical patterns on this structure, and then it can materialize in our reality. Enlightened beings can do this instantaneously – we mere mortals need to keep practising!' It's Bill's belief, he explained, that true adepts and higher-dimensional beings can help 'set' major events on this lattice grid years and even centuries before they manifest in this reality. And he added that if psychics and seers access specific wavelengths within the vacuum level, they can pick up information about specific future events from the lattice – though he pointed out that they are often incorrect in predicting precise dates, because they are usually receiving communication from sources outside our space-time. 'Spirits have little concept of time or space,' he explained, 'because their domains of experience are all frequency domains.'

Bill is keen for us all to appreciate that anyone who wants to manifest an event in this reality first needs to create, via intention, a coupling of the two distinct levels (the slower-than-light electric atom/molecule physical level and the faster-than-light magnetic information wave level). Otherwise, he says, we can wish for things till the cows come home, but nothing will happen. And we will know if this coupling has occurred, as our intuition will become much sharper and more reliable. 'Over time,' he explained to me, 'you will come to know whether something is emanating from your ego (conscious) mind, or from the subconscious mind, which is linked to the mind domain lattice grid. This comes with practice. It's essential to first "couple" with this lattice grid if you want things to happen – and this is where films like *The Secret* and *What the Bleep Do We Know?* got it somewhat wrong.'

'So, what's the secret to coupling and manifesting our dreams?' I asked in haste.

'Practice, practice and more practice, with plenty of patience.' He laughed before continuing, 'In my scientific model, powerful emotions trigger the release of "deltrons" from the emotion domain –'

'And,' I interjected yet again, 'are deltrons things?'

Bill smiled at the simplicity of my question. 'Basically, deltrons are consciousness "entities" that we can interact with. There are deltrons in everything; consciousness is everywhere, it is just not activated. And deltrons act like the toner on a copying machine, allowing the faster-than-light magnetic stuff to "couple" with the electric atom/molecule slower-than-light world and thus imprint upon this reality. If you greatly desire an event to happen, not only do you need to visualize it, to ask for the higher dimensions to assist in the process, but you also need to *feel* it and *sustain* the heartfelt intention. This triggers more deltrons to be produced – the more deltrons, the better the coupling and the faster your intention can happen. *Belief and intention are crucial to any desired outcome.* Again, I reiterate, the higher realms will assist you to a point, but you most definitely need to do your part.

'Remember, the majority of our sustained conscious thoughts build a pattern in the mind-level lattice. And once these repetitive thoughts become set on your individual lattice grid, then no matter how much you want "the universe" or "the higher realms" or your "angel guides" to help you manifest, your unconscious filters will let in only the stuff that you have imprinted. If, for example, the great majority of your daily thoughts have a similar theme – such as "I never have any good luck" or "I'm not good enough" – then no matter how much you desire to have good luck, the right partner or whatever it is you want, your conscious mind only allows in what has been "set" on your individual grid. In this case, you need to be far more disciplined and positive with your thoughts and build a new pattern, unique to you, on your grid. Once an intention is set, it has the potential to remain in place for years, but if you stop placing your attention and emotional output on it, it will dissipate over time.'

Now, you may believe Bill's science or you may dismiss it; I repeat, you need to find your own truth. Yet for years scientists have been making statements similar to his. Back in 1994, in a magazine called *Science of Mind*, I read an interview with Beverly Rubik PhD, a biophysicist trained at Berkeley who at that time was director of the Center for Frontier Sciences at Temple University in Philadelphia. Like Professor Tiller, this lady knows her stuff. Through their thought experiments, her team demonstrated that there is a definite interaction between consciousness and matter. Dr Rubik stated, 'The research has shown a significant relationship between what we intend in consciousness and what we experience. Of course, if our intention is not clear, the results we get will be muddled by deeper, subconscious inclinations that may even work *in the opposite direction*. But when we do have a clear intention for something to occur and it is not blocked by contrary subconscious thinking or a feeling that we don't deserve it, our thought does tend to create results we desire. Thought matters, thought materializes. A clear intention can create a reality.'

If I had a pound for every time I have read such claims, I would now be wealthy. For years the anecdotal evidence has been in place, but now, thanks to Tiller and others, emerging science is finally uncovering *how* these results are produced and how they can be validated. Bill and his team have developed a feedback device that will allow us to measure our levels of intention. The rest of his research is, for the moment, a closely guarded secret!

'And how big,' I asked Bill, 'is the invisible lattice? Are you saying that we each have an individual lattice, which is somehow attached to the "mainframe"?'

'Think of the physical Internet,' he said. 'It contains massive amounts of information, and we can retrieve this information by accessing a variety of servers – grids – which in turn connect us to the mainframe.'

Bill's words made me smile. During my experience, I had felt 'plugged in' that very same way, as though my small, limited-reality mind was connected to an ultimate supercomputer that held all knowledge. Anything I needed to know, in the moment I needed to know it – I knew!

'The metaphysical mind domain lattice grid is huge, beyond our normal imagining,' Bill went on. 'It is where the Akashic records, as I mentioned yesterday, are thought to be stored. And *all* our sustained thoughts, plus unimaginable amounts of data, are ultimately stored on this "mainframe".

'If small black boxes can "communicate" across both small and huge distances through a new type of physics, then we have helped to demonstrate in principle how remote viewing works, how telepathy works, how a prayer or a curse can reach a specific person or target a specific location – either across a room or on the other side of the world – and how we can have access to the past and the future.'

'And,' I continued, 'if an enlightened man or woman converts water to wine or to oil – as I myself have seen – these phenomena are the same in principle as what you have shown though your pH intention experiments, which changed the water's structure at its vacuum level.'

'You got it,' said Bill.

It was almost time for him to leave, so I asked him to summarize for me what these ideas might mean for our world. 'Once we learn how to "couple" more efficiently and gradually become more coherent at every level,' he began, 'we will develop incredible memories, as we will have better access to the Akashic records – *the* ultimate Internet. Our psychic and healing abilities will expand. Computers will become capable of interfacing with thought patterns, our ability to change our appearance through intention will increase, and frequency-based medicines and treatments will become more commonplace. We are already hearing more about the "Crystal Children", a new generation of sensitive beings who can, for instance, read the contents of a book if it's placed under their feet. Edgar Cayce, the revered psychic, who died in 1945, had similar abilities, but now they are becoming more apparent. Slowly but surely, many people are becoming more coherent.

'Interestingly, Cayce long ago warned us that even if we *subconsciously* absorb the seemingly endless negative news from media sources, we could be contributing to materializing more negative situations in our future. Through our experiments, we can now surmise that if enough people are thinking something, *even at a subconscious level,* then this too could be imprinting on the invisible lattice grid. Therefore it's vital that no matter what is happening, we all make the effort to remain as positive as possible.'

As I walked him to his car and we hugged farewell, Bill reiterated, 'Humanity needs to think more with their hearts as well as their heads. They need to work on "coupling" with the magnetic information wave level, build coherence on a personal and collective basis and intend for the good of the Whole. Whatever future outcomes we show through science, there is now no doubt that our thoughts count at every level. We need to have more "good" goals and use the proper heartfelt means to achieve these goals. Collectively we are all responsible for co-creating our future on this planet – one that we would be happy to see our children and grandchildren live in. We have an opportunity to learn how to do it right at this simplest level of reality. If we do, our souls may be more prepared for the forth-coming epochs of experience as we continue to ride the river of life together, on our journey home to total coherence at all levels of reality!'

A lovely man – who without doubt in my mind is working for the good of the Whole! If you would like more information on his experiments, articles or science books, log on to www.tiller.org. I particularly recommend Bill's DVD *Psychoenergetic Science,* recorded over two days at the University of Denver.

Some of you may find it hard to visualize how different your life could be if you lived at a 'coupled' level even a fraction of the time – but after reading on about my experiences in Sedona, which I later dubbed 'Superworld', you will be left in no doubt as to its implications for you and for us all . . .

Chapter Seven

Superworld

The spirit world are potentially
always players in the game if they
choose to be.

– Professor William Tiller

May 2007 – Sedona, Arizona

W<small>HEN</small> I <small>LEFT MY PHYSICAL BODY</small> on that fateful Saturday in 1998 and found 'myself' looking down at a drama unfolding below me, it took what felt like a few seconds to realize that the 'body' I could see below me was me! I, my consciousness, 'me' and all that entails – minus my physical shell – had watched with fascinated detachment as the doctor held 'my' hand. It was like watching a movie. There was no desire to return to that body – I was completely free. No more pain and confusion ... just freedom and clarity.

Over the years, I often wondered what I had become in that moment. In what medium might it possible for my consciousness to exist outside my physical body?

I was about to find out.

Fast-forward to March 2007, when a friend sent me an e-mail advertising the world's first-ever conference on the emerging phenomenon of Orbs, which was due to take place in Sedona, Arizona, two months later. At that time I had never heard of Orbs, yet my intuition told me I absolutely had to attend the conference. As he often has over the years, my wonderful husband once more concluded I had lost the plot. Yet again, I was being invited to choose.

Sedona is a magical city situated two hours' drive north of Phoenix and 300 miles south of the Grand Canyon, with several major energy vortices within its bounds. For centuries, various indigenous tribes lived in the harsh yet spectacular desert landscape, which is studded with impressive towering red rock formations. Now, several hundred Orb enthusiasts and several highly accredited scientists had arrived at Sedona from more than 16 countries to share their unfolding knowledge in this dramatic setting.

By the time I arrived in Arizona, I had Googled the subject of Orbs and learned they are strange spheres of light that have in recent years begun appearing on digital photographs all over the globe. Some sites claimed that the Orbs were E.T. come to visit us, others surmised they might be angels – but the sites I found most interesting were those of retired physicist Dr Klaus Heinemann and theologian Dr Miceal Ledwith, both authorities on the Orb phenomenon who were due to speak at the conference. If the higher realms are ever to be taken seriously by the masses, I have no doubt it will be through science.

Shaman and medical anthropologist Dr Alberto Villoldo (whom you'll meet again in chapter 9) opened the conference on a cool spring Friday evening, telling us that the medicine men and women of the Andes have known about Orbs for thousands of years. He explained that at the moment of physical death, all the information within our seven chakras – the metaphysical energy vortices in our bodies that act like a coupling device between this reality and others – downloads into an eighth chakra situated above our heads to become a nonphysical being – an Orb. In the moment he shared this truth, a light went on in my head and I knew that my decision to attend had been right.

As Bill Tiller told me, when you join a like-minded group, you amplify the 'coupling' effect. So it was in Sedona. Earlier that day I had spotted Professor Tiller and his wife, Jean, and had joined them for a quick chat. At that time, I was seriously considering making a film of my '98 experiences and had approached a few TV producers and filmmakers. Over breakfast I shared my ideas with Bill.

He told me that two days earlier a New York–based TV producer and his partner, who were making a film about the accelerating incidence of Spiritual Emergencies and the phenomena surrounding them, had interviewed Bill about his scientific conclusions. I jokingly replied, 'It's a pity I did not meet them, as I could have told them my story.' He promised to look for the couple's business cards upon returning home from the conference and to put me in touch. Thinking little more about his promise, I got on with my day.

The conference organizers had arranged for me to briefly meet Joan Ocean (her real name!), a psychologist whose life was transformed after an encounter with a whale in 1984 that led her, eventually, to work with Orbs as well. Joan is a very bubbly lady whose eyes sparkle with a joy at being alive. They lit up as I asked to know more about the whale incident.

'It was in 1984, when I was forty-four. At the time I was working in a very stressful environment, counselling women in an abortion clinic, and I desperately needed some peace and quiet. When a friend told me he was going on a camping trip on an island off British Columbia to watch whales for a month, the thought of being in nature sounded very appealing – even though I was afraid of water and could not swim – and I went along.'

One day when walking alone near the shoreline, Joan made eye contact with a lone female grey whale. 'I just stood there enthralled,' she recalled, 'and as I looked into the whale's eye, intense feelings of what I can only describe as pure love washed over me and filled me with peace.'

This incident inspired Joan to learn two important things: how to swim, and how to work with sound holography in order to study whales and dolphins. And over the years, as digital cameras became available, she started to notice Orbs on pictures taken near her subjects.

The following morning at her lecture, Joan shared slides showing near-transparent spheres of light – of many sizes, shapes and colours and in myriad locations – telling us that they were higher-dimensional beings existing on different frequencies and that their world would seem as real to them as ours is to us. Some may suggest that Orbs are either fakes or flukes, but Joan's examples were convincing – especially the pictures where an Orb was eclipsed by an object between it and the camera, which wouldn't happen if the Orb were just a speck on the lens.

Joan spoke of parallel universes, extraterrestrials and Bigfoot. To a person without a spiritual bent, her lecture would have sounded completely 'off the wall', yet she balanced her information with some interesting facts. I learned that digital technology is more sensitive to the near-infrared range of the visible spectrum than regular film cameras and that Orbs tend to show up predominantly in this spectrum. Again we were reminded that our physical eyes operate only within a very limited range of the electromagnetic spectrum – the visible-light spectrum – and that the infrared frequency realm is normally beyond our capacity to see, though some other animals, such as horses and dogs, can apparently see spectra of light that are invisible to us.

Digital technology converts normally invisible low-infrared light into a higher frequency of light and colour that *is* visible to human beings. It can also be used to heighten contrast and enhance the appearance of something that would otherwise be difficult to see. When photographed with older cameras, Orbs might not have been noticed even if they were actually present in the photo; with the new technology, we are able to see features that were previously invisible to us.

These days Joan works with groups who want to experience being with whales, dolphins and Orbs. You can find out more at www.joanocean.com.

At coffee time, along with 300 other people, I made my way to the exit to buy a drink, thinking that sceptics would have a field day with the whole Orb thing, yet I remained open-minded and keen to find out more. Out of the throng a young woman approached me, asking, 'May I speak with you?'

'About what'? I asked.

'Well, you have an interesting field,' she said. 'I was drawn to you.'

I was starting to think 'Cuckoo' ... as in One Flew Over The! 'So, what can I do for you?'

'My partner and I are making a film about intense spiritual awakenings ... '

The penny dropped. 'Was it you who filmed Bill Tiller a couple of days ago?'

'Yes, why?'

Presuming they had met Bill that morning and heard of my interest, I queried, 'Have you seen him today?'

She frowned, looking genuinely surprised. 'Is he at the conference?'

This was a surreal conversation. 'Why did you choose to speak to me, then?'

'My intuition, it's quite strong ... '

'Er, out of three hundred people?'

'Yes,' she replied.

Some intuition.

During the lunch break, the young woman, a TV producer, and her associate, a 30-something filmmaker, recorded me talking about my Spiritual Emergency on camera. The sceptics will dismiss this event, but it struck me as a pretty incredible 'coincidence'. The couple told me that they had decided to pop into the Orbs conference for a day at the last moment, as they were in the area. They assured me that Bill had not mentioned my name – they were simply hoping to find others who had interesting stories to tell.

Over the years I have met quite a few people who can, during quiet moments, retrieve extremely accurate information that is attached to the 'grid' that Bill Tiller described. Dr Deepak Chopra once told me how he had been keen to contact an old college friend, so he tuned in and a number came to him. And it was the right number. Once you are totally 'on line', I can assure you that any fact you need to know, you *can* know. It happened to me in '98. And the knowledge you have access to is neutral; it's what you do with it that counts! Most crucially, once you can intuit your way through your life by coupling with the magnetic information wave level that Bill spoke of so passionately in chapter 6, you are far more likely to end up in the right place at the right time. Listening to your 'inner voice' could save your life.

On 10 September 2001, I was definitely not listening to my inner voice. I was due to fly to New York to meet with Oprah Winfrey's colleague Gayle King, Oprah's close friend and the editor of O magazine, in the hope of persuading her to write about my spiritual experiences. It had taken six months of persistent phone calls to arrange that meeting.

Two days prior to my scheduled departure, I fell awkwardly and sprained my ankle, which left me in considerable pain and on crutches.

My wonderful husband suggested I should cancel my flight to the Big Apple. Was he crazy – after all my efforts?

Because my flight was due to leave London early on 10 September, I stayed in a hotel near the airport. Just before leaving the hotel, I made my way onto a small balcony for some air. The wind slammed the door shut behind me – and it would not open! I finally extricated myself after much shouting and banging, by which time my adrenaline was pumping – which, unless dispersed by exercise, causes one's blood to thicken, which in turn contributes to hardening of the arteries. It was definitely a time to practise some deep breathing. Thankfully, the kindly check-in lady at the airport arranged for me to be taken to a lounge, telling me that someone would collect me at the appropriate time. I began to calm down.

An hour or so later, when no-one materialized, I hobbled over to the information desk and was told that my flight had closed. Another adrenalin rush kicked in. 'How can that be?' I asked in none-too-polite tones. 'My luggage is on that plane!' Urgent calls were made and eventually I was taken to the aircraft – which was then delayed on the tarmac. And so the saga went on.

What would you have done?

The eleventh of September 2001 dawned a brilliant sunny day in New York as I carefully prepared for my important meeting. Within an hour the first of the Twin Towers was hit and events that had only minutes earlier seemed important suddenly became insignificant.

As Bill Tiller had reminded me time and again, the spirit world are always players in the game if they choose to be – and the more right things you do with the right motives, the more spirit is likely to assist the process. My motive for travelling to New York was based in ego. Even so, spirit did not abandon me. I ignored the signals – it's called free will. I wasn't listening. Most people don't even know that they need to listen.

Yet if I had been more 'coupled' – more coherent – then instead of being stranded for a week in a devastated city in mourning, I could have been at home. A powerful example of what Professor Tiller meant when he talked about our 'uncoupled' existence. Ninety-nine per cent of us remain in an uncoupled state. It's time to change. If we are to return to coherence, we need to listen more to the echoes of the eternal mind, which is always 'on line', and think less with our ego minds.

Back in Sedona, I was discovering just how 'on line' it was possible to be. The organizers of the conference, Robin and Cody Haines Johnson, had also arranged for me to interview physicist Dr Klaus Heinemann, who was due to speak on Sunday evening. Yet every time I called his room to arrange a chat, he was out. By Saturday afternoon I was becoming concerned that the interview might never happen. Silly me.

As I walked through the lobby late that afternoon, I once more bumped into Bill and Jean Tiller. When I told Bill about meeting the young filmmakers, even he was astonished, and believe me, it takes a lot to astonish Bill. Laughing, he said, 'You see, we are all here for the same purpose – we are creating a conditioned space. We have a strong collective heartfelt intention for the spirit world, including the Orbs, to join us, and they are obviously assisting in our endeavours.'

I joked that I was having problems meeting the elusive Dr Heinemann and perhaps the spirit world could help.

'Maybe they can,' said Bill, looking over my shoulder. 'If you turn around I'll introduce you.'

To my utter astonishment, walking in through the doors were Dr Klaus Heinemann and his wife, Gundi. My camera came out to record the moment for posterity (see plate 2) – and we decided there was no time like the present.

The German-born Heinemann is a retired experimental physicist who, like Tiller, spent years researching and teaching at Stanford. Heinemann studied surface physics, fluid dynamics, nanotechnology and electron microscopy; some of his work involved research into how various metals, such as those on the space shuttle, reacted in space and in other applications. He went on to form his own research company, now run by his son, which helps devise the space technology of the future for NASA.

How on earth had such a distinguished scientist become involved with Orbs? Over several cups of herbal tea, I found out.

'If anyone,' Klaus began, 'had predicted six years ago that I would become involved in research into what I believe are "other-worldly phenomena", as a sceptical physicist I would have reacted with flat-out disbelief. Yet today there is no doubt in my mind that Orbs may well be among the most significant "outside of this reality" phenomena mankind at large has ever witnessed.'

Well, he was certainly sticking his head above the parapet!

His fascination with Orbs began in 2004 when he and Gundi, an educator and energy healer, took photographs at a conference on energy medicine using digital cameras. When he uploaded the images onto his computer, Klaus discovered a clearly defined bright disk in one picture. Like most people, he assumed that the camera was faulty or that dust particles or stray light had caused the effect.

'I was sufficiently intrigued to return to the conference room to see if I could find any obvious explanation for the light sphere,' he told me. 'There was none. Gundi and I started taking hundreds of random pictures to see if the mysterious spheres might appear again, and to our astonishment they did. This prompted me to see if anyone else had reported similar phenomena. At that time there were only small amounts of information dating from the late '90s reporting light forms which were being called Orbs. Until that moment, an orb to me was just something like a halo in a Renaissance painting.'

'So, what happened next?'

'As a scientist used to working with sophisticated techniques such as electron spectroscopy – which can detect details down to the atomic level of optical resolution – I began examining my Orb pictures and found that the spheres had intricate geometric patterns inside, resembling computer circuit boards or mandalas, and that every interior was unique.

'More research was obviously needed. I was taught that to prove any theorem it must be verified through numerous reproducible, independently verifiable experiments. But when one gets to the borderline of our physical reality, the realms of subtle energy – sometimes called the paranormal – orthodox research methods often go out the window.'

For the umpteenth time, I was reminded that what we see with our physical eyes is only a minuscule fraction of what we term reality. I nodded politely as Klaus reiterated that radio waves carrying information into TVs or mobile phones exist, yet we cannot see them. I knew that well, and I understood that humans, animals and plants are transmitters and receivers of energy – which is information – in the same way.

I could sense Klaus's excitement about the Orb phenomenon as he continued. 'In the early days, we were quickly able to eliminate a host of likely causes, including the common problems associated with photography, as well as dust, water droplets, pollen and reflections of various kinds. Of course it would be easy to fake a few pictures, and I realize that stubborn sceptics may never be convinced, yet thousands of people are reporting similar phenomena on their digital pictures.'

And most of them, I had noted, seemed to be at the conference!

'Over time,' Klaus went on, 'I took hundreds of sequential pictures of the same Orb, under scientifically sound conditions, in rapid succession, and I demonstrated that they are capable of moving very fast, up to 500 miles per hour or more. They can also change size and orientation almost instantaneously. Most astonishingly, Gundi and I found that if you "ask" Orbs to appear, they definitely show up more often in your photos, especially at happy gatherings. Also, our analysis – far beyond what one can call random occurrence – shows that they appear to want to communicate by the *location* where they appear in photos. For instance, a woman in the UK whose eighteen-year-old son died in 2007 sent me pictures of her daughter's wedding day. These pictures clearly show a bright Orb close behind the bride. Like thousands of people who have seen Orbs in their pictures after losing a loved one, she believes that this was her son letting her know that he was there for his sister's very special day.'

'Are you saying, as a scientist,' I asked, 'that the Orbs are souls of people who have passed on?'

Klaus took his time in responding. 'Orb research is in its infancy and far more work needs to be done, but my working theory is that Orbs are indeed emanations from spirit beings. There has always been a huge body of anecdotal evidence that the spirit world exists, that consciousness survives physical death, but now, thanks to digital photo technology, we believe we are seeing it. The consensus from the scientists currently at work in this field is that the Orbs are nonphysical, albeit real, phenomena – they are plasma-like balls of subtle energy, but an energy that can now be detected by physical means. The implications for the way we view our world and physical death are enormous.' (*See* Klaus Heinemann's Orbs pictures – plates 4 and 5.)

As I listened to Klaus and recalled my out-of-body near-death experience yet again, perhaps, I reflected, we really do become Orbs .... For 12 years I have reported research demonstrating that consciousness survives physical death. Now it struck me that the tables are about to turn. The veils between this world and others are lifting, and I hope that within my lifetime, the onus to prove that our consciousness does *not* live on will be placed firmly back in the laps of the sceptics.

'So,' I continued, 'if these beings are indeed spirits of those who have passed on, are you saying they are intelligent?'

'I would say so, yes. After carrying out hundreds of dual-camera experiments in which I photographed the same Orb with two cameras from the same and varying locations and angles, I concluded that Orbs are conscious and have intelligence.'

With a growing sense of anticipation, I asked, 'Are Orbs loving, or might they be harmful to us? After all, there are good ghosts and downright bad ones. I have always thought that just as there are kind, loving people in life, those who are plain nasty or even evil surely don't change overnight when they move on to the spirit world.'

'Well,' said the scientist, 'first, let me tell you that the coloured "light" Orbs not only change size and shape very quickly, they also *emit* a specific type of light known as *coherent* light. Basically this means they emit laser-like light in very specific directions, which is possible only if they *choose* to do this. Now that we are able to "see" different frequencies, many realms that have been going about their business for eons are still doing so, but I do believe they are keen to interact with us. The coloured Orbs that *emit* light seem to be the "good guys"; they appear at happy gatherings and by the thousands at places of learning such as museums. From the growing body of evidence, I would say that some of them are indeed our loved ones who have moved on, as you asked. I have seen faces very clearly within the Orbs. They may also be souls of those waiting to be born, existing for the moment outside our space-time reality. Conversely, I have seen darker Orbs at the sites of supposed hauntings, but dark Orbs *absorb* rather than emit light. Globally there has been a huge increase in the incidence of light-emitting Orbs, whilst dark ones are pretty rare. What's more, I have never seen dark Orbs in the presence of their lighter counterparts, which leads me to conclude that dark spirits do not feel welcome near the light-emitting Orbs.'

As afternoon drifted into early evening, my grumbling stomach reminded me it needed nourishment, and I realized it had been such an exciting day that I had hardly eaten since breakfast. The food at our hotel was processed rubbish, virtually no fresh fruit or vegetables, let alone a decent cup of tea. Perhaps, I mused, spirit could conjure up a fabulous meal . . . .

Before I took my leave of Dr Heinemann, he showed me Orb pictures taken near the Brazilian healer John of God. Klaus is working on the theory that certain Orbs assist in psychic surgery – a procedure John of God is known for, in which a healer enters a trance and allows spirit guides to work through him or her, thus enabling the healer to 'operate' on patients. Although many psychic surgeons have been shown to be fakes, John of God has been widely studied by medical professionals and scientists alike.

The connection with Orbs made sense to me. If Orbs are indeed spirit beings, they would not be limited by our space-time domain, but operating from a frequency domain, and so would easily be able to permeate anything – including our energy fields and bodies. Individual Orbs entering one's energy field would also help explain spirit 'walk-ins', such as the one I experienced in 1998, and perhaps some cases of multiple personality disorder. More on this concept in chapter 12.

I still needed a decent meal. Happily, I had a congenial companion. When I had arrived from London on Thursday evening, I had met a spiritual teacher from Scotland, Dawn Flockhart, and we had taken to sitting together in the conference. She was great fun and invited me out for supper that night.

As we drove to the restaurant in town, which offered spectacular views over the red rocks, Dawn related some of the content of a fascinating lecture I had missed by Miceal Ledwith, a theologian whose insight I had admired in the hit film *What the Bleep Do We Know?* She was a bit envious that I had briefly met Ledwith earlier in the day and that I was due to interview him early the next morning. 'Now, there's a man you could talk to for hours,' Dawn said wistfully. 'A lot more to him than meets the eye. How I would love to meet him one to one.'

As we sat ordering our meal, Dawn's eyes widened in surprise. You have guessed: in through the door had walked Dr Ledwith. And because I had met him earlier, I was able to introduce him to Dawn.

No wonder I dubbed Sedona 'Superworld'. It was coming to the point that every wish we voiced was coming true within minutes. It was as if we had left what most people term 'this world' and entered another like Alice in Wonderland!

Miceal (pronounced *Mihaul*) Ledwith is a former professor of theology who for ten years was President of Maynooth College at the National University of Ireland. He was also a member of the International Commission at the Vatican, which advises the Pope on various theological issues. He had first heard about Orbs in 2002 when he visited the Ramtha spiritual school in the US as part of his research into the thousands of doctrines, beliefs and religions currently practised in the world. As we ate and relaxed, I asked him if Orbs could be some huge practical joke.

In his soft Irish lilt, Ledwith told us, 'My dears, in 1861 Dr Ignaz Semmelweis demonstrated that when physicians went from performing autopsies to delivering babies without washing their hands in between, there was a high rate of infant mortality. His mainstream colleagues ridiculed him, yet he had found the first evidence of what later became known as bacteria. Most great discoveries throughout history were ridiculed at first.

To my mind, there is no doubt that the Orb phenomenon is real and deserves to be taken seriously. There are not just a few pictures of Orbs – those could easily be faked – but thousands upon thousands from all over the world. In fact, I have the largest private collection in the world, over a hundred thousand pictures.'

We chatted about the dozens of opinions voiced on Orbs and how some of the attendees claimed to be communicating telepathically with them, whilst others categorically stated they had seen the unique faces of their loved ones within specific spheres.

'There is no validation in science as yet for such claims,' Ledwith cautioned. 'To say the Orbs are only spirits of the deceased is an oversimplification. I believe they could be many things. Indeed, they may turn out to be the spirits of those who have passed on; or, as some spiritual teachers state, they might be spirits waiting to be born into a physical body. They may also be, or represent, a host of other intelligences, from nature spirits to beings of pure energy that have never incarnated in a physical form. There are literally hundreds of types of Orbs, which at times have even been seen forming vortex-like structures.' (*See* plate 5.)

And what about their purpose? Ledwith commented that audiences regularly ask him, 'What are the Orbs here to do for us?' – an egocentric question, in his opinion. Over the best homemade apple pie I have ever tasted, he told us, 'The Orbs have always been here and are an everyday part of reality as much as we are. Their world may be as real as ours; it simply exists on different frequencies. If you change your TV channel, you switch to different frequencies, which contain different information. It's illogical to think that what we cannot see is not real. For too long we have tended to dismiss anything we cannot see as paranormal – ghostly –which is absurd.'

I could not have agreed more. Dawn had said that Ledwith was a man you could talk to all day, and I wished we had more time to delve into that mine of information. I would get my chance a year later, when we met again in Wells in the UK and he shared some of the astonishing misinterpretations he has uncovered in various holy books during 35 years of academic research. Riveting stuff – and you can read it in chapter 14.

The following morning, the organizers invited attendees to share any pictures taken during the conference that showed Orbs. There were hundreds, including virtually every picture that Dawn had taken. In the months following this conference I was to meet a host of people who had photographed Orbs, many after losing a child or a partner, and in every case the Orbs' appearance gave them comfort. The following year in Glastonbury I was to see them with my own eyes.

So what do Orbs have to do with our journey to coherence? For starters, as Klaus Heinemann explained, the majority of Orbs emit 'coherent' light. Furthermore, an enormous body of evidence indicates that some of our loved ones who have passed on are more coherent than most of us here are. As Bill Tiller stated, this coarse physical reality is at a point of minimal coherence. When we lose our physical shell, depending on our level of consciousness, we become somewhat more coherent, and as our consciousness evolves it 'climbs' ever higher up the ladder back towards home. Orbs represent levels of consciousness that we can now 'see' – good evidence of higher-dimensional realities.

If you would like to know more about Orbs, I suggest you read Dr Ledwith and Dr Heinemann's fascinating book *The Orb Project*. You can also visit Dr Miceal Ledwith's website at www.hamburgeruniverse.com (Miceal has also made a DVD about his Orb experiences) and Dr Klaus Heinemann's site at www.acviews.com/kh/klaus.htm.

So many synchronicities have occurred in the writing of this book – those you've read about in this chapter are just a few – that I have been left in no doubt that the universe has an underlying intelligence. Something, somewhere, has wanted me to experience that intelligence at work. As enlightened men and women have told me over the years, it's one thing to talk about something but quite another to *experience* it.

Now prepare to understand the scope of what that 'something, somewhere' truly is . . .

Chapter Eight

Infinity and Beyond

The reason people who have near-death experiences 'see the light' is because they are able to see more of the light that is always and has always been there. Everything in the universe is glowing all the time. Darkness is an illusion – death is an illusion. This is a huge take-home message.

– **Professor Gary E Schwartz**

2007 and 2009 – Tucson, Arizona

IF YOU ARE READING THESE WORDS, you are without a doubt some way along your spiritual path – and I wonder if by now you may have changed your views on survival of consciousness after reading about the Orbs. And who or what do you consider God to be? Perhaps some kind of supercomputer being run by E.T. that 'projects' what we think of as our reality, or perhaps a bearded man residing in Heaven? Or are you like myself and Tiller, who think that we are not yet sufficiently conscious to even speculate as to what God really is?

As I have already mentioned, several highly accredited scientists, including Bernard Carr, professor of mathematics and astronomy at Queen Mary University of London, state that any mechanism that can produce one universe is likely to generate other universes, and there are several theories being openly discussed and researched in mainstream science on multiverses. As this debate unfolds, Professor Nick Bostrum, head of the Department of Philosophy at Oxford University, has published a scientific paper entitled 'Are You Living in a Computer Simulation?' He writes: 'At our current stage of technological development, we have neither sufficiently powerful hardware nor the requisite software to create conscious minds in computers. But persuasive arguments have been given to the effect that *if* technological progress continues unabated *then* these shortcomings will eventually be overcome.'

Even open-minded folk such as myself find it incredible to think that one day an artificial 'mind' could be constructed capable of creating worlds such as ours. Yet on the shores of Lake Geneva, neuroscientist Professor Henry Markram at the Brain Mind Institute of the École Polytechnique Fédérale de Lausanne is using a huge parallel computer known as Blue Gene to construct a functioning structure similar to our cerebral cortex – the grey matter that makes up 80 per cent of the brain and is responsible for our ability to think, reflect, communicate and plan – *inside* a computer. Markram says that the our brains can outperform, by a factor of a million or more, any current known computer – so his Blue Brain Project is building a billion-dollar machine in an attempt to recreate a sentient, conscious mind. By 2015 he and his team aim to have a functioning partial 'mind' ready for use in medical research.

Makes you think, doesn't it? Yet if we begin to consider that we are part of God and all parts make the Whole, then as we grow in coherence why should we not become co-creators? It's our birthright.

During my investigations for this book, I enjoyed a number of thought-provoking discussions on this issue – as well as questions such as whether consciousness survives physical death and how it's possible to store information within inanimate objects – with my old friend Gary Schwartz. Gary, a Harvard-trained scientist, a former professor at Yale, and the author of five books, is currently professor of psychology, neurology and psychiatry at the University of Arizona. We met in October 2003 in Tucson when I took part in Gary's Afterlife Experiments, in which he used highly trained mediums to access specific information from various 'deceased' people – the accuracy of which was verified time after time after time. In total, he and his team have carried out more than 1,400 such trials under ever more stringently controlled conditions.

When I had first contacted him in the summer of 2003 claiming that I had been 'possessed' for some months by a high-profile woman who was tragically killed in August 1997, he was dubious, and rightly so. Yet after reading my story in my book *Divine Intervention* he had finally agreed to test my claims using scientific protocols. The experiments, documented in my book *The Evidence for the Sixth Sense,* were so successful that Gary went on to write the foreword for that book.

During my visits to Tucson, I was lucky to stay at the luxurious Ventana Canyon Resort, where, enjoying yet another all-American breakfast in May 2009, I shared with Gary my ideas for this book and the questions I raised at the start of this chapter. I reminded him that he had once compared God to an ultimate mind, as being in the deepest sense like a supercomputer, and I asked him to expand.

'Well, I would need to begin by defining certain qualities of such a hypothetical "mind",' he said. 'Firstly, such a mind would have to be "big enough" to encompass all that we mean by the concept of the infinite. I don't mean just physically big. It would have to be big enough conceptually to encompass what we mean by the infinite, which includes an infinite number of infinites. And this quality of mind would also need to be big enough not merely to exist in space and time, but to *transcend* space and time, and even to have been "big enough" to have *created* space and time!

'This mind would also have to be big enough to encompass everything that we have learned about the evolution of the universe. This mind must encompass what we mean by "holographic in nature", in that you need to imagine infinite complexity simultaneously being present everywhere – which is why I use the metaphor of a supercomputer, or parallel processor, as many scientists do, including Nick Bostrum and astrobiologist Paul Davies at Arizona State University.'

I was frowning to try to understand the complexity of what Gary was telling me. Realizing that I was no computer buff, he smiled. 'Let's make this easier. Imagine that you have an orchestra with an infinite number of musicians; you have an infinite number of players and instruments, and all of these instruments are simultaneously playing their unique melodies and harmonies. How does this gigantic orchestra ever play as an organized whole?'

'With a good conductor,' I suggested.

'Exactly. It needs some sort of central organizing process that can convey signals that can reach each and every one of this infinite number of musicians and facilitate their capacity to play in harmony. And not only do you need a conductor who reflects that level of infinite coordination, but you also have to have a composer sophisticated enough to create all these melodies and harmonies. This is why I refer to God as the Guiding Organizing Designer.

'Another quality of this mind is that it would have to be based on what we know – infinite compassion and infinite caring – to the point that it could give us every level of such abilities to various degrees, plus relative flexibility or freedom, within certain bounds, to be able to make "our own" choices. I put "our own" in quotes, because every choice that we make is within boundaries. In the physical body, for example, we can choose whether we want to breathe on a given breath, but unless we are fully coherent, fully enlightened at every level, we don't have a choice about whether we stop breathing for an hour. We exercise *relative* choice, upon which the system then takes over. We can choose to eat or not to eat certain foods on a moment-to-moment basis, but our short-term or long-term health can be dictated not by what we want, but ultimately by how the system is designed and by its limitations. At every level we are given the choice to either optimize what we have or minimize it.'

As Gary said these words, I was sitting in the sunshine eating a buckwheat pancake with fresh blueberries – and was on the verge of adding maple syrup. Yet when he spoke of 'choice' and of 'optimizing', I thought it better to give the sugary syrup a miss for the sake of my bio-bodysuit.

Gary's lecture continued. 'And, if Mind has "infinite" energy, that is just what it is – it is that which can create infinite everything, including manifesting all the energy and matter in our universe, which is, relatively speaking, trivial, because It has infinite capability.'

'But surely,' I proposed, 'any such mind or "supercomputer" must be enormous beyond our capability to imagine it?'

'Big and small are relative terms. Until you have a thing with particular dimensions, it has no "thing-ness", so it is neither small nor huge. Size only makes sense in the context of space and time. Let me repeat a phrase I use often with my students: the All is in the small and the small is in the All. Why am I reiterating this now?'

I shrugged – then thought about it and announced, 'Because we are part of this huge infinite supercomputer-like mind, which means that *we* are like biological computers.'

'*Now* you are starting to get it,' Gary said, smiling broadly. 'We'll come back to the biological computers in a moment, but first I need to quickly mention the "observer effect". In quantum physics, scientists have demonstrated that quantum particles – minuscule particles of matter – do not come into existence until they are *observed*.'

I had long ago read about these experiments, which I had problems getting my head around. Leading-edge scientists now state that the transition from potentiality to wave function, to the manifestation of the particle (matter), which they had previously termed the 'collapse' of the wave function, is in reality not a collapse at all; instead, the wave function appears to become *coherent* through the process of observation. In simple terms, scientists have found that *it's the observation itself* that brings something into reality, which we can then experience.

Keeping these findings in mind, I argued, 'But Mount Everest was there long before I was born, and all the people around the world are as we speak seeing lots of different things that I'm not seeing.'

'Absolutely correct,' Gary agreed. 'But if, as quantum physics dictates, that observation is required before *anything* can come into existence – where does the observation come from?'

'Your super parallel computer – God.'

'And that's the crux of everything. It could be the *most profound* thing that people can ever read and truly get their heads around.'

I waited ...

'*If* the infinite mind is like a parallel processing computer and *if* it is infinitely conscious – this means that *it* is simultaneously observing *everything*. This is a metaphor, but, I repeat, if our universe and everything in it is being sustained by observation – then it would have to be *the continuous observation of an infinite and conscious mind*.'

When Gary first made this statement, I did not fully register the implications of his words, but once the tapes had been typed up and I read his words again, they leapt out at me. You too may be asking, 'What's the big deal?' I'll tell you what the big deal is. Most people on a spiritual path have long realized that we are all part of God and all parts make the Whole – but how many of us have truly understood, let alone experienced, that we are existing *inside* an infinite mind? An infinite mind that encompasses multiple levels of reality, of consciousness and of coherence. God's house does indeed have many mansions.

Make yourself a cup of tea, walk in a garden, look at the sky, the animals, the trees; think of the Orbs, the spirit world and other realms going about their business. Think of the planets, the sheer vastness of this physical universe, and consider that you are living *inside* what even the great theoretical physicist Stephen Hawking describes as a 'bubble' formed over eons of physical time, after an indeterminate amount of energy 'escaped' by exploding from a black hole. When you consider such possibilities, it seems we are indeed akin to seven billion holograms of the Whole. Yet we are real. Everything is a paradox.

What is crucial here – the take-home message, as Gary would say – is that we exist *inside* God. Consciousness is everywhere, at every level. It's inside and outside everything. When you speak ill of someone, at an ultimate level you are speaking of yourself. When you forgive someone, at an ultimate level you are forgiving yourself.

The 'enlightened beings' Arten and Pursah that author Gary Renard claims to communicate with state, 'Nothing is real but God.' Ultimately, they are right: there is no 'you and me', only the Ultimate I. But imagine making such statements to fanatics or fundamentalists – or indeed to the many people in the world who have not yet given spirituality a thought! When I mentioned this to Professor Schwartz, he cautioned, 'This return to coherence, which your book is all about, is a possibility for *some* of our futures, but you only have to watch the daily news to realize how much mass consciousness still needs to be raised. I have told you before that if we all became even partially enlightened at once and started experimenting with what we could materialize, there would be total and utter chaos.

'If we want this coherence,' Gary continued, 'and this access to infinite intelligence and power, then we first need to learn infinite responsibility and wisdom. And infinite wisdom includes not doing everything all at once and not being selfish. Infinite wisdom and infinite compassion are about caring for everything and everyone simultaneously. We all have the capacity to pursue our dreams with relative freedom – but no-one should wish to wake up tomorrow as a fully enlightened being unless he or she is mature enough *at all levels*.'

After what I went through in 1998, and thinking of all the people I have met and interviewed who have gone through, or are going through, their own unique spiritual awakenings, I totally agreed with Gary's heartfelt sentiments.

Finally we returned to the concept of biological computers. 'The body is a tool of the mind,' Gary explained. 'Our down-to-earth ego mind, plus the Guiding Organizing Designing mind. As Tiller calls it, this "bio-bodysuit" that we need in order to interact with this physical reality is like an outrageously complex supercomputer itself. It has trillions of cells which are engaged in very complex computations. And these trillions of cells communicate via photons of light – as does everything in our universe – but not visible light. The Big Bang birthed both visible and invisible (to us) spectra of light. If you could truly "see" all the spectra, you would see that everything in our world and our universe is glowing – you would be blinded by the light. There is no darkness; it's an illusion. For instance, what happens to starlight during the day?'

There was no time for me to comment, as Gary answered his own question. 'Has it disappeared? Of course not – the sun's light is just so much brighter than the starlight. Same when we physically "die" – we no longer have our bio-bodysuit, but our light, our field of information, remains. Just because most people can't see that light doesn't mean it's not there. Same if you amputate someone's leg or arm – its field of information remains in place for some time before dispersing, and this is part of the reason why some amputees suffer "phantom pain". Same if you receive someone's heart, liver, lungs or whatever – you are receiving a field of information. This is why many transplant patients start exhibiting the traits and memories of the people whose organs they receive. They receive a group of cells, made up of molecules, which are made up of atoms – which are made up of energy and information. Frequencies.'

This rang a bell with me. Biophysicist Dr Harry Oldfield, whom you may remember from chapter 6, has over the years shown me dozens of his PIP scans – images of people's energy fields – which clearly demonstrate Gary's point, such as a scan of a subject with an amputated arm that shows a clearly defined field in the shape of the missing limb (*see* plate 8A). I even have a PIP scan film from Dr Oldfield that clearly shows our chakras as whirling vortices of energy and the kundalini energy channel emanating from our base chakras (even in animals). Oldfield has demonstrated that light enters our energy field from our environment, interacts with our fields on a subtle level and bounces back out into the environment again. As he once joked with me, 'Pain does not stop at your skin, and neither do your thoughts.' He has also shown me scans of ghostlike figures, which underline another point Gary has often made: even though we vacate our physical bodies when we 'die', our energy and information goes on. Discover more information about Harry Oldfield at www.electrocrystal.com.

Another chat with Gary in Arizona had taken up this very point from a different angle as we talked about his research into psychometry, in which highly sensitive mediums 'pick up' information from personal objects such as watches – and even from structures such as Stonehenge and the Pyramids. 'How was this possible?', I asked.

'Let's start with an analogy,' Gary said. 'You turn on your central heating and you set the thermostat. When the temperature drops, the thermostat tells the heating to switch on, and once the required temperature is reached, the heating switches off again. This is what you would call a feedback loop.

'Now let's go back to atoms, which are the fundamental building blocks of our universe. Everything that exists in our physical universe functions as a system composed of two or more parts that share information and energy. Within an atom you have electrons, which look like a "cloud" in the centre of which is a nucleus. Electrons "pull" on the nucleus and the nucleus pulls on the electrons, which means you have a feedback loop. In scientific terms there are many more components to this whole scenario, but in essence it means that a "system" is a whole composed of parts. So I'm a system composed of organs – I am a whole composed of parts – and you are a system, a whole composed of parts. But you and I are also simultaneously part of a larger system. We are friends; you send me information and I send it back. We form a feedback loop.'

This all made a fair amount of sense.

'Getting back to your question,' Gary continued, 'when you have any system at any level – whether it's a subatomic particle, a nucleus, an atom, a molecule, a cell, an organ, an organism, people, the earth, the solar system, a galaxy, it doesn't matter what level you are looking at – it is a system and it has circulating feedback. To put it another way, it has memory.'

'So,' I mused, 'what you are saying is that atoms, which make up everything – us, the Pyramids, everything – are storing information? Atoms have memory?'

'Yes – what stores memory is feedback, and everything that exists has feedback. In addition, at every level – within the nucleus of the atom and also at the vacuum level, the so-called empty space within every atom – feedback operates. What goes around *stays* around and *evolves* around. In practically every spiritual book you read, the author will tell you that you could have atoms within you now that might once have made up Jesus or a road sweeper or whomever.'

'The trick, I presume, is to become so sensitive, so coherent, that you are able to retrieve the information held within the atoms?'

'Absolutely,' said Gary.

'But,' I pressed, 'are we exchanging actual atoms with a pyramid or a watch, for instance – as our bodies are renewing themselves all the time?'

Gary shook his head. 'You are sitting on a chair, but you are not exchanging actual atoms with the chair. Most of the communication involves sharing the energy and information being emitted by the atoms in the chair and in you, not sharing atoms themselves.'

'Yet you just said that atoms that were once in Jesus or whoever could now be in this very room or even be in our bodies,' I argued.

'We exchange atoms with our environment through oxygen,' Gary explained. 'We are constantly breathing in oxygen and breathing out carbon dioxide. I am now breathing in what you have just breathed out; we are not necessarily exchanging atoms, but we are exchanging energy and information, the heart or essence of feedback. But yes, we can and do exchange some atoms.'

'And what about the atoms in the watch or the pyramid?'

'Solid structures are more stable than we are. We are not made of stone; their atoms generally stay where they are. When you are near a pyramid or a standing stone or holding someone else's watch, then generally what you are exchanging is energy and information, because such structures act like tuning forks. Everything is vibrating, every atom is extending energy and information into space and every atom is receiving energy and information.'

'So you are stating that it's possible to "implant" information into stone, crystals or whatever, which could potentially remain in place for thousands of years?'

Gary smiled knowingly. 'Yes, this is one potential. Lots of things could happen, and if you want to spend a few months in my classes I'll go through them one by one!'

Though I could have listened to Gary for days, I didn't have time to go into quite *that* much depth ... But I was keen to ask him more about his work, which is revealing evidence for the survival of consciousness – a subject near to my heart from my experience in 1998, which was what had first brought Gary and me together in 2003 when he put my story to the test. He recalled the details, some of which he recounted in the foreword he wrote for *The Evidence for the Sixth Sense*.

'For those controlled experiments I invited two highly experienced mediums, Allison Dubois (the TV series *Medium* was based on Allison's abilities) and Laurie Campbell, to meet a stranger (Hazel) and to see "who" they might independently receive information from in the spirit world. Remember, the individual spirit can choose whether to communicate or not, it can choose whether to be truthful or not, and we have also had instances in which a "spirit" claims to be a specific soul – but we have later discovered is an impersonator. Finding the truth is not always easy.

'Anyway, for Hazel's experiments neither medium knew which country the sitter (Hazel) would be coming from, nor did they know her gender, her name or age. And when they met separately, Hazel was forbidden to utter a word, nor use any facial expressions. The readings were filmed and the evidence from those readings was surprising, highly emotional, very specific and extremely convincing. From my perspective – as a sceptical scientist – the readings in October 2003 were jaw-dropping in their accuracy.'

Gary and his team have done a great deal of exciting research into survival of consciousness. I took advantage of this opportunity to ask him again if he truly believes that our consciousness survives physical death.

'Well, I would have to say if you look at the totality of the evidence from a host of sources – including my laboratory at the University of Arizona, plus the Division of Perceptual Studies in the Department of Psychiatry at the University of Virginia, and the independent Windbridge Institute here in Tucson – then I would say it is not just beyond reasonable doubt, it is *far* beyond reasonable doubt.'

'And are you personally convinced that all sentient life, including animals, survives physical death – that consciousness is primary?'

His reply was exactly what I wanted to hear. 'Yes, I do, and I go further by reiterating it's now the turn of the sceptics to prove that consciousness does *not* go on. After all, for over a decade we have been receiving, via highly trained mediums, unique information and evidence under ever more stringent conditions that is regularly seventy to ninety per cent accurate.'

And the evidence they had received while investigating my case supported what I believed – that the spirit I was in contact with in 1998 was Princess Diana. During several controlled experiments with Gary, all the mediums involved independently brought through messages for me from Diana – whom I had met several times before she died in August '97, which gave me some verification for my experience. I hope that mentioning her name will not destroy my credibility in your eyes. My interlude with the spirit of Diana almost cost me my life; I paid a huge price in my health and for some time lost credibility as a serious journalist. Yet early on in my experience, I realized that the spirit of Diana and others before her had agreed to act as spiritual spokespersons for a time – as they are determined to demonstrate that we do indeed live on, and a famous 'voice' is more likely to be heard.

Even today, although I no longer even attempt to 'hear' Diana, I recall 'her' words in my head during 1998 advising me to practise unconditional forgiveness just as Gary Renard recommends in his books. Her spirit also reminded me that too many people are 'held back' by the burden of guilt, and that if we want to be at peace, then we need to let go of guilt – another concept that Renard advocates.

And when I had argued with Renard back in Stockholm that such teachings might tempt one person to harm another without the need to feel any guilt, he had agreed, saying, 'Sure – and many people do kill without remorse of any kind. But most people on a true spiritual journey are not into violence. They want to live in peace with themselves and others; they understand that what goes around comes around. And if we can all join together as one mind by using true forgiveness and letting go of guilt, then our consciousness will merge back into the Whole Mind from which we "think" we have separated.'

Gary Schwartz, meanwhile, had told me that when we 'die' and shed our physical bodies, the trillions of atoms that make up our bodies go on to become part of a plant, an animal, a rock or another human being. We do indeed, quite literally, merge back into the Whole.

For the moment, please consider the trillions of atoms that make up your body and your surroundings right now – which are *all* exchanging energy and information and have been doing so since the beginning of time. *All that knowledge is within you.* The All is in the small and the small is in the All. Sure makes you think, doesn't it? Meanwhile, you will read more of Gary Schwartz's wisdom in chapter 11. For more information on his ongoing research, visit www.drgaryschwartz.com or read his books, including *The Afterlife Experiments, The G.O.D Experiments* and *The Energy Healing Experiments.*

Chapter Nine

The Shaman, Scientist and Shape-Shifter

Having the courage to dream means following your calling today, in some way, despite the facts in your life that seem to be unmovable obstacles. And then, if your canvas is unfinished at the moment you die, at least you'll have died an artist instead of a dabbler who talks about how she or he would truly like to live.

– Alberto Villoldo PhD

Late April 2009 – The Mandarin Oriental Hotel, Hyde Park, London

To hear another fascinating perspective on who we truly are, where we are going, and how our journey back to coherence will unfold, I arranged to meet an enlightened shaman who's also an accredited scientist. After 25 years of research, Alberto Villoldo has gathered an encyclopaedic knowledge of ancient rituals, including healing, altered states, shape-shifting, kundalini awakening, the effects of mind-altering plants, possession, spirit guides and Orbs – which he now shares through his worldwide lectures and his organization, The Four Winds Society, which he founded in 1984 to bring the ancient knowledge to others.

Here is a man who not only understands the science of miracles but has also experienced them firsthand from some of the world's most powerful shamans and medicine men and women. We had first met very briefly at the Orbs conference back in 2007 and I had always felt that we were destined to meet again. And I was right.

We had agreed to meet in The Park, a restaurant in the heart of London's fashionable Knightsbridge that overlooks the unfolding seasonal grandeur of Hyde Park. The room was almost deserted apart from a small party of Japanese tourists enjoying the ritual of an English afternoon tea. My guest was nowhere to be seen, which gave me an opportunity to reread my notes and marvel at the breadth of knowledge within the man I was about to meet.

Alberto Villoldo PhD was born in Cuba, studied psychology in California and went on to earn a doctorate in medical anthropology. As the youngest clinical professor at San Francisco State University, in 1982, he founded the Biological Self-Regulation Lab, which studied how energy medicine and the power of the mind could alter brain chemistry. He and his colleagues found that we are capable of increasing production of endorphins – natural brain chemicals that reduce pain and create ecstatic states – by almost 50 per cent utilizing the techniques of energy healing.

'Then one day,' he writes on his website, 'I realized that the microscope was the wrong instrument to answer the questions I was asking.' Anthropological stories hinted that there were people around the globe, including the Inka descendants in Peru, who could effect what we in the West would term miracles. What they claimed to know, he wanted to learn as well.

Much to the astonishment of his scientific colleagues, Villoldo resigned his promising career and went to study among healers and shamans in the jungles of South America. He spent almost ten years in the Amazon, training in ancient shamanic traditions, before travelling extensively in Peru, from the Andes to the site of the Nazca lines and on to the fabled Shimbe lagoons, home to some of the world's most renowned sorcerers.

'I discovered a set of ancient technologies that had been lost to the Western world,' his notes continue. 'These people knew five thousand years ago about our luminous energy field (LEF), commonly known as the auric field, whose source is in infinity. They knew that the LEF is a matrix that contains the body's blueprint, not only of the physical body but also of our emotional and spiritual destinies.'

By now it was past the time we'd arranged to meet. I checked my watch and looked around the restaurant, wondering if he might have been delayed by the ever-present London traffic. Much to my astonishment, when I looked once more, there was the Professor sitting quietly working on his computer.

'Have you been here long?' I enquired, wondering how he could have appeared without my noticing, concerned he might think *I* was late for our appointment.

'Oh, an hour or so,' he said. 'It's given me time to do some work.'

How could this be? I had looked carefully around the restaurant 15 minutes earlier, yet apart from the Japanese family I had seen no-one.

The Professor simply smiled knowingly.

We ordered a light meal, as Villoldo was going on to give an evening lecture immediately after our meeting. Time was limited, so I began by asking if any of this 5,000-year-old knowledge had been recorded.

'Mainly it's been passed down orally through generations of shamans and sages,' he replied. 'But it was also recorded in carvings, textiles, cave paintings and so on and is far more ancient than most people realize. Some is prophetical, before humans, before linear time began.'

I thought of what Bill Tiller had told me only three weeks earlier in Arizona, of nonphysical societies that existed before our physical world was even birthed. 'So, do you believe that we are returning to nonphysical states of being?'

'Yes, I do. We are gradually evolving from *Homo sapiens* into *Homo "luminous"* beings. It will take time, but already there are growing numbers of people who can "read" an individual's luminous energy field, or LEF. Science and the public are finally getting the message that we are far more than simply transient physical bodies.'

I presumed Villoldo could read anyone's energy field – and probably, as I once had, their thoughts too. It had been amazing to be able to compare what came out of people's mouths to what they were actually thinking. As we shared some mango tea, I made a mental note to be careful with my thoughts.

'A good shaman,' continued my guest, 'can interpret your LEF, which is a field of electromagnetic information encoded into your energy field as a holographic image. Based on the principle of like attracting like on a frequency level, this determines which types of people you will meet, whom you will marry, the work you will do and how you are likely to die.'

'In other words,' I interjected, 'shamans like yourself are super-psychic in that you can see and hear more frequencies than the rest of us?'

'That's part of it, and keep in mind that highly experienced shamans and sages have had years of training. The LEF is the software, an information field; DNA is the hardware. And the shaman' – he pronounces it *sharman* with his gentle accent – 'understands that we manifest our reality via four different levels: the level of the body, the level of mind, the level of soul and the level of spirit. For instance, at a spirit level there is truly only one of us in this room, but there are several distinctly different souls in very different bodies.'

I knew he was reading my field when he asked, 'Would you have chosen to marry your first husband knowing what you know now?'

His question made me sit up sharply. Over the years I have met numerous fascinating teachers – yet even now, it's one thing to be *told* about their knowledge and quite another to *experience* it on a personal level!

He smiled. 'All the information about you,' he said, 'everything from your past to your health, who you are and your current level of consciousness, is encoded in your LEF. Old patterns leave an imprint, and if you want to change your probable futures or behaviour patterns that are not serving you, this needs to be done at the matrix level.'

Thinking about several of my behaviour patterns that definitely need changing, I asked tentatively, 'Do you know how I am going to die? Many spiritual teachers state that our physical death date is set in stone and that we "choose" the circumstances of our death before incarnating, whilst a few enlightened men and women have told me the date of one's ego death – at the moment of enlightenment – is set, but not necessarily one's physical death. And we know now that on a physical level, even the likely results of inherited genetic weaknesses can often be changed if we live a different life to that of our parents and grandparents.'

Alberto listened patiently to my lengthy question. 'I believe that our death date is not set in stone,' he replied thoughtfully, 'but the circumstances of our death are preordained in *probability*.'

'Even a car crash?' I countered.

'A person may have been very angry or tired and taken his or her mind off the road. The car crash is simply a detail resulting from this – but when and if you become more conscious, you can then clear such a potential future from your LEF and it doesn't have to happen.'

Just as I wrote in chapter 4 – if I had been more 'conscious', more spiritually advanced, when I fell so badly on my back in 2007, I would not have been in any hurry and therefore I would not have fallen!

Alberto added, 'If you are more "conscious", more connected, then I believe you will always be at the best place at the right time. Conversely, if you're not "conscious", you may often feel that you're in the wrong place at the wrong time.'

After what happened to me en route to New York before 9/11, I could not have agreed more!

'It's important to realize that most decisions are made unconsciously,' he went on. 'But if, for instance, you were born with a genetic predisposition to heart disease, which killed your father and grandfather, you can change the outcome in *your* life by consciously changing many of your habits. No-one is necessarily doomed to a specific genetic karma.'

Again I was amazed. Even if he had read my books, he might have known how my father died – at 50 of a heart attack – but I have never mentioned my grandfather.

His words reminded me of just how often we make choices that we know full well are not the healthiest or wisest, like eating too much saturated fat or smoking – yet we do it anyway. I don't smoke, but I love homemade cakes. And after years as a health writer I'm fully aware of how stress can thicken the blood and make it more acid, which contributes to hardening of the arteries – thus increasing the risk for heart attacks, strokes, and inflammatory conditions like arthritis – yet being a typical Type A person, I'm always on the run. Yes, I meditate, but not often enough. Yes, I eat plenty of healthy food and take regular exercise, but I also enjoy treats, sometimes more than I know is sensible. And Alberto was gently nudging me towards an even healthier potential future – based upon the imprints in my energy field. There was obviously little that I could hide from this man.

He seemed to sense my thoughts as he continued. 'Shamans can travel along timelines, both forwards and backwards in time, which is not linear like an arrow, as most people think it is. They understand how and why people are the way they are; they can see probable outcomes and then help people – if they choose to – change potential negative scenarios.

'But,' he warned, 'for a person to choose an alternate destiny line can be hard, as it can, depending on the person's circumstances, mean changing up to ninety-eight per cent of one's habits and way of life. It can be done, but a person would need to be very committed and disciplined to do it.'

'What about someone like the teacher Ram Dass, who has suffered hugely in his physical body from strokes and intense pain – why would he not have created another reality?'

'Because,' Alberto replied emphatically, as if he had heard similar questions many times, 'Ram Dass does not consider healing primarily at the level of the physical, but at the level of spirit – and at that level he is completely healed. Everyone needs to think on multiple levels, not only the physical, but also the emotional, mental, soul and spirit levels.

'Shamans are men and women who mediate between the visible and the invisible world,' he went on. 'Your choices prior to your experience in 1998 were made unconsciously, for once people become more conscious of why they do what they do, they can *consciously* choose to change old imprints in their LEF and create a new reality or timeline. I teach people how to dream a new life and way of being into this physical world. And if you don't dream or realize that you can be a creator, then you have to settle for the dreams that are created by the media or your karma. As Oscar Wilde said, "Action is the last resource of those who know not how to dream."'

'You talk of altering the imprints on the matrix, and so is what you term the matrix part of God?'

'The concept of an all-seeing man sitting in Heaven, looking down on us, is a Western notion of God which doesn't exist in the indigenous traditions. Indigenous peoples have recognized and celebrated the forces of nature, personified them and worshipped them, but they view the conscious creation itself as a macroorganism, and in its *entirety* it is what we call the Creator.

'The matrix is really the invisible fabric of creation, the unmanifest from which everything is born, so the matrix is both the acorn and the oak tree and the idea of an acorn and the idea of an oak tree.'

'So, from your perspective as a shaman, what happens to the luminous energy field when we "die" in physical terms?'

'We have an eighth chakra situated above our physical bodies but inside our luminous energy field,' he explained. 'This eighth chakra is our soul. When we die, all of our other chakras download their information into the eighth chakra, and in the majority of cases we are drawn towards the frequency of existence and reality that suits the level of consciousness we have attained during that lifetime.'

This, I remembered, was what Villoldo had told us when I first heard him speak in Sedona – that the eighth chakra might appear as an Orb!

'Then when the time is right, our spirit heads towards the families that offer the greatest learning, and the information within the eighth chakra is downloaded into a new body and we are born again.'

'And who decides where and as whom we incarnate again?' I enquired.

In answer the shaman looked me straight in the eye and said, '*You* do, of course. Whatever your recent experiences have been – not necessarily your immediate last life, but the most vivid experiences and memories that you have – they propel you towards the parents who can continue those lessons. But it's crucial to realize that once you become totally coherent, totally enlightened, then you can "individuate" and thus become truly immortal. At such a point, you would not necessarily need to reincarnate; rather, you could consciously choose whether and how to return.'

When I had first heard Alberto speak in Sedona, he had shown us an amazing picture of a large Orb, saying it was a group soul. Wistfully I recalled my near death over Easter of 1998, when I felt as free as a bird, looking down at my shrivelled body below me. I was still 'me' – but had I become something like that radiant sphere? Now I had my chance to ask. 'Had I truly in that moment of physical death become an Orb?'

'Orbs, as you have already told your readers, are many things,' Alberto answered. 'They can indeed be what in shamanic terms we term the "luminous rod" of an individual soul that has departed from this world or other worlds, or they can be part of a group soul. For instance, most animals, except dolphins and whales, belong to group souls. Orbs can also represent lineages of great masters, or elemental spirits of water, fire, earth and wind – or even our children's children, calling out to us from our future, inviting us to create a more harmonious world in which they can be born.

'And when we have ritual ceremonies in the jungle honouring our ancestors,' he went on, 'we create a sacred space through which the Orbs can appear. Quite often a large group-soul Orb appears and you can clearly see on digital photographs that these spirits are absorbing the energy emitted from our prayers.'

His words made perfect sense to me. Scientists such as Professor Gary Schwartz at the University of Arizona, parapsychologist Dr Serena Roney-Dougal and biophysicist Dr Harry Oldfield – to name but a few – now maintain that even when we 'shed' our physical body, our unique field of information is still 'out there' for a time, perhaps for several incarnations. But not indefinitely, as Alberto was keen to point out. 'It's important for people to realize that if they don't evolve spiritually towards coherence, then for the majority, as the luminous rod or field of information becomes weaker, it will eventually dissipate and merge back into the vast sea of consciousness.'

Of course, there are multiple explanations of what happens to the soul after physical death – several of which are discussed in my book *The Evidence for the Sixth Sense* – but Alberto only had an hour or so, not a week, and I was keen to move on to subjects such as spiritual walk-ins, multiple personalities, shape-shifting, and how social drugs such as cannabis, crack and

Ecstasy are contributing to the huge growth in mental-health problems. Since going through my own spiritual breakthrough, I had heard from many people who had attempted to accelerate their spiritual growth by experimenting with such drugs, and I had also realized just how many young people using 'social' drugs ended up having intense spiritual and psychotic episodes.

Eyeing the scones on our table with a longing akin to needing my own 'fix' (of wheat and sugar), I asked Alberto if he had ever taken ayahuasca, the South American plant extract used by medicine people to induce higher states of awareness.

'Indeed, I have tried it many times,' he said, 'but only in the right setting and circumstances and with the right master, and I only know two or three "right masters". At such times the results can be extraordinary.

'The problem today,' he went on, 'is that some people on their spiritual journeys tend to be rather naïve and have rose-tinted expectations as to what might happen when and if their kundalini energy awakens. And they are travelling to the Amazon on spiritual package tours offering ayahuasca, sometimes organized by people who themselves have only a limited knowledge of what they are getting their "clients" into. Unsuspecting men and women may try this most powerful neurochemical hallucinogen without due care, not realizing that its misuse can be dangerous. When I take people on my annual trips to Peru and the Amazon, I never include use of such drugs.'

I was delighted to hear that Alberto did not advocate using drugs of any kind to heighten a spiritual experience. Almost rhetorically I asked, 'In what way can they be dangerous?' I knew only too well that such brain-chemistry-altering substances can trigger intense kundalini awakenings, which in many cases can invite negative entities into our energy fields.

'For starters,' he replied, 'the majority of drug users initially experience an intense feeling of euphoria, but a week, a month or a year or two later their LEFs can collapse, causing huge health problems, mental and physical.'

He really is not kidding – anyone out there who thinks that taking drugs is 'cool' should have a look at the picture taken by physicist Harry Oldfield (*see* plate 6), which clearly shows the wild-looking eyes of a young crack addict whose kundalini has blown, as mine did without drugs in 1998. As you can see, her brow and crown chakras are wide open.

'You don't want to scare people,' Alberto went on, 'but they need to really understand that certain circumstances – such as drug use, long-term stress, shock, extreme spiritual practices and so on – can cause instability in a person's field, which can trigger psychotic-type episodes. Such instability leaves a field very permeable, at which time a spirit or another consciousness can intrude into the field and merge with it. This is a walk-in scenario.'

This sounded exactly what had happened to me back in 1998. Briefly I related my story and asked if this could be true in my case.

'Absolutely,' agreed Alberto. 'You have told me that you were under considerable stress at that time, which alters brain chemistry, and your field became highly unstable. I teach my students how to perform "extractions" in such cases. For instance I had a patient who came into my office saying, "The witch is dead ... " Apparently she hated her mother and called her a witch, yet since her mother had "died" the woman had not felt well. And I could clearly see her mother walking right behind her. There was a cord attached to my patient's solar plexus, connecting her to the mother, who was caught between this world and the next and was draining her daughter's energy. Once I released the attachment, the health problems cleared.'

'So, let me be clear,' I pressed. 'When the kundalini blows suddenly and unexpectedly, as mine did back in '98, does a person automatically get attachments? And is this where multiple-personality symptoms emanate from?'

My guest took a deep breath. 'Firstly, I need to clarify that if people make time for regular spiritual practices with occasional help from a trusted teacher, then their kundalini opens slowly over time; the process is more controlled, and this is always the best and safest route towards becoming who they really are. But yes, if the kundalini blows suddenly for whatever reason, then there will be attachments, and in some cases such attachments are very destabilizing and can indeed be a factor in multiple-personality disorders. Multiple personalities can also have other causes, such as chemical imbalances in the brain or former lifetimes that have reawakened in a person's unconscious.'

Having recently spoken to several men and women who had been committed to psychiatric hospitals because they were displaying multiple personalities, I prayed as I listened to Alberto that more psychiatrists and doctors could open their minds and understand that we truly are spirit having a physical experience. The Spiritual Crisis Network in the UK are doing great work to raise awareness in this area: www.spiritualcrisisnetwork.org.uk.

Over the years, spiritual teachers and enlightened men and women have advised me again and again that the safest way to become enlightened is to take your time and raise your consciousness gradually. How do you do this? By being honest and honourable; by caring for yourself, others and your environment; by learning to discriminate between New Age gobbledegook and truth; by assimilating and learning to work with more pure energies – and, in time, by aligning and becoming at one with the All That Is.

Alberto chimed in once again. 'Energetically, the more elevated your consciousness becomes, the more likely you are to attract – both on a physical and on a metaphysical level – an elevated spirit or person that you can resonate with that supports you in some way. Like attracts like.'

As we chatted, a second pot of hot tea arrived – now there's a panacea if ever there was one. My brain was also craving some glucose as nourishment, and I finally succumbed and ate a scone. It was fabulous.

But my time with Alberto was running out, and I was keen to pose one more important – and, I hoped, not too impertinent – question. 'Can you shape-shift?'

'Oh, on a good day,' he replied with a twinkle in his eyes. 'After all, you did not see me when you arrived!'

His eyes were mesmerizing. I got the distinct impression that this man can do many strange and wonderful things that he generally keeps to himself.

'Even today,' he continued, 'there are sages who can shape-shift, especially among the Laika women, who are descendants of the Inka, but these people lived outside the empires in which high priests wanted control and power over the masses. I have walked past shamans in the jungle thinking I'm passing a tree and then I get a tap on the shoulder and they say hello. There are individuals who can shift into the body of an eagle, a condor, a hawk or an owl. This is not myth – it's real and I have witnessed it many times. These great sages know how to transcend the physical body, beyond space and time; they understand how to walk between worlds, and they can change their frequency and vibration, which enables them to appear as they wish to appear.'

I realize that such a concept may seem incredible to you – yet I believe it to be totally true. Only a few weeks earlier, Professor Tiller had told me that as we grow in coherence, our ability to change our physical appearance by intention will grow. And at the risk of becoming a bore, I can only quote from my own experience yet again. In 1998 I asked a colleague to watch as I consciously drained the strange and powerful energies that were flooding like a river through my whole being down into the ground. She was incredulous as I began to appear to her like an aged crone. Then I consciously brought the energy back up from my feet and became an energetic young woman with different coloured eyes. My 'trick' felt like an innocent game to me at the time, but the poor woman was mildly terrified!

As Professor Tiller has told me more than once, when you become totally coherent, anything is possible – *anything*.

Alberto and I stood to leave and walked together out to his cab. As we said goodbye, he was keen to add one last word. 'Above all else, remind your readers that the best way to help heal themselves and this world – and to evolve into luminous beings who are totally at one with the great mind which underlies all of life – is by working on raising their own level of consciousness as much as they can within their life's circumstances. Part of us is always "at home", and we are all good enough – we just need to know it.'

A fascinating man. If you want to know more about his courses, lectures or workshops or his several books (*Courageous Dreaming* is my personal favourite), visit www.thefourwinds.com.

Chapter Ten

Soul Choices and Challenges

As our souls evolve, the more
challenging our challenges become.

– Robert Schwartz

October 2009 – Henley-on-Thames, Oxfordshire

Do you find it hard to believe that you may have chosen a great majority of your current life events before you were born and that some aspects of your future may already be set? I have always believed that certain events, such as my near-death experience back in '98, were predestined for my soul's growth – but, as Alberto says, not at a conscious level. Yet many events in my life have also come about because of my conscious, though not necessarily always wise, choices.

Ever since I have become fascinated with spiritual issues, when I share certain incidents in my life with like-minded friends, there's a good chance that one of them will spout, 'Oh, Hazel, why not view this as another *wonderful* growth opportunity?' To which I retort, 'I'm done with "effing" growth opportunities!' I'll bet there are many days when you feel the same.

However, there is a growing body of fascinating anecdotal evidence – some of which I'll share in a moment, based on research done by Robert Schwartz, author of *Your Soul's Plan: Discovering the Real Meaning of the Life You Planned Before You Were Born* – that at a *soul* level we do indeed choose much of this life prior to our physical birth, including preordaining our physical death in probability. In fact, you are most probably doing your soul's chosen work right now and you don't even know it – yet!

With your current life's circumstances, do you find this hard to believe, and do you wonder what this concept has to do with returning to coherence? All will be revealed as you read on.

To many people, subjects such as pre-life choices, life after physical death, and the possibility of returning for multiple lifetimes are dismissed out of hand as quackery. Yet as Professor Gary Schwartz (no relation to Robert) once asked me somewhat tongue in cheek, 'Hazel, if something looks like a duck, walks like a duck and sounds like a duck, would you consider that it's more than likely to be ... a duck?'

Of course I would.

Gary's point being that if you hear 'facts' from one source that you disbelieve or disagree with, then if you are open-minded you may listen to another scientist coming from a different perspective, and then another, and another. Yet when you start to hear and see similar results and conclusions over and over again from a broad spectrum of authoritative sources – surely you must eventually conclude that the simplest explanation is, in the majority of cases, the obvious answer.

On the subject of reincarnation alone, I have read and interviewed myriad highly accredited scientists and researchers who conclude from their studies that reincarnation is not a theory, but a fact – and that we bring into this incarnation, as Professor Villoldo states, our most vivid experiences, emotions and memories from past lives, whether lived in this dimension or in others. The late Ian Stevenson, who was a professor of psychiatry at the University of Virginia and a renowned pioneer in reincarnation research, documented over 3,000 remarkable cases offering the strongest available evidence that we live multiple lives. Like many others, when he examined the totality of the evidence, Stevenson too concluded that we do indeed choose our parents and when and where we will be born.

And when a multimillion-selling author such as Dan Brown (of *Da Vinci Code* fame) writes a book entitled *The Lost Symbol*, relating a thrilling story with fictional characters that weaves in considerable amounts of real published scientific evidence, demonstrating that we create our own reality through intention, that consciousness survives physical death and, most magically for me, that we are all divine beings in a physical shell – then *surely* the time is upon us when even die-hard sceptics and fundamentalist religious fanatics may slowly but surely reconsider certain preconceived ideas.

Hence why I reiterate Gary Schwartz's words: 'If something walks like a duck, sounds like a duck and looks like a duck – do you think it's a duck?' What do you think? I think all the 'stuff' that I and others are writing about and experiencing is very, very real and deserves to become more widely known.

Enter my next guest. Back in 2003, Robert Schwartz was working as a communications consultant in Cleveland, Ohio. He was a high-flying businessman, but an unhappy one. 'I was basically floundering,' he told me in the autumn of 2009. 'I had this innate desire to make some kind of difference, but had no idea how to go about it or what form it would take.'

Within days of his deciding that he wanted to make a positive contribution to people's lives, an idea 'popped' into Robert's head – to consult a good medium.

Although highly sceptical, he felt he had nothing to lose and began searching for a suitably experienced practitioner. He was totally astonished by what happened during their first meeting.

'The medium,' he recalled, 'began channelling my spirit guides, who through her gave me incredibly accurate information known only to me. *Exact* words that I had spoken in desperation five years earlier were mirrored back to me. My guides informed me that I had planned several major challenges before I was born – not for the purpose of suffering, but for my soul's growth.'

'And what,' I interrupted, 'is your definition of "soul"?'

'Soul is the spark of God – a portion of God's energy placed inside a physical body. Yet the soul is already merged with God. There is only a perceived separation on the part of the individual ego personality – but, as you know, this is an illusion.'

From Robert's reply, I knew we were coming from the same perspective. He continued, 'After that reading I started to "remember" things at a soul level and to feel unconditional love for everyone and everything. I decided that if people could realize why they have chosen this lifetime, their attitudes could change and they could get on with consciously learning the lessons and having the experiences they chose to aid their souls' growth. And so I left my job and began a whole new chapter in my life that I hoped would also help others.'

Robert's new career eventually became his wonderful book, in which he shares numerous real-life case studies illustrating why people chose their lifetimes. His stories gave me several surprises. For instance, he relates the story of Jennifer Stewart, a Florida woman raising three children on her own, two of whom are handicapped. Her son Ryan has Asperger's syndrome and also suffers from bipolar disorder and ADD. Her second son, Bradley, is severely autistic and blind. Both sons have considerable problems communicating. Jennifer says, 'After studying psychology in high school I became interested in autism, years before my sons were even born. For some reason I was fascinated by varying levels of communication. Ryan, my oldest son, has an amazing brain and can remember incredible facts, even though he struggles to have a normal conversation – and since childhood he has been fascinated by politics and the weather. Bradley, meanwhile, only has a vocabulary of about twenty words.'

There were many days, says Jennifer, when if she had allowed herself to cry, the tears would have never stopped – yet somewhere deep within herself she felt that there was a reason why her children were born disabled. That's why she offered to take part in Robert's research when he advertised for subjects to study.

Robert arranged for Jennifer to have a session with medium Corbie Mitleid in New York, who told her that in the 1930s she had been a Jewish reporter based in Washington. Jennifer had received information about what was really happening in the concentration camps – but no-one wanted to print that information, which later was proven to the world to be true.

Corbie also relayed to Jennifer that her two sons had worked together for the Nazis, writing and disseminating propaganda. The sons had therefore planned *this* lifetime to learn the value of truthful communication. They had sought their handicaps to foster their spiritual evolution. And Jennifer had agreed to be their mother, both to teach them how to communicate and to teach her own soul the art of patience. Although she had no way to verify the facts told her during her soul readings, Jennifer says the story resonates with her and has made a profoundly positive difference in the way she views her sons' current lives and her own.

As I read Jennifer's story, I recalled how furious I had been in 1991 – after I had slipped on ice and fallen under a train (thankfully, a stationary train) at Euston Station in London, breaking my leg – when a therapist suggested that I had invited this event into my life. As it turned out, though, breaking my leg forced me to scale back a hectic work schedule and thereby gave me the space and time to visit my mother daily for months as she lay dying of cancer. We cannot know the bigger picture – we can only see a small part of it.

Years later, my housekeeper made me laugh when she asked, 'Do you remember how, the week before you broke your leg, you told me that you were sick and tired of doing so much travelling?'

'Did I really?' I responded, somewhat taken aback.

'Yes,' she proclaimed. 'You have often told me to be careful what we wish for, as it may come true but not in ways that we expected!'

Indeed I had.

On this theme, Robert commented, 'I honestly believe that things can only happen to us if our vibration allows it into our experience. You magnetize events and people into your life depending on the range of frequencies that you are emitting at any specific time.'

Everyone I have spoken to agrees with Robert on this subject – and it certainly rang true for me. When I slipped on the platform, I was stressed, in a hurry, late for the train and trying to be all things to all people! What you give out is what you get back.

This sounded like karma, so I asked Robert's views on that concept as well. 'Most people,' he said, 'consider karma to be some kind of cosmic debt, but I think of karma more as unbalanced energy. For example, let's say that two people had a life together in which one was a loving caregiver for the other, who was chronically ill. And when they move into spirit, there might be a sense of having had an unbalanced relationship which they decide to rebalance in their next lifetime – simply by swapping roles. In this way I think of karma as being totally "neutral".'

I found his use of the word *neutral* very appropriate, as anyone who has been in the presence of a truly enlightened being has realized that most of the time these men and women are not only fully coherent at every level of being – but they are also completely 'neutral' themselves. Nothing is 'good' or bad' in their eyes, it just 'is'. They judge no-one, they love unconditionally, they have no fear. Believe me, it's an amazing space to be in. Thankfully, it's where we are all headed!

Robert's view of karma as 'neutral' was also interesting to me because it resonated with a description I had heard from

Professor Fred Travis, who has studied the science of enlighten-ment and brain coherence for more than 30 years (and from whom you'll hear more in chapter 12). Fred had told me that at the moment of total enlightenment, all karma from all lifetimes, at all levels of being, is 'wiped clean' and from that moment you can start afresh. It's like pressing a reset button. All parts of the Whole Mind of which you are a fragment, which exists in all dimensions at all levels of reality simultaneously, come together as one, so that any karmic 'debt'– or imbalance, in Robert's terms – is cancelled out. This may help you to further understand how you and all of us are a part, or an aspect, of one Ultimate Mind that exists everywhere.

As always, there are a host of possible realities. While chatting with Robert, I also mentioned my meeting with Dr Michael Newton, a clinical hypnotherapist and psychologist with over 20 years of experience in clinical practice in America and author of two best-selling books, *Journey of Souls* and *Life Between Lives*. In his practice, Michael found while conducting past-life regressions under hypnosis that sometimes his patients' previous lives had been cut short, which had not been part of their blueprint.

'Indeed, it appears that our soul's plans can go awry,' Robert agreed. 'In my book I relate the story of Bob Feinstein from New York, who was born blind. The medium who worked with Bob was Staci Wells, based in Arizona. Prior to her soul readings for Bob, we informed Staci that he had been born prematurely and that excess oxygen in his incubator had caused his blindness. Staci went on to tell Bob that his guides were with him when the blindness was triggered in the incubator, and that his soul self was given the choice to stay in his body and remain blind for a lifetime or to leave and then choose another body. But as his soul's intention for this life had been to achieve emotional independence, Bob's spirit decided to stay. In other words, being blind had not originally been part of his blueprint, yet because of an error in this reality, he became blind.'

'So,' I interrupted, 'you are basically saying that there are no victims?'

'Yes. Not so much on a physical level, but more on an unconscious soul level. And, like you, I also remind people that whatever you are giving out via your sustained thoughts and actions has the potential to magnetize the same experience into this and other lifetimes.'

I totally agreed.

By the way, do you consider yourself to be an 'old soul' or a 'young soul'? When I posed this question to a highly sceptical friend who thinks that anything spiritual is out-and-out wacky, she wryly commented, 'Well ... I have no idea, but I certainly know a few a——souls!' Her retort made me laugh – even though I was thinking that even 'r-souls' are coherent at a certain level of being. After all, you *are* soul.

I was keen to hear Robert's comments on this subject. 'From my experiments with several highly experienced mediums and multiple "sitters",' Robert replied, 'I believe that frequently, as our souls evolve, the more challenging our challenges become. This is why when I meet someone who is dying of AIDS, someone homeless living on the streets, a disabled person or one who seems to experience seemingly endless negative challenges – whereas previously I might in some situations have judged them – now I do not. I feel compassion and deep respect for them, as they may be very old, highly evolved souls who no longer incarnate to experience wealth, success or transient fame, but have chosen their challenges in order to grow at a soul level.'

As he spoke, I thought of Nelson Mandela. Could it be that at a soul level he chose to suffer the terrible hardships he experienced at the hands of apartheid in South Africa, so that in the winter of his life he could emerge to change a nation's history?

'Yet surely,' I argued, 'at times, social, economic or world events might change a single soul's plan. They may indeed at a soul level have planned some events, but not all. And don't most people have varying degrees of free will according to their life's circumstances?'

'Absolutely,' Robert agreed, 'yet the more I do this work – and the more conscious I see people becoming – the less randomness and the more order I witness.'

'So, do you agree that at a soul level we are all working our way through our experiences back towards a state of coherence, which is pure order? And as our souls experience all that there is to experience, there will come a time when we will no longer need to, unless we choose to, reincarnate in a physical body at all?'

'Pretty much,' he replied. 'However, during one of these readings, an angelic being also explained to us that chaos is fertile ground for growth; we cannot understand the whole picture without polarities. The soul learns by experiencing opposites, masculine/feminine, light/dark, sorrow/joy and so on. And as we experience opposites or dualities, we automatically have a sense of separation. But as we become more coherent at all levels of being, as we move from judgement to discernment, then our ego mind will begin to more fully appreciate the inter-relationships between all things.'

Returning to Robert's book, I found one of his most fascinating concepts to be that it may be possible for souls to reincarnate at any period in time – the present, past or even other dimensions. The implications are mind-boggling – yet the more I thought about everything I had learned, the more feasible such a concept became.

To help me try and grasp such a scenario, I turned to para-psychologist Dr Serena Roney-Dougal, who suggested I draw a straight line and mark the centre of that line as 'today'. The past I marked as 'backwards', to my left, and the future was marked by an arrow going 'forwards', to my right. Serena then told me to join the two ends of my straight line together to make a circle, so that the point where I had marked my 'today' was now both the beginning and the end – *as was every other part of the circle.*

To clarify, Serena reminded me that at *this* level of linear-time reality, we absolutely do have a past, present and future where our futures exist as probabilities. But *outside* our space-time reality, at the holographic level where there is no space or time, it's not that 'time' has already happened – it simply does not exist!

How many times have you read about living 'in the now', the Golden Present? All enlightened men and women speak in such terms.

Taking this concept one step further, I invite you to imagine that you have died, left your physical body, and are now floating as an Orb, a soul being, no longer constricted by a body or linear time. Now, imagine that 'you' can choose where and when to 'insert' your soul self into a new physical reality at *any* point on what Schwartz describes as the 'web' of time. I picture this web as a sort of bubble-like structure that is an 'offshoot' from the Core (which is God). Schwartz likens it to an incomprehensibly vast flow chart – an elaborate series of decision points or if/then scenarios, each of which propels us onto a new strand of the web. Alberto Villoldo calls these strands 'timelines'.

Imagine yourself existing inside a bubble-like balloon, and imagine that all around you are timelines existing at various locations within the balloon. Now, let's say that as a soul being, which, remember, is part of the Whole, I choose to insert myself into the appropriate timeline as Elizabeth I. Don't laugh! After all, once you access the vacuum level of reality, linear time as we understand it no longer applies.

And so my soul with all its experiences enters the body of baby Elizabeth inside her mother, Anne Boleyn. It's 1533 – and voilà, my soul becomes Queen Elizabeth and 'I' experience her life. I exist as Elizabeth in her 'now' on her timeline. Her lifetime then becomes another of my soul's realities, another movie to add to my collection of incarnations. At this point my rational mind says, 'Don't be ridiculous – Queen Elizabeth died five hundred years ago. Ashes to ashes and all that.' But most souls tend to 'forget' previous existences and realities when they move from one dimension to another – though some, especially young children, may remember them either partially or very clearly. My hypothetical scenario makes perfect sense when you consider that every single 'separate' soul originally emanated from a single unified source that exists in all realities, in all things, *simultaneously* – and that 'little you' is a part of it all.

Such a scenario would also imply that we, as souls, might have the potential to go back and change the past – which of course could potentially change our reality today. But historical fact is fact – right? Incredibly, Dr Serena Roney-Dougal has shared with me research that shows it might indeed be possible to alter *certain* events in the past that would affect the present. You will read more on this subject later, along with other experts' views on the nature of time and even our potential to travel within it.

Robert was keen to add, 'I have also found that when a really strong emotion is involved, at a time when a person makes a really life-changing decision, there can be a "bleed-through" into other dimensions. This might manifest if a person, for nonspecific or nonrational physical reasons, suddenly experiences, for example, overwhelming sadness or great joy.'

Back in Arizona, Professor Tiller had told me that 'causes' at one level of reality can, if sufficient emotion is involved, have an effect in other levels of reality. At the time I had found this theory difficult to grasp, yet listening to Robert, perhaps it was time to reconsider.

I had one more important question for Robert. Had he found that we also choose the date and manner of our physical death?

'That's a big question,' he sighed. 'My current understanding is that souls plan several "exit points". There comes a time when either the soul feels that it has done everything that it needs to do, or it concludes that it will not, for whatever reason, be *able* to do what it came to do, and then it will choose an exit point.'

At this time there is plenty of evidence to show that consciousness survives physical death, but no definitive scientific evidence to show that we preordain our death's time and circumstances. Having posed this question to mediums, enlightened men and women and a host of spiritual teachers, I conclude yet again that there are many possible realities, and that our physical death may indeed be preordained, but only in probability. Our choices at every level have the potential to change our outcomes.

Death is a fraught issue indeed. Yet after undergoing an intense near-death experience myself, I now have much less fear of physical death, as I have a firm belief that we all go on. We are eternal – so we need to concentrate more on living this life rather than worrying about the next!

———— ∞ ————

Yet sometimes even I find myself asking, 'What's the use of knowing all this stuff? After all, grasping the idea that the Ultimate I exists in multiple dimensions, within everything, doesn't really help me type this page or pay my bills right now in this dimension, does it?' In fact, nothing would please me more, in this moment, than to have two enlightened beings appear before me – and dictate the rest of this book. Wouldn't that be great? Yet, as Professor Tiller told me, 'Spirit can and will assist you in the process, but you have to do your part . . . .'

Listening to Robert Schwartz helped me to reaffirm what I have long felt – that I actually chose at a soul level to do what I am now doing – and I am thankful, most of the time, to have found my life's purpose and to have the opportunity to practise it. Yes, I sometimes fleetingly fantasize that instead of typing hour after hour, I could spend my life eating fresh, warm homemade cakes served by George Clooney. Of course I have some choices and a degree of free will. Unfortunately, so does Mr Clooney!

Joking aside, perhaps you too are starting to see your life differently. Has your attitude towards your circumstances and challenges begun to change? Do you find yourself considering cause and effect at all levels and taking more responsibility for your actions? Have you begun to shift your thoughts towards what you need more of in your life, rather than what you don't? Most importantly, are you working on a daily basis at forgiving yourself and others?

If you were not already pursuing a spiritual practice such as qi gong, chanting or meditation when you started this book, perhaps by this point you have begun to – and if not, I hope you will consider doing so. Meditation alone, if practised regularly, especially in groups, will help your brain to function more coherently on all levels. It also aids sleep, balances hormones, lowers blood pressure, improves your body's ability to cope with stress – and has been shown to slow the aging process and make you more intelligent as well.

Over time your natural psychic abilities will begin to awaken and improve, and, with discernment, you should soon begin using your intuition to help you to be more often in the right place at the right time. More synchronicities will begin appearing in your life – some that will take your breath away – once you begin living with the intention to align with the coherent whole mind of which you are a part.

In the meantime, if you want to know more about Robert Schwartz's work, lectures and books, visit his website at: www.yoursoulsplan.com.

Chapter Eleven

Premonitions, Predictions and Planets

People always find it easier to be a
result of the past, rather than a cause
of the future.

– Anonymous

October 2009 – Henley-on-Thames, Tucson and New York

IF YOU COULD SEE THE FUTURE, what would you envisage and what would you wish for?

For eons, sages, shamans and oracles have used various methods to see what lies ahead. On 27 June 1558, the seer Nostradamus, who used deep meditative states and astrology to arrive at his predictions, sent a letter to Henry II of France with this quatrain: *The Lion shall overcome the Old on the field of war in a single combat. He will pierce his eyes in a cage of Gold. This is the first of two lappings, then he dies a cruel death.* A year later, on 30 June 1559, ignoring the prediction, Henry took part in a joust and was mortally wounded when his younger opponent's wooden lance pierced his headgear and entered his eye. The King attempted to keep going, but soon collapsed and took 11 days to die in agony.

Today, more than 70 per cent of people consult psychics at some point in their lives, wondering what their future may hold. There are those who believe, like author Gary Renard, that we are living in a movie that is simply repeating itself. Conversely, several highly accredited scientists have told me that our potential futures are not completely 'set', but constantly co-created by our thoughts and actions.

The preponderance of evidence shows that we exist in a probabilistic universe where nothing is 100 per cent determined. Parapsychologist Dr Serena Roney-Dougal helped clarify this point when she told me, 'Even though – thanks to our genetic makeup, life's circumstances, soul choices, diet, thoughts and so on – some things might be ninety-nine per cent determined, or as you say "set in stone", there is always that possibility of a shift, always that edge where things can be changed.'

During my stay in Phoenix, Professor Tiller had told me that our sustained, focused intentions eventually reach a plateau and thus become attached to the mind lattice grid in geometric patterns. His theory is that very powerful intentions/events could have been 'set' on the grid hundreds or even thousands of years earlier, and that sensitives such as Nostradamus can retrieve information from the grid the way the rest of us retrieve information from the Internet. Imagine a scenario in which several dozen terrorists are making plans for a negative outcome – such as 9/11. They are concentrating, their minds are highly focused, and as their thoughts become more coherent, they eventually attach to the grid. In the course of his research into telepathy, biologist Rupert Sheldrake found several people who had without any doubt predicted the catastrophe of 9/11 in their dreams – some months, weeks or days ahead of time. 'Although the problem with predictions,' he told me, 'is that you have no idea if they are correct or not – until they actually happen!'

A dilemma indeed. Dozens of people predicted John F Kennedy's death; even more predicted Princess Diana's. If the police, MI6 or the FBI acted upon every prediction they received, it's unlikely they would get any other work done. Sometimes, though, they do listen ...

Christopher Robinson of the UK is known as 'Premonition Man', and through his precognitive dreams he has helped to save lives. Now in his 50s, Chris – whom I met through my good friend Professor Gary Schwartz at the University of Arizona – started dreaming the future over 20 years ago when he worked with a national newspaper gathering information on crimes. Following a near-death experience which doctors linked to a mild heart attack, Chris began dreaming of 'crimes' before they had happened.

Over time his police friends began to take a greater interest in Chris's predictive dreams when they materialized precisely as he had foretold. In early December 1998 he warned the author-ities that a bomb was going to be placed on a plane at Heathrow; that same night, an airliner blew up over Lockerbie in Scotland, killing everyone on board.

On 6 June 1999 he reported to British Intelligence another vivid dream in which Muslim terrorists hijacked planes and crashed them into a city. Unfortunately, he did not 'see' a date. As Bill Tiller explained to me, when you access information stored outside our space-time at the vacuum level of physical reality, precise dates are often elusive.

Chris has hundreds of fascinating recorded predictions to share, many of which have come true – but even more interest-ing, his abilities have been tested using scientific protocols by Gary Schwartz in Arizona. On the phone from his home in Tucson, Gary recalled the mind-blowing experiments: 'When Chris first contacted me in April 2001, his claims were fairly outrageous, and as a clinical psychologist, I needed several phone conversations with Chris to determine that he was neither a schizophrenic nor a pathological liar. Eventually, I agreed to design a controlled experiment to take place here in Arizona, which I believed would prove impossible for Chris to achieve. I was in for some amazing surprises.

'The basis of the experiment was that Chris should try to predict ten random locations we would visit on ten consecutive days, which I would pre-select. By the time Chris arrived in Tucson in August, I had listed twenty possible locations in southern Arizona – choices known only to me – which I printed on separate pieces of paper. I placed each sheet in a blank envelope, then sealed and shuffled them. They were then shipped by courier to a colleague, who handed them to a third party not known to me. Of these locations, we were going to pick one at random to visit on each day for ten successive days.

'As Chris has spent years documenting his dreams, he began in May of that year recording where he thought we might visit on each of the ten days. He repeated this ritual three times before flying to Arizona. When he arrived, I was reluctant to read his predictions, still believing that it would be impossible for anyone, no matter how psychic, to correctly predict all ten locations.

'On day one, 2 August 2001 – having asked Chris to dream where we might visit the next morning – I filmed his raw information from his previous night's dream plus a summary of his three dreams from the previous months. For day one he predicted "holes, lots of holes, along with a basin empty of water".

'With the camera still running, I then called my colleague in California, who asked the third party to reshuffle the twenty envelopes and randomly choose one. The contents as I had written them months earlier were "Desert Museum/Animals".

'As we drove off, I did not share with Christopher where we were going, nor did I tell my colleague what Christopher had predicted. When we arrived at the museum, we found it surrounded by a huge variety of holes, ranging from caves to tunnels to animal dens. And it's located in an area where, millions of years ago, there was an ocean . . . a basin empty of water. Chris was spot on.'

By this time, as you can doubtless imagine, I was longing to meet Chris!

'We continued for another nine days,' Gary went on, 'and I became ever more nonplussed at Chris's accuracy. Most astonishingly, on the final day, my schedule was suddenly changed, which meant I had to remain on the campus after 11am. My jaw literally fell open when the tenth envelope was opened, again randomly from the 11 remaining envelopes. On the paper inside I had written "Campus Museum". Christopher had predicted we would visit a museum in the morning, but that he would also spend much of the day by a pool, and he did. His hotel pool.'

Chris's amazing feat is documented in detail in Gary's book *The G.O.D. Experiments*. Needless to say, I was keen to meet Chris. Thankfully, Gary gave me his phone number.

Before contacting Chris, I wanted to know more from the learned professor about the implications of his findings. 'So, this experiment,' I prompted, 'gave you evidence that demonstrated not only a higher intelligence but also that our futures may to some extent be pre-determined and not simply random occurrences or pure potential?'

'I would go as far as to say that the combination of scientific evidence and logic leads to the paradigm-shifting conclusion that there is no such thing as pure randomness. As far as I can tell, there *is* a Guiding Organizing Designer everywhere and in everything,' Gary replied. 'And obviously no-one would see any kind of future if it was *all* only in potential! But tests such as this also help us to understand that our universe, which is part of a "whole mind", has a destiny or an agenda. Without doubt certain aspects of the future are set; the problem for the seer is *discernment*.'

His words touched a nerve. Back in November 2003, a well-intentioned astrologer friend told me that 'without doubt' the Houses of Parliament were going to be attacked during the State Opening of Parliament, scheduled for the following day. Taking her warning seriously, I called a high-ranking friend linked to the Government to warn him. Thankfully, nothing happened – but talk about mountains of egg on my face! Discernment is indeed the key.

'In small ways I could predict the future right now,' Gary went on. 'I could drop my pen and know one hundred per cent it's going to fall to the floor; I also know that the sun will come up tomorrow and the next day and the next, unless of course we blow ourselves to bits in a moment of madness. Most of us have clues as to what may be ahead for us based upon our genetic makeup, lifestyle and so on. It's as if everything is in spirals and most of us in this reality cannot "see" around the corners. Others, like Chris, with practice and experience can "see" somewhat farther, as can those in the spirit world.'

Imagine that 20 people dream scenarios, but only one of them comes true. That's a 1-in-20 chance. Dr Serena Roney-Dougal suggests, 'What the other 19 people may have done is either picked up some emotions from their own subconscious that evoked a symbolic story to help them deal with what was going on in their lives at that moment, or picked up various thoughts that were becoming set on what you term the matrix or grid.'

The more firmly 'set' an event is, the more it comes into psychic focus. Research has shown that as many as 80 per cent of people who experience precognition 'see' events that are going to happen within the next 24 to 48 hours, as these have become crystallized in this reality and are therefore highly likely to occur. 'It's like remembering the future in a way similar to recalling the past,' Serena explains. 'And the bigger the event, the bigger the shadow it casts – in every direction.'

In our conversation, Gary took the analogy further. 'Think of lightning during a storm. First we see the flash of lightning, then after some time we hear the thunder, and then we feel the vibration. The light is travelling faster than the sound and the sound is travelling faster than the vibration of the earth. Therefore, the light reaches us before the physical effect: energy precedes the physical. I am not a physicist, but the manifestation of anything into this reality goes through a process – it moves from consciousness, to information, to energy, to matter. Consciousness is primary.'

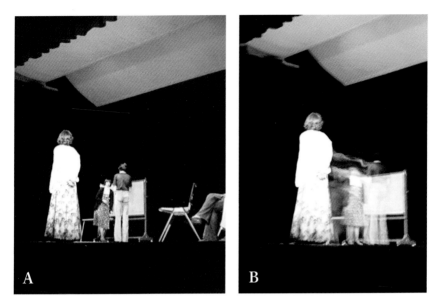

Plate 1: Picture A taken during scientifically controlled experiments using a non-digital Kodak camera in which you can clearly see Uri Geller's back. Picture B, using the same camera sensitized by researcher Stanislav O'Jack, which then operates at a 'coupled' state – you can 'see through' Geller's body to the blackboard. Courtesy of Tiller Foundation.

Plate 2: At the world's first Orb Conference, Sedona, May 2007. The author Hazel Courteney with Dr Miceal Ledwith, Jean Tiller, Professor William A. Tiller, Dr Klaus Heinemann and Gundi Heinemann.

Plate 3: Part of the spectacular Hall of the Earth, one of the nine incredible underground Temples of Humankind built by the people of Damanhur near Turin. Courtesy of Esperide Ananas and Cosm Press.

Plate 4: A night shot clearly showing Orbs. Courtesy of Dr Klaus Heinemann.

Plate 5: A rare picture showing Orbs in the process of forming a vortex near Dr Miceal Ledwith. Courtesy of Dr Miceal F. Ledwith.

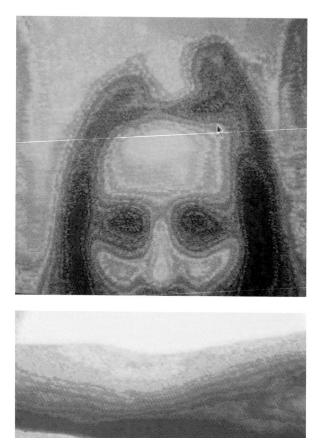

Plate 6: A 15 yr old crack addict whose kundalini energy has been released triggering a spiritual emergency. Her brow and crown chakras are wide open - this is one of the reasons why taking drugs is extremely dangerous. Courtesy of Oldfield Systems.

Plate 7: You can clearly distinguish the meridian energy channels in my arm – as the blue, yellow, green and red lines. Courtesy of Oldfield Systems.

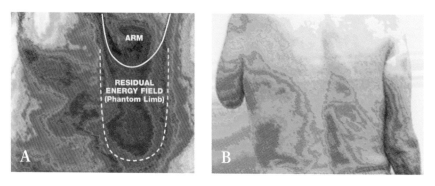

Plate 8: Picture 'A' A man who has had his left arm amputated and is suffering phantom limb pain, which is clearly shown in red in the shape of an arm where it used to be. Courtesy of Oldfield Systems.

Picture 'B' After calming frequencies are applied to the red area – the pain (previously in the shape of an arm) begins to disperse. Courtesy of Oldfield Systems.

A few weeks earlier I had watched a fascinating programme on the Discovery Channel in which three university graduates shared their experiences in Glastonbury Abbey, Somerset, where, as they attempted to 'tune in' and visualize how the abbey would have looked hundreds of years earlier, they saw a hooded monk running up some stairs. Their immediate reaction was to follow the monk, yet as they ran towards the stairs, they found only 'empty space' and fell head over heels. They later learned that the stairs, which had looked very real, had been destroyed 400 years earlier ... I shared this with Gary, keen to ask him about 'seeing' the past. 'Do you believe that we may be able to travel into the past, as well as into potential futures, via our minds – and possibly even in our physical bodies?'

He thought for a moment. "Remember what I told you about atoms having feedback and thus memory? And the majority of atoms have been recycled for almost fourteen billion years. So the past is always present *in* the present. Back in the '70s at the CIA-funded Stanford Research Institute, highly trained psychics such as Russell Targ and Ingo Swann were able to "remote view" specific co-ordinates and describe intimate details at these locations which were later found to have been correct *fifty years earlier.*

'You can travel into the past and potential futures via your *mind*,' he continued, 'but not, I and most of my scientific colleagues believe, in your physical body. Those students in Glastonbury for a few seconds saw a movie of the past that is playing in the present. It is like a hologram ... '

Back to the hologram again. 'Do you mean everything is an illusion?'

'I mean that if you tune in to the information that is always and has always been inside the atoms, then all kinds of memories are stored in them *holographically.* So, in a deep sense, everything is like an illusion, but – and this is important – an illusion is nothing more than a *limited perception* of what's really present, a *false interpretation* of reality.'

Listening to Gary, I felt that we could all drive ourselves to distraction trying to make sense of so much information and so many possibilities. And when I finally met Chris Robinson at my home in Oxfordshire the following weekend, I was keen to know how he had learned to sort the wheat from the chaff.

Over a delicious winter chicken stew, Chris told me, 'All my life I have had an innate desire to help solve crimes. This was why I began working with a newspaper, helping them collate information on crimes. After my near-death experience, my dreams became an extension of my passion. And, over time, as some events in my dreams began to come true, I started to record more and more details, even things that did not make sense at the time. Eventually a psychologist and I went through all my notes – and realized that certain symbols in dreams denoted certain outcomes.'

'Such as?'

'Well, I learned that if a dog appeared in my dreams, it symbolized that I was "seeing" a potential future act of terrorism, and if snow also appeared, this meant the event was imminent. And if I saw meat or a butcher's shop within a dream, I knew that people were going to die, but not necessarily from terrorism – it might have been a natural disaster or a gas explosion. Over the years I have developed a strong gut instinct as to whether events in a dream are indeed a potential future event – or simply a dream.'

Listening to Chris, I wondered what most people request from his prophetic dreams. He smiled. 'I have lost count of the numbers of people who have asked me to dream the winning lottery numbers or which horse will win a particular race.'

Why was I not surprised? If you ask most people what they would love in their future, they usually say more money, or more time to do what they love to do, or, if they are sick, better health. Very few, as I surmised in chapter 2, would say, 'I'd love to become enlightened and return home to coherence!'

Yet looking back on my experience, I feel that I won the spiritual lottery, which is worth far more than physical money could ever buy. Of course, there is nothing wrong with being wealthy in monetary terms – after all, think of all the good you could do with it, and go shopping too!

Chris laughed when I told him this. 'Over the years I have found that the more we set an intention to contribute to helping others rather than helping ourselves – even if it's only in a small way – then what we need will come to us.'

As we moved on to a dish of stewed winter fruits, I asked Chris, 'So, how do you do what you do?'

'Well, when Gary asked me to dream where we might visit on each of the ten days of our experiment, I began to build a picture of myself as being in Tucson and visualizing each destination. I placed myself at a mind level *into* the situations, which creates a kind of feedback loop. Basically I bring an event onto my radar screen and then see what appears in my dreams.'

'And what about random dreams, when you have not visualized anything beforehand?'

'It depends on the size of the event,' he said. 'As Dr Roney-Dougal says, the bigger events cast a bigger shadow. Or you could say I feel the energy first, then the event materializes.'

'So,' I asked, as many undoubtedly had before me, 'why don't your dreams give you exact dates so that you can prevent more crimes?'

'Sometimes they do,' Chris replied. 'In 1991 I dreamt of an IRA bombing that was going to take place in a bank in

St Albans on a specific Friday night and I immediately alerted Scotland Yard. They asked me on a scale of one to ten how likely the event was to happen – and I predicted a nine. I had no idea that The Blues and Royals military band were playing in St Albans that night, but the police did. Anyway, they staked out the town centre, and sure enough they saw the bomber dropping a parcel through a bank letter box. The bomb went off, killing the bomber, but no innocent person was injured.'

'Yet have you ever thought of your gift as a curse?'

'Never.' He smiled. 'It's what I came to do. Like you, I believe that sometimes certain events are meant to be, but we cannot know the bigger picture all the time.'

'But do you get frustrated?' I pressed.

Looking pensive, Chris replied, 'When I dreamt that someone was planning to kill a minor royal' – Sophie Rhys-Jones, then Prince Edward's fiancée – 'I clearly saw that someone would murder Jill Dando, the well known BBC-TV *Crimewatch* presenter, by mistake. They looked so alike. And I reported that dream to the police six weeks before Jill was killed in April '99. That incident was very frustrating, as Jill might have been saved.'

Thinking how many deaths could possibly be prevented that weren't, I asked, 'Do you sometimes feel like giving up?'

Cheerfully he responded, 'Life can be very frustrating for anyone. That's life. But as I know with my whole heart that I'm doing what I chose to do, I'll keep going. Saving any life has to be worth it. I do lots of TV and many people still think that what I do is some kind of trick, but now that scientists like Gary and Rupert Sheldrake and others are finally demonstrating through science how these types of phenomena are possible, slowly but surely the public at large will realize that we are capable of much more than is generally accepted. And one day I believe many more people will be saved.'

Couldn't have said it better myself. Back in 1998, as I briefly became incredibly telepathic, I intuitively knew what people were thinking and what they were wishing for. And for a brief time I was also able to 'see' some of our potential futures. Some were dire, whilst others were wonderful, and my spirit guides constantly reminded me that what we experience in our futures is based on what we do and think today.

In chapter 9, Professor Villoldo advised, 'If you don't realize that you can be a creator, then you have to settle for the dreams that are created by the media or your karma.' How true.

Before Chris left, I asked what he sees our future may hold in this reality. Suddenly he looked more serious. 'I firmly believe that fanaticism from any source is going to become our biggest headache. If people plot to kill, and eventually carry out such plots, they have to take responsibility for that. What goes around comes around. I'm not saying "an eye for an eye" because, as Gandhi said, that leaves everyone blind – but such people need to open their minds.'

Chris is a wonderful human being, and we could do with many more like him. Find Chris via www.dream-detective.com.

After Chris left, I went back to my office and began sifting through other predictions that had arrived several months earlier from my girlfriend Linda Joyce in New York, a renowned astrologer. They had turned out to be spot on, and I decided to give her a call and ask how she was able to predict specific events that had indeed occurred within days of her predictions. What tools was *she* using to tap into the underlying intelligence of the universe?

Like Chris, Linda is always upbeat and very cheerful. She told me that astrology is a system of moving symbols (planets) and it is the relationship of these symbols by mathematical angle and degree that describes in detail the energy that is coming into our lives.

'Predictions are really probabilities,' she explained. 'An astrologer sees them as events either coming from you to impact your world or coming towards you to trigger change in your life. For instance if the planet Uranus is in your tenth house of career, then the chances are you'll either leave or get fired from your job – that is, if you don't listen to your instincts and bring in change yourself.

'When clients ask a specific question about the future, we look to the planets and houses that rule that question and see if there is any activity there that would trigger things to happen. In time it's amazing how accurate one's interpretations can become.'

'But how do you know,' I asked, 'how difficult or easy it is going to be for people to have what they desire?'

'By doing the maths and looking at the angles created by the moving planets to their positions in a person's unique chart. For instance, a one-hundred-twenty-degree angle in a person's chart denotes that a situation will be flowing and easy, whereas a ninety-degree angle is the angle of a square, which indicates that a new direction or some kind of change is required before the person can move forward. Many people wonder about whether free will is incompatible with astrology, and the answer is simple: when you merely respond to life without awareness, there is little or no free will. You are carried along by what is happening around you rather than paddling your own canoe! However, the more you become aware that you have choices in a situation, the more you move out of fate and into free will. When you're conscious about where you are and what you want to accomplish, you have choice; when you are not conscious, old patterns or other people take over and make your choices for you.'

How many times have I said it? The more coherent you become, the more connected and aligned to the Source you become, the more the Universal Mind can flow through you, and the more effortless your life will become.

Meanwhile, I was keen to understand more about world events and the planets. Thinking of an example, I asked Linda if she had known that Barack Obama would become President of the United States.

'Well,' she laughed, 'when it comes to world events, things can be more difficult, because there are usually more factors to consider and some information is simply not available. However, it wasn't difficult for me to decide between Obama and McCain, as when I looked at the cycle of Pluto in Capricorn, it was a happening that only occurs every two hundred and fifty years. The last time Pluto was in Capricorn, the United States was being created, and it began as a slave-owning nation. As Pluto reached each of the other two earth signs, major advancements were made when it came to racial equality: Pluto in Taurus (1851–1882) brought the Civil War and freedom from slavery; Pluto in Virgo (1956–1972) passed laws that ended segregation. And so the final step, the return of Pluto to Capricorn after a journey of two hundred and fifty years, showed that an African American would emerge in a high position. That's how astrology makes predictions.'

Before saying goodbye, I was keen for Linda to go 'on the record' with a few predictions based on the positions of planets in the coming years.

There was a lengthy silence before she spoke again. 'Throughout history,' she began, 'there have been countless predictions of "end of the world" scenarios, most recently around 2012, yet we are all still here! The Mayan Calendar ends on 21 December 2012, which points to a turning point in human consciousness. Astrologically this change has already begun with the transit of Pluto into Capricorn in January 2008. The length of the stay is almost sixteen years. Pluto in this earth sign, which represents our institutions, banks and government, quickly revealed during 2008 and 2009 which of those supposedly invincible facades were illusions, and which were based on some semblance of truth. However, change is never easy to implement; therefore the years 2010–2013 will put us through several false starts in which the media will declare the recession is over many times before it actually is. But it will end.'

As Linda spoke, I was reminded once again of how disconnected our existence has become, especially in the West, as we have come to rely ever more on technology rather than on our intuition, to navigate our world. 'That's true,' agreed Linda. 'When the twelve-hour/sixty-minute clock was created in the 1600s, we took our first steps towards relying on a machine for something we used to find within ourselves and nature. Now, with Blackberrys, cell phones and technology constantly improving, we have never been more connected to the physical world, yet less connected to our intuition and each other.

'With Pluto in Capricorn we are finally discovering the need to return home to the spiritual core of our being – a need which is felt by many – and this feeling will grow in intensity. The first step has already happened; the centre of power has shifted, and although many are holding on for dear life, trying to undermine the changes that are inevitable, given enough time the old will loosen its grip and pass away. There is a yearning to reconnect to old ideals, to a moral code that serves us, rather than destroys us, and now we must manifest these ideals through conscious choice.'

I hope you are starting to understand that you are a co-creator.

'And,' Linda further predicted, 'from April 2011, when Neptune moves into Pisces, our yearning for spirituality will increase because faith will suddenly become more essential to our survival. This necessity could be brought about by natural disasters that bring us together, or a mass spiritual sighting, discovery or experience that heralds a new reality. Science and the metaphysical world will begin to mirror each other as new information and knowledge bring them closer together. The union of these two opposing perspectives is the beginning of a new world vision. Many leaders will be further humbled as they are forced to realize that nature, the earth, has more power than they do and that they must listen to what it tells us that we need or there will be consequences that are irreversible.'

Within three months of my chat with Linda, a massive earthquake would devastate Haiti, and within another month a quake would hit Chile as well, followed by another in China. And world leaders and the public alike were indeed later reminded of nature's awesome powers when all aircraft were grounded in the UK and around Europe after the Eyjafjallajokull volcano erupted in Iceland.

'So, my prediction for the coming years,' Linda concluded, 'is a return home – a letting go of what has blocked the way to living harmoniously with each other and nature. And whatever is in the way will not survive, because the choice is no longer entirely in our hands.'

When I told her that my book was entitled *Countdown to Coherence*, Linda laughed. 'We cannot avoid our destiny. We are indeed on our way home, but we can, through making better choices from this moment, help the ride to be a less bumpy one.'

Prophetic indeed! We are, after all, co-creating our future in every moment. Through our actions, reactions, thoughts and attitudes we can indeed decide whether our transition is going to be easy or difficult. If you would like to know more about astrology, you can read Linda's book *The Day You Were Born* or visit www.lindajoyce.com.

Are you starting to believe, as Gary Schwartz suggests, that the Whole Mind of which we are a part does indeed have an 'agenda' – and that its agenda for *us* is to make our way back to coherence, back home? At the individual level, the first signs of becoming more coherent manifest in the physical brain, and some people do have bumpier rides than others; after what I had gone through in '98, I knew this to be true. As my journey unfolded, I was keen to know more about what happens in our brains and bodies as we grow in coherence – which could help us prepare ourselves better and thus enjoy a smoother transition. Several more aha moments awaited me as I pursued this inquiry with the help of a very 'awake' scientist.

Chapter Twelve

Spiritual Breakthroughs, Spontaneous Healing and a Saintly Scientist

You are gods.

– Psalm 82; John 10:34

Before enlightenment a man chops wood and carries water, after enlightenment he chops wood and carries water.

– Buddhist saying

1 November 2009 – London and Fairfield, Iowa

I DISTINCTLY RECALL walking down a busy London street at the height of my spiritual experience in 1998 thinking, 'These people think I'm like them, but they have no idea how *special* I have become.' I truly *felt* 'godlike'; I was telepathic, incredibly psychic and at times manifesting ash (as some spiritual teachers do). My eyes continually changed colour, I was affecting and being affected by electricity, and I could 'see' and hear other realities – including 'dead' people. At times I had incredible physical strength, at others I was as weak as a kitten. And I thought I *knew everything* – a big mistake. When I interviewed Hollywood star Whoopi Goldberg for my *Sunday Times* column, she seemed to sense I was in trouble, as she advised me, 'There is nothing you cannot do if you keep calm and go forward.' Today, some of these memories make me cringe, whilst others make me laugh – but I wasn't laughing back then.

After meeting dozens of ordinary people who have also gone through their own unique awakenings, I have been fortunate in being able to discuss their experiences with psychiatrists and scientists as well as with enlightened spiritual teachers. I have learned that the triggers for spontaneous awakenings vary greatly; they include prolonged stress or a sudden intense shock, the intervention of an enlightened man or woman, spiritual practices, certain drugs and even intense orgasm. The range of reported symptoms is equally wide. As parapsychologist Dr Serena Roney-Dougal explains, 'With spiritual "breakthroughs", your experience and symptoms can depend on a host of factors: your background, your beliefs – especially religious beliefs, your diet, the state of your physical body and mind, your stress levels, whether you have taken drugs and so on.'

Symptoms of intense breakthroughs are diverse and wide-ranging; this is an abbreviated version. The body may experience muscle tremors, fever or cold. Some people hear voices or, depending on their culture and beliefs, see visions of angels, demons or archetypal animals. You may undergo a physical near-death experience or a symbolic feeling of death and rebirth. There might also be a sense of having 'married God', or even that little you is the reincarnation of Jesus, Buddha or the like. You might manifest objects such as holy ash or phenomena such as stigmata. Can you imagine an orthodox doctor's reaction to such a roster of complaints?

Whatever your personality is, at the time of a spiritual breakthrough it becomes hugely amplified. Feelings of humility alternate with a belief that you are a super-being; you may wonder, 'Why doesn't everyone want to listen to *meeeeee?*' You may believe that you can fly, or have a sense that you have become indestructible, or feel unconditional love interspersed with episodes of panic. Quite inadvertently, Nelson Mandela summarized how such intense moments can affect us when he said, 'In a moment we can catch a glimpse of all that we can be and in a moment we can lose it to fear.'

You may be wondering how long such a roller coaster of symptoms might last. It could be ten seconds, ten minutes, ten hours, ten months or even ten years. Yet the more prepared one is, the easier the transition. And the healthier and more spiritually aware one becomes, the more unlikely any negative episodes. Several psychologists have concluded that some spontaneous kundalini experiences are linked to a cry for help from a broken nervous system – which was certainly correct in my case.

Once my experience faded and my physical body recovered, for some time afterwards I asked myself, 'How come I felt so special, but looked the same? How come I still needed to clean my teeth and take a bath?' Anything to do with the physical aspects of myself had seemed so mundane! In those moments, it was my inflated sense of ego – in other words, duality – that prevented me from realizing the truth of what was happening.

Conversely, during moments of pure bliss, when I felt like everyone's mother and father and yet completely humble, I would happily have given my life to save another. I knew that all consciousness was part of me and I was part of it. In such moments there was no duality, no ego. Just me. Little me and Bigger Me became as one. Atonement. At-One-Ment. Many people are learning to be, as I glimpsed in those moments, in this world but not *of* this world, and as we grow in coherence we will learn how to literally 'walk between worlds'.

But how do *you* think a god should look or act? Centuries ago Eastern potentates and emperors were considered divine beings. Popes, priests, saints and royalty have been referred to throughout history as being God's chosen earthly representatives.

Now, I invite you to go and look into your *own* eyes in a mirror – have a good long look. In 1998, when I looked into my own or others' eyes, the pain at times was excruciating. Why? Because I was so full of light I was fit to explode with it – and in looking into other people's eyes I could feel and see the light being emitted from within them. I didn't need to 'receive' any more light, as I was *becoming* the light. Eventually I figured out that when and if it was appropriate, I needed to transfer some of that light which is energy and information, which pulsed through and around me, into other people's eyes in order to share the light with them. In the East, this practice of spiritual blessing is known as Darshan.

Imagine now for a few minutes that you are like a god in a physical body, with all its good points and bad! Put your ego to one side and sit quietly. Stop worrying about how you look, any aches and pains, what you will wear today, if little Johnny will pass his exams and so on. Instead just *be* for 10 or 15 minutes. Totally surrender into aligning with God. Don't *try* to do it, simply take a deep breath and let go. Unburden yourself of it all. Simply be in the Golden Present.

Then slowly imagine that you are in some small way merging with God and that you have access to some of his/her powers. What might be your first command? World peace, a pizza, a lottery win? Would you forgive yourself your 'sins'? Would you heal yourself and others? Or perhaps let go of your guilt or make up with someone you had cross words with?

And what would I command? Well, initially, little me would indeed intend world peace, which would free up lots of money to help save, feed and educate more people.

Unfortunately little me remains in a physical body with an ego mind – and all that this entails. Even a fully enlightened master of the self in a physical body can utilize only a *fraction* of the potential power that emanates from the Whole, which is manifesting and working through him or her. Enlightened men and women may have access to the Whole, but the expression of it in this space-time reality has its limits! So, all little me can do is begin by working on myself – by bringing my *attention* to an *intention* to align with coherence. Or as my next guest, Professor Frederick Travis, would say, by 'having an intention to align with the field of universal intelligence that underlies all of life'.

———— ⋙⋘ ————

Fred Travis is a professor of Vedic science who has spent more than 30 years studying the science of consciousness, altered states, and how they affect the physical brain. As head of the Center for Brain, Consciousness, and Cognition at the Maharishi University of Management in Fairfield, Iowa – an accredited institution offering traditional degree programs with a distinctive focus on developing human potential – Fred is pioneering the science of enlightenment. He and his colleagues have documented the existence of what ancient traditions have spoken of for thousands of years as a state of enlightenment – a state of total brain functioning – and 47 of his scientific research papers have been published. Thankfully, after years of regular meditation, Travis also has the patience of a saint.

In chapter 6, I mentioned the measurable positive effects that group intention can have in war zones, demonstrated in more than 50 verified, validated scientific trials. Professor Travis has often reiterated that if we are willing to sit quietly and through meditation become more coherent, then in time that coherence will affect our psyche, health and outlook in positive ways – but it will also affect others and the local environment. As Bill Tiller said, coherence is catching.

On a sunny afternoon, marvelling at the autumn colours unfolding outside my study window, I settled in with a steaming mug of organic Earl Grey tea and dialled up Professor Travis via Skype on my computer.

I began by asking Fred about research claiming that if one in every hundred people could meditate regularly, then their contact with this pure intelligence would help to 'unfreeze' the expression of pure intelligence everywhere on the planet. I wondered if such research implied a critical-mass-type scenario that could potentially create panic if everyone had a spontaneous awakening at once.

Fred smiled at my question. 'Obviously if everyone had a spontaneous kundalini awakening,' he responded, 'as you have pointed out, it would cause pandemonium in an unprepared body; the nervous system would not be able or ready to cope. But in my opinion this simply won't happen.'

'So how do you see this growing coherence unfolding?'

'I don't see what's unfolding in spiritual terms as a wham-bam shift,' he replied. 'It's a one-by-one process. I believe we are indeed heading back towards coherence, but as each person contributes and adds their individual unit of consciousness to the process, the collective consciousness is enhanced.

'Every single one of us counts, and someone out there could be the one person who tips the balance. In time, as our consciousness aligns with the underlying field of intelligence, there will be greater calls for peace. On the surface everything will look the same, but our inner quality of life will be different. Every single act will become more in tune with all other parts of life. The media will start reporting more good news, rather than bad, as negativity begins to dissipate. In terms of world events, specifically as people begin to understand how we are all linked, we will see more cooperation among nations. There will be a flowering of the arts and creativity, working with nature rather than against it – this is starting to happen through the "green" movements. In other words, our motivation for doing things will change from "What's in it for me?" to "How can I help make a difference to the Whole?"'

I can't wait. Imagine switching on the news or picking up the newspaper and seeing only stories that lift your spirits! More good news encourages us to think, and ideally act, more positively – and if we can sustain this 'feel-good' factor, it will attach to the grid and thus become our reality. We *are* co-creators.

And little me in my physical body can aid this process by choosing to eat more of the foods that I know suit my constitution, that are literally 'on my wavelength'. I can also have some fun; after all, life is all about balance! I can choose, and take more responsibility for my choices at all levels of being. I can choose my thoughts – though some days are still better than others.

I can choose to imagine a fantastic future for myself and mankind. I can choose to change my reaction and attitude to external events. I can choose to help others when I can. I can choose to forgive myself and others, especially those who 'know not what they do'. Most of the world's population are 'conscious' in that they walk, talk, go to work, have children and go about their lives – yet they are not truly 'awake' at all. So I can choose to judge someone – or not, as I don't know their whole physical or soul story. We are all little me's who need to realize that we are also part of a Bigger Me – we *are* all connected.

And finally, I can choose not to beat myself up or feel sorry for myself if I become ill – and even consider new avenues for healing. His Holiness Satguru Shree Shivkrupanandji, an enlightened teacher based in India, whom I have interviewed several times, once became quite irritated when I moaned about my back pain. 'If you could concentrate wholeheartedly on God,' he told me, 'your pain would melt away.' At the time, I was in such discomfort that his words simply added to my frustration. Yet during an interview I conducted with Professor Travis for my book *The Evidence for the Sixth Sense,* the professor told me that during moments of total brain coherence, this coherence automatically transfers to every cell in the body, which can trigger a spontaneous healing.

Most doctors still cannot explain such phenomena, yet there are plenty of scientists who can. As this knowledge spreads through authoritative books such as *The Biology of Belief* by cell biologist Bruce Lipton PhD – which documents numerous cases of how the mind affects the body – I believe that cases of spontaneous healing and other 'miracles' associated with enlightenment will become far more commonplace.

I was keen to learn more from Fred about what happens in our brains as we work our way towards enlightenment, a state of totally coherent brain functioning. But first, I wanted to touch on the growing belief I had discussed with several of my expert sources – that what we see as our physical world is nothing more than a hologram and that our reality only becomes real or 'set' when we observe it.

Fred smiled on my computer screen. 'The key point for your readers to keep in mind is that knowledge is different in different states of consciousness. In one state of consciousness, we are a hologram, and in another state we are not. You use the term *God*, which is fine, whereas I term it the *underlying intelligence;* and that field of underlying intelligence, as Professor Gary Schwartz has told you, is everywhere, in everything, and therefore is holographic in nature. But you as Hazel and I as Fred inside this space-time reality view the world from our different perspectives.

'And as we begin to grow in coherence, we start "seeing" the world differently, still through our same physical eyes, but from ever-changing perspectives. And our experiences at an ego-mind level reflect back into the holographic whole and thus all our experiences whilst in this physical body contribute to the Whole – which is growing via its experiences through us.

'And as people evolve towards higher states of consciousness – as their whole brains begin to synchronize – the outside world remains the same, but it is the *consciousness* projecting though our physical computers, our brains, which change. This is when our higher self-consciousness (the holographic part of us) comes together with our outer sensory perception, through our eyes, touch, feeling and so on, to create our final experience.'

Back in 1998, the world had indeed looked the same – yet all my senses became super-heightened immediately following my initial experience in Harrods, when I felt as if a volcano had erupted inside my body. Therefore I was keen to hear Fred's opinion as to what he might have seen on his specialized brain-imaging equipment at such a moment.

'There is no doubt that if we could have measured your brainwaves around the time of your spontaneous "awakening", we would have seen a coherent increase of activity in *all* parts of your brain, as you would have started processing information differently.'

'But,' I interjected, 'another scientist has told me that although most of us only utilize about four per cent of our brain's total potential capabilities and even the greatest masters of self are only using about ten per cent. Now you say that we do in fact use our whole brains all the time. Which is correct?'

Another patient smile. 'Both are correct. Your physical brain is always active, and on a brain scan you would see activity throughout the whole brain. The point about the four per cent is that your potential activity has to be coordinated. Right now, as you are listening to me, the part of your brain related to hearing – the thalamus in the centre of your brain and the auditory cortex, behind the ears – is more active by two to three per cent, whilst the rest of your brain is taking care of balance, monitoring hunger and thirst, scanning your environment for other things that are happening. So yes, the brain itself is always active.

'Returning to your question about what happened to you physically in Harrods, it's important to reiterate that the meta-physical kundalini – the fine "pipe" or channel that starts at the base of the spine and runs through to the top of your head – can open and activate slowly over time if a person regularly meditates, chants, does yogic breathing and so on. However, during a spontaneous kundalini awakening, higher-dimensional energies flood up the neural pathways in the spine, like a dam bursting, and surge into the thalamus in the centre of the brain. Such a situation triggers a chemical imbalance and a *huge* heightening of the senses, as the thalamus controls sensory awareness, sight, touch, smell and so forth, as well as regulating sleep and wakefulness. And this is why, as your kundalini flooded, your senses became super-heightened.'

Crikey. No wonder I had been able to smell more, hear more, see more and sleep less. At times I felt like a mini-car that had inadvertently been filled with rocket fuel. And listening to Fred, I understood better why a person's underlying personality becomes so amplified during a spontaneous awakening. We don't have a specific sixth sense as such – it's more that we suddenly develop a greater awareness of all our previously muted senses!

'So,' I clarified with Fred, 'are you saying the thalamus is like the "G spot" for enlightenment – not the pineal gland, which has long been thought of as the "seat of the soul"?'

'Yes, I am,' he replied. 'The pineal gland was long thought to be the "third eye", as it's the only structure in the brain that is not paired with a mirror structure. In fact, the pineal gland actually works by responding to light coming in through the eyes; and light, depending on its intensity, slows or stops production of the hormone melatonin, which induces sleep. Hence, during winter months, when there is less daylight, the pineal gland automatically secretes more melatonin, which makes us feel more sleepy. This is the basis of SAD, or seasonal affective disorder, syndrome.

'But,' he added, 'a master of the self has spent years learning how to control, integrate and work with these powerful energies. This is why people should never try and accelerate their spiritual awakening by using drugs such as cannabis and cocaine or hallucinogens such as LSD and ayahausca.'

I was delighted to hear Fred say this, as it echoed what Alberto Villoldo had told me and what I had long believed. 'How, specifically,' I asked, 'do these drugs affect the brain?'

'These types of drugs block the uptake of neurotransmitters. Within the brain you have "pleasure circuits" which fire when you eat a favourite food, such as chocolate, or you see a fabulous sunset. The neurotransmitter dopamine is released and travels to the receiving part of a cell, where it is held for a moment, then "let go" and recycled and taken back up by the neuron that fired it. But if you take a drug like cocaine, it fills up the reuptake receptors, and the dopamine just sits in the space between the two cells, so the receptors just keep firing. That is the basis of the "rush" that users experience.'

'Which causes what to happen in the long term?'

'The dopamine circuits can eventually be destroyed,' Fred said. 'Users no longer enjoy such intense highs on a single dose, so they take more and more drugs to feel that rush again. This spiral takes them ever further away from living a stable life as their brains suffer more and more damage.'

Though I knew of the damage these drugs could do, I was keen to hear from Fred the types of symptoms they induce.

'Psychosis, depression, suicidal tendencies, sometimes multiple personality disorders, schizophrenia ... '

I thought of what Professor Villoldo had told me – that if, for whatever reason, a person experiences a 'walk-in', it is possible for a discarnate spirit to enter the person's energy field. I myself had 'heard' or felt specific voices in my head and had the experience of two distinct personalities existing in one body – mine! Yet I inherently felt that I was not schizophrenic. I asked Fred if he believed that people suffering from multiple-personality disorder might have multiple walk-ins.

He looked thoughtful. 'This is a highly complex subject and we could spend weeks discussing various realities, but in this context, let me keep it simple by saying there are numerous well-documented cases of people with multiple-personality disorders.

In some cases, when a specific personality becomes dominant, the patient may exhibit physical symptoms of diabetes, for example, or cancer; yet when another personality becomes dominant, he or she is perfectly healthy.

'To explain such phenomena, let's return to the analogy that we are all a reflection of the Whole from our own perspective. And the whole underlying field of intelligence contains every aspect of all of us – every trait and thought imaginable. We have found in the brains of schizophrenics, for example, a thinning of the brain cortex, which means they have less grey matter and fewer cortical connections. Therefore they find it difficult to maintain a coherent sense of individualized "self" – as they cannot integrate thinking, feeling and a sense of self at the same time – and can easily become disoriented into other levels of feeling and of reality. A shaman might term such events a spirit "walk-in", but I would say that such people are "picking up" energetic aspects of the Whole and therefore becoming confused in their everyday reality. Their brains are simply flooded with information. This also helps explain phenomena like speaking in tongues: at times of intense religious experiences, people may link to the universal field which contains all knowledge, and since their brains cannot process so much information, it comes out as a garbled mess!'

I knew Fred was not kidding. There were times in '98 when I spoke a fair amount of rubbish – and I well knew how disorienting the whole experience could be. In the years since, I have met many people who believe they have become spiritually attached to a person who has 'died', whilst others are seeing demons or angelic beings or believe they themselves are superbeings, even gods. For a time, I too lost my sense of self – as I no longer knew who 'I' was!

Allow me save you a lot of heartache and much confusion. You are a part of God and all parts make the Whole. And if you should experience sudden heightened states as I once did, I hope the information in this book will help you through them.

On a physical level, I found that eating sugar helped calm my brain, which felt as if it was 'cooking' when in fact it was just calling for more fuel in the form of glucose. Over several months, as my experience took its natural course, by trial and error and receiving advice from nutritionists and healers, I eventually realized that my physical body was desperate for more nutrients – B vitamins to nourish my nerves, calcium and magnesium to reduce the constant muscle tremors, and essential fats such as fish oils and evening primrose oil to help me think more clearly, as our brains are approximately 60 per cent essential fats. Foods like porridge and stews rich in earthy vegetables, as well as literally lying on the ground, helped to bring me 'back to earth'. Salt baths and seawater were very grounding as well. Hands-on energy healing helped by balancing my energy field, and over time – with the help of good friends, healers and my husband – I finally became me again.

Towards the end of my experience I was told about the work of Stanislav Grof MD, a retired professor of psychiatry once based at the world-famous Johns Hopkins School of Medicine in Baltimore, Maryland. In 2003 I interviewed Grof at length – a fascinating man who has spent over 60 years studying altered states after experiencing them himself while researching LSD for a pharmaceutical company in his early medical career. When he began seeing patients who had never taken drugs but were experiencing altered states, he realized that access to what he termed, after Jung, the 'collective unconscious' is part of our birthright. Today, in his 80s, he still lectures around the globe on the transformative potential of altered states via his holotropic breathing techniques. He and his wife, Christina, coined the term 'Spiritual Emergency', and his book *The Stormy Search for the Self* was a godsend. You can find out more at www.stanislavgrof.com.

Fred and I had been talking for almost an hour, and I needed to stretch my legs. We agreed to a recess. With another mug of tea in my hand, I walked in the fading light and took a few deep breaths, not only to alkalize my blood but also to oxygenate my brain and consider the subjects I was still keen to discuss – among them dreaming, ageing, the reptilian brain, and what happens within our brains as we slowly become more coherent.

Prior to calling Fred back, I scanned some of the facts he had shared with me over the years. Apparently, when we are born, our physical brains are 'unassembled', and during our first 25 years of life a huge maturation process takes place. By the mid-teens most brain cells are fully myelinated – insulated in fatty tissue – which allows information to pass more quickly to other cells. However, our connections to the frontal parts of our brain – the prefrontal cortex – where our planning, decision making, moral reasoning and sense of self are located, does not mature until later. This is why teenagers tend to do silly things without thinking them through first. They are like cars without brakes!

And when we are asleep, under hypnosis or in a trance state, these frontal lobes become disconnected, which explains why if woken suddenly we are somewhat disoriented until our frontal lobes come back 'on line'. But during meditation, if we can access the vacuum level of reality in the space between our thoughts, the frontal lobes remain connected and the quality of functioning within the brain changes – which not only triggers an array of health benefits but also heightens our senses.

So I was quite interested to return to an earlier subject and hear what happens in the thalamus as we meditate. As Fred's friendly face reappeared on my screen, I posed my question.

'During meditation,' came his response, 'as you detach from your ego self, the frontal lobes become more active, and the switching function within the thalamus operates at a higher level, which means that your senses begin to function more optimally.'

'Meaning we become more intuitive?'

'Basically, yes. But as always it takes time to learn to trust your intuition, your heightening sense of awareness!'

Realizing that our chat could go on indefinitely, I was keen to know more about our ancient reptilian brain. According to Darwin's theory of evolution, which despite some detractors has long been confirmed through science, eons ago our ancestors were reptiles. As numerous people I have interviewed have distinct memories of being 'lizard-like', I wondered what mechanism made the connection. I said to Fred, 'Professor Schwartz has told me that most of the atoms here today have been around for over fourteen billion years – and atoms have memory. So, in heightened states of awareness, are we simply retrieving ancient reptilian memories from within our atoms, or are we accessing ancient parts of our *brains?*'

'That's truly a thought-provoking question,' Fred replied, smiling. 'I have no idea if we are retrieving information from atoms, but I can share information about the reptilian brain which is linked to dreaming.'

A synchronicity indeed – as dreams were to have been my next question.

Fred elaborated. 'During sleeping and waking hours, certain cells in the midbrain, part of the reptilian brain, are completely silent. This part of the brain "wakes up" when we dream and activates our visual system, our emotional system and our motor system, which moves our limbs. So when we are asleep, most of our brains are active, except for the frontal lobes. However, this brain activity is driven by random firing from the brain stem, so dreams are very visual, full of emotion, and involve plenty of movement – it's like throwing a pot of paint on a canvas and trying to make sense of it.'

'But,' I countered, 'some people, like Chris Robinson, dream actual events in the future. In my dreams, I often see places that I, Hazel, could never imagine in this lifetime. And what about astral travel?'

Fred laughed and suggested I slow down. 'This is an important point,' he said. 'EEG research suggests that in the moments between sleeping and waking and in the moments between sleeping and dreaming, as the activity of mind and body settles somewhat, *we pass through the field of universal intelligence that administers all of life.* Several times a night, we pass through this basic level of reality, in which we have access to all information independent of time and space.'

I was blown away. In one simple paragraph, so much was finally explained. And I barely had time to reflect on the implications, as it was almost time for us to call it a day. Before saying goodbye, I wanted to clarify with Fred that masters of the self have integrated all realities and so have access all the time to that level the rest of us only pass through – to all knowledge stored within the underlying field of intelligence.

'They do indeed,' he confirmed. 'Once people become thus enlightened, they are still different, and the Whole works through each one in a way that is most appropriate for their physiology.'

'And what subtle changes will people on their spiritual journey begin to notice as they grow in coherence?', I asked.

'They become much calmer, less "involved", less affected by external events. Their perceptions change. And when life presents challenges, solutions pop into their heads. Life becomes altogether smoother and joyful. High blood pressure can be lowered, thus reducing the risk for heart disease and strokes. Production of the stress hormones cortisol and adrenalin is reduced, which means a regular meditator can handle stress more effectively and for longer periods and therefore can age more slowly. If you meditate regularly for seven to twelve years, your biological age at the end will be twelve years younger than your chronological age. And the more you meditate, the more creative and intelligent you become.'

The Professor had certainly given me much to consider, and as I thanked him profusely and cut our connection, I thought of the message from the Gospel of Luke – to go within, 'for the kingdom of God is within you.'

The next morning, with my mind still buzzing from my chat with Professor Travis, I was due to fly to the ancient city of Turin to meet an alchemist who has created his own template for such a kingdom – an amazing community of people that may give us a glimpse of our own enlightened future.

If you would like to read more from Professor Travis on the science of enlightenment, visit www.fredtravis.com.

Chapter Thirteen

The Alchemist, the Temples and the Nature of Time

Time is a space you can navigate –
if you know how.

– Oberto Airaudi

November 2009 – Turin

PROFESSOR TRAVIS FORETELLS that as we align with the universal intelligence that underlies all of life and begin to more fully understand who we truly are, we will witness greater cooperation between peoples and nations, there will be a flowering of the arts and creativity and every act will be in tune with all other aspects of life. During the past decade I have visited or read of numerous and diverse spiritual communities springing up around the globe to bring this vision into being – from ashrams in India to yoga-based communities in America to Findhorn in Scotland and healing centres in South Africa. All have their unique ways of living yet adhere to a central theme of respect for each other and our planet. But nowhere have I seen Travis's vision so completely encompassed as in the community of Damanhur.

Nestling in the foothills of the Alps in northern Italy, 45 kilometres from the ancient city of Turin, lies the valley of Valchiusella, peppered with quaint, rustic medieval villages. Some 1,000 Damanhurians from more than 17 countries and all walks of life live peacefully in 80 settlements within the valley. But the story of how the community of Damanhur – which has taken its name, meaning 'City of Light', from the ancient subterranean Egyptian temple to Horus – came into being in the late '70s includes intrigue worthy of a Hollywood movie, and the spectacular geography of Valchiusella holds a secret that has earned the title of the Eighth Wonder of the World.

Damanhurians pay Italian taxes, but they also choose to give a percentage of their income to help support community projects. They are doctors, lawyers, bakers, bankers, architects, farmers, artists, healers, plumbers, electricians – a hugely diverse group. Some live and work within the community, whilst others work outside yet live within and contribute to it. No matter what, everyone who has chosen to become a citizen of Damanhur offers a few hours of time each month to community projects.

Thanks to this 'spirit' of connection and cooperation, Damanhur has its own Open University offering courses in subjects ranging from spiritual physics and astral travel to healing, lateral thinking and creating sustainable communities. Its state-of-the-art school is attended by some of the best-behaved, most well-travelled pupils I have ever met. Within the community are also organic supermarkets, cafés, vineyards, farms and bakeries. Damanhur even has its own currency, which encourages people to spend their money on local produce, helping the community to thrive.

The Foundation for Environmental Education has recognized Damanhur with an award for its inspired eco-homes. In 2005 a UN committee voted Damanhur a model for new sustainable communities. Politicians from several countries have visited to learn about the infrastructure, and Damanhur is fast becoming a template for a new way of living – both physically and spiritually.

Most fascinating of all, it has the most elaborate spiritual 'town hall' imaginable. Weaving their way underneath a hillside are nine ornate temples on five different levels, linked by hundreds of metres of tunnels – more than 8,500 cubic metres of space in all – constructed like a three-dimensional book that narrates the history of humanity through all types of art. These unique Temples of Humankind have been built entirely underground by the people of Damanhur.

This was my second visit to the community and I was looking forward to chatting once again with its founder, Oberto Airaudi. Known as Falco within the community, this modest man in his 50s is like a modern-day alchemist. The dictionary defines alchemy as 'a medieval forerunner of chemistry, the pursuit of transmutation of baser metals into gold or silver'. Yet Falco is more interested in helping *us* transform from ordinary human beings into divine ones and thus have the ability to create miracles for ourselves! During our first meeting two years earlier I had been impressed by Falco's self-effacing humility and appreciated his wry sense of humour, yet I sensed that he was a fully enlightened being with much wisdom to share, and I was keen to hear more of it.

Two years earlier, Falco had shared the incredible story of how Damanhur came into being. It began in 1960 when he was ten years old – and highly psychic. 'From an early age,' he told me, 'I experienced detailed memories of what I believe was a past life in a place like Atlantis, in which there were amazing temples containing futuristic healing technologies, which were also transmitters and receivers of information. Around these temples lived highly evolved spiritual communities that enjoyed an idyllic, peaceful existence in which all the people worked for the good of the whole community. Even though science and science fiction were my passion, these remembrances went far beyond a child's vivid imagination.

'When I was young,' he continued, 'I thought that everyone could do what I presumed was normal. At school, my classmates wanted to play with me because I would share "tricks" like levitation with them. I could direct my mind to "see" inside closed buildings and describe in detail what was happening there, just as physicists did at the Stanford Research Institute in America during the '70s and '80s. As I grew older, I learned to be a lot more discreet with my inherent abilities.'

Can you blame him? Ignorance, misunderstanding and fear of the unknown have caused so much unnecessary judgement and even death down the centuries. One young mother I met attempted suicide after being forcibly committed to a psychiatric ward because she could see and hear 'dead' people. It was only after her attempt failed that her grandmother revealed that she too had this ability. The poor girl was a natural medium, but no-one had told her. Many enlightened men and women have been persecuted for such abilities – *to which we all have access.*

I asked how Falco's parents had viewed his 'gifts'. 'My parents were naturally extremely perturbed,' he told me, 'but eventually my mother began to document my experiments and we converted some rooms in our large home into laboratories, where I also began sketching blueprints for the underground structures from my memories. My goal was to recreate the temples from my visions alongside a new society in which people respected and cared for the planet and each other.'

As he grew into adulthood and began a career as an insurance broker, Falco kept searching for the perfect site to found his new society. In 1977, he found it on a remote hillside in an area where Eurasian and African plates had thrown up over millennia the mineral mylonite, an ancient ore that Falco felt would sustain the large underground structures he had in mind. On a clear night in August 1978, he and his companions saw a bright meteor with stardust in its wake speeding across the heavens and agreed this was an auspicious moment to begin their secret project.

During that first night, using only hammers and picks, they dug over a metre down into the rock. Simultaneously, they began restoration work on an old house above ground to hide what was being constructed underneath. As the project grew, volunteers worked in four-hour shifts digging deeper day and night, year after year – for 16 years. Astonishingly, no geologists were consulted and there were no formal plans other than Falco's sketches and visions.

Some of the volunteers trained as electricians, whilst other aspiring artisans learned to work with glass, sculpt stone, and paint. They began buying homes within the valley, and eventually, to earn their living, they set up small cooperative businesses to meet not only their burgeoning spiritual community's needs but also those of the valley's long-time residents. In this way the Damanhurians built thriving bakeries, vineyards, publishing houses and furniture workshops. House builders, artists, farmers and jewellers ran their businesses during the day and dug quietly when time allowed. What they have created is a modern miracle, complete with stunning three-dimensional murals, fine mosaics, statues, tons of inlaid marble and hydraulics that work secret doors – all of which are nowadays open by appointment to those who feel drawn here.

Before being taken into the temples, guests are shown a few Damanhurian homes, which are beautifully painted with oversized scenes from nature to remind us of its enormity. Our guide and interpreter, Esperide Ananas, an author with degrees from New York University and Milan University who has lived in the community since 1993, also showed us Falco's prolific paintings, full of symbolism designed to aid spiritual growth. Yet none of the above, inspiring though it all is, prepared me or my companion, my assistant Lindsay, for what lay beneath.

When the predominantly Catholic Italian government first learned of the temples in July 1992, helicopter gunships and armed police were dispatched at dawn to 'force' Damanhurians to reveal their secrets. On the belief that something unholy was happening underground, the state prosecutor threatened to dynamite the entire hillside – yet when the policemen saw what had been achieved, some were in tears. I can understand why. It is extraordinary to step through an innocuous door in the side of a small house, then travel down in a lift to alight in another world!

Lindsay and I made our way along a passageway decorated with Egyptian hieroglyphs and found ourselves in the Hall of the

Earth: a circular chamber 8 metres in diameter in which a sculpted column depicting a three-dimensional man and woman supported a ceiling of intricately painted glass portraying the explosive birth of the universe. Set against this backdrop, bright stars glowed, depicting how cosmologists say the night sky would have looked 22,000 years ago, when Atlantis, according to Damanhurians, was at its height.

On the walls a huge mural in vivid colours showed the diversity of nature on our planet, complete with paintings of endangered species, like an underground Noah's Ark. Among them were portraits of Damanhurians as representatives of humanity, symbolizing that we are all divine beings who reincarnate through several lifetimes and that the human body is a temple for a divine essence (*see* plate 3). Underfoot, intricate mosaics depicted the different ages of human life in images of men and women at play. In the Hall of Water, I saw for the first time the Selfica healing structures built by Falco from the information he 'saw' in other worlds – masses of intricately woven metals, mainly copper, set with crystals, like something out of a Jules Verne film set.

Back in Arizona, Professor Tiller had spoken of 'conditioned' or sacred spaces, such as those found in the Pyramids, that act as 'coupling' devices between our electric atom/molecule physical reality and the invisible (to us) magnetic information wave level. As I stood marvelling at what had been achieved in these temples, I truly began to understand that they act as transmitters and receivers of information between realities. The temples are in effect a giant coupling device!

Recalling this experience, and armed with a notepad full of questions, Lindsay and I returned to Damanhur on a grey, windswept November morning. We met our old friend Esperide, who was once again to act as our interpreter, and at Damanhur's welcome centre Falco joined us with warm smiles of greeting all round. Through Esperide, I shared the concept of this book and began by asking Falco if he believes that humanity is indeed 'going home' to coherence.

'Well, I would say that whilst a small part of humanity is evolving towards who they really are, a huge proportion are devolving,' he replied. 'This is like a selection process. We tend to confuse progress with evolution. This process of evolving cannot be externally evidenced, as it is an internal process. Many religions and dogmas are trying to make spiritual growth into a commercial enterprise, as the old ways of living are beginning to crumble. Many people are clinging on by their fingernails. It's time to let go. Consciousness is dividing – this has been happening for some time.'

His words echoed many of my beliefs and reminded me of Bill Tiller's comments back in Arizona: that it's our consciousness that is 'going home' to merge back from whence it came, and that a 'split' in consciousness is going to occur. Falco was speaking in general terms when he said that this ongoing process cannot be evidenced externally; this is because we still look the same. But as more and more of us grow in coherence by aligning with the intelligence that underlies all of life, as Fred Travis states, the way we think, feel and act will change, which in turn will change our physical reality for the better. Gary Schwartz had reiterated that we live in a probabilistic universe – that we are co-creators, that every thought and action counts, and that going home to coherence is a potential probability for all our futures, but not everyone may decide to take such a path. That's their choice. At its core, the underlying intelligence may be totally coherent – in phase – but at this coarse physical level, we are far from perfect and urgently need to change. And because coherence is catching, the more we can increase our individual levels of coherence, the faster this transition can happen.

Hoping that Falco might offer a sweeping statement that would encourage more people to change, I asked, 'If you were now addressing a body such as the United Nations and you only had a few minutes to speak, what would you recommend?'

He looked thoughtful before responding. 'I would advise them not to be lazy and to stop pretending to be something they are not. They should look at themselves every day in the mirror and ask, "Did I do what needed to be done today or just what was convenient to me?" Quite often the interests of an individual state are not the interests of its people. Most politicians do not think at higher levels of being in a spiritual sense. You only have to see what is going on in the world to realize that our present systems are not working. Instead of moaning about what's wrong with our societies, *all people need to take action to help make this reality a better place.* Actions always speak louder than words!'

How right he is.

'At Damanhur,' Falco continued, 'there is a sense of community – without looking for personal reward. We work hard at creating a spirit of service that much of humanity lacks. We build eco-friendly homes, we grow our own organic crops, we support and trust each other, we practise our 'inner work', we acknowledge the existence of other realms and intelligences.'

I realize that some of you reading his words might wonder if Damanhur is some kind of cult. But cults are most definitely not coherent; they are coercive and negative and often riddled with fear. Falco is not trying to formulate a religion. He is not a teacher with a big ego, trying to impose his will on others. Damanhurians are open and friendly and are free to come and go as they wish.

'People try to categorize us, but find they cannot,' added Falco as if he were reading my mind. 'There are aspects of many ancient religions in our art and beliefs, and our concept has been to create a community that lives to help others.'

I decided it was time to hear more about those beliefs and the esoteric side of Damanhur. 'Do you truly consider that you have seen the fabled Atlantis and its people?' I asked. 'And were they physical or nonphysical beings?'

'Their world and many others are as real to the people existing in them as our world appears to us. As you have realized, we have both physical and nonphysical aspects that make up what we term the "self". And, yes, I believe I have seen Atlantis and other places too. It is no longer existing on our timeline, yet on other timelines it is still in existence – *time is a space that you can navigate.*'

The silence between us was palpable as his statement hung in the air, reminding me of what Professors Tiller and Villoldo had told me back in Arizona, that potentially there are many realities existing alongside this one.

Esperide broke the silence to tell me more about their theories on Atlantis. 'We believe that Atlantis was a civilization that existed on our planet until around 20,000 years ago,' she said, 'and that Atlanteans grew part of their crops near the Nile. And when the main continent of Atlantis was destroyed, maybe by volcanic explosions or meteorites, some of the remaining Atlanteans migrated to Egypt and took their knowledge with them.'

To the sceptic, I realize her words are total supposition – yet Egyptologists have never been able to fully explain where such an advanced civilization sprang from. Archaeologists have discovered that some temples are much older than structures such as the Sphinx, which is generally dated at 4,500 years old.

For instance, at Abydos there are three temples, one of which, the Osireion, archaeologists now believe is around 12,500 years old, built at a time when sea levels were hundreds of feet lower than they are today. Remnants of ancient, highly sophisticated cultures have been found by divers off Malta, Japan, India and Cuba. Mythology may not be myth after all.

And can you even begin to imagine how amazing it would be to have the ability to navigate through time?

Months earlier, during my stay in Arizona, a Native American shaman descended from the Hualapai Tribe had told me that people can be 'led' by their spirit guides to 'star gates' through which they can physically travel in time. He emphasized that 'time travellers' cannot interfere with the past, but they could leave a 'signature' such as a rock formation or a carving – something seemingly innocuous which could be found later and puzzled over. At the time, I had dismissed his claim as nonsense. Yet theoretical physicist Michio Kaku in his book *Parallel Worlds*, when writing about the possibility that only a single quantum event may separate two worlds, states that 'to slip between these worlds *is* within the laws of physics.'

If you also consider that within a temple in Abydos in Egypt there are carvings 3,000 years old of what appear to be a helicopter, an aircraft and a submarine, that a modern-looking rocket is carved on the 1,300-year-old Mayan sarcophagus of King Pakul, or that Leonardo da Vinci around 1490 sketched helicopter-like machines and what look strikingly similar to stealth aircraft – you might now consider such anomalies from a new perspective. Perhaps the artists were living at that time, but had 'memories' of future lives that they had lived on other timelines. Or, perhaps, such artists were indeed time travellers who decided to leave messages, just as people today sadly carve their names onto buildings to say 'we were here'. I realize such concepts are highly controversial – but one day I believe science will validate them.

In Damanhur, after seeing the complex temple structures and the Selfica healing technology, I found myself asking the inevitable question – could Falco travel through time in his physical body?

Smiling enigmatically, he said, 'Anything could be possible once you know how. We exist in a virtual reality and time is indeed like a web of potential. Other civilizations and realities exist alongside our own. It's like switching channels on the TV or radio – you could potentially instantly "be" in that place ... '

His eyes are deep and knowing and the silence of his unfinished sentence told me more than any words could have done. At the height of my experience, I had intuitively felt it was possible to travel in time, but fear prevented me from experimenting, thinking that I might not return! Yet once we can learn to completely detach, let go of fear and align with other frequency domains, I firmly believe we will physically travel in time. But, as there is currently no definitive, documented, scientific evidence on physical time travel, there was little point in pressing Falco further – even though I was longing to hear more.

Again he seemed to sense my thoughts. 'Most people would consider time travel in one's physical body impossible, yet certain evolved individuals have always had this ability. Orthodox science is only just waking up to realities which have always been there.'

He is right. And that's what this book is all about, our potential capabilities and thinking 'outside the box'. Many times I have suggested that our universe and everything in it exists 'inside' what people term God, which is growing in experience through us, and that consciousness is *everywhere simultaneously*. And little you, at a certain level, is part of a Bigger You.

From there, it's not hard to conclude that everything could indeed be happening at once; but our existence in linear time creates the illusion that it is not! The Core from which we emanate, though, is not linear. It's everywhere – all the 'time'.

Staying with this theme, I was keen to hear Falco's views on the theory that it is possible to reincarnate into any time period as a specific person. In my case, I had joked about becoming Elizabeth I.

'It's entirely feasible that we could reincarnate at any period in time,' he replied. 'This would not be your ego's choice, but your soul's choice. And, in the simplest terms – as like attracts like at all levels – you would only reincarnate on a similar wavelength or level of consciousness, resonance, to your previous life. It's like taking a lift and alighting at the correct floor! You cannot conceive of such events by thinking in terms of linear time; you have to think more about resonance.

'Once people reach higher levels of consciousness,' he went on, 'this allows them, as part of the Whole, to choose where and when they will reincarnate in service to humanity. They have the ability to consciously choose when to leave a physical shell, and they can take their knowledge and wisdom with them back into their race, their community, and help that community to grow spiritually. One person can only achieve so much, but once you come together and form communities of like-minded people, you create a larger "spirit" of community. If you connect to and work in harmony with what we term the Divinities – multidimensional beings with higher levels of consciousness that can affect events within this space-time – then you can make a greater impact on the Whole, which is what we are working towards here.'

'So, do people within this community – when they die physically – consciously choose to rebirth here?' I asked.

'Yes, we have had many such cases.'

'And what about being able to experience consciousness in other forms?'

'Once you learn how to coherently direct your mind, yes, you can place your consciousness into an animal, a tree or another person's energy field – but it is essential that an individual attempting this *not* attempt to superimpose his or her individual consciousness or ego onto another, which can cause damage.'

We agreed that the Whole Mind, of which we are all a part, perceives through the senses of every creature from ants to elephants – and how profoundly our perception would change if we could 'see' life from other perspectives and levels of consciousness. But we all smiled as Falco added, 'Imagine if you suffered from vertigo and you were to merge your consciousness with a bird. If you were not completely detached from your ego mind, where might the poor bird end up?'

Moving on, I asked Falco if each of us, as an individual consciousness, can reincarnate infinite times.

'Absolutely not,' came his emphatic response. 'Everyone has to build his or her own inner temple and we only have a few lifetimes in which to do this.'

'And what happens if we don't build our inner temples?'

'Then we become a failed experiment!'

On many days, when I watch the news, I have reached the same conclusion!

Falco went on to suggest, as shaman-scientist Alberto Villoldo had, that an individual consciousness can indeed be retained for up to seven or eight lifetimes – but if an individual soul does not grow in spiritual awareness, then the luminous rod at its core will eventually weaken until it dissipates completely back into the vast sea of consciousness and becomes 'fertilizer' for other life.

As Falco prepared to leave, he added, 'It's important to reiterate that if you are linked to a "people" or group of like-minded spiritual people, you can retain your unique soul with its *knowledge and wisdom* for far longer, through a larger structure or "group mind" that links to the divine. If we were all linked in this way, we could evolve far more quickly. Also, being alive is a form of karmic responsibility; every person has talents which are precious gifts, yet not everyone invests in their talents. Those who use their gifts for the good of all are more likely to be allowed to choose when and where they return.'

I had one more question. As he stood up to leave, I asked, 'What's God to you?'

With a childlike grin, he mused, 'I would say ... God is like a bubble of patience!'

On this magical note, Lindsay, Esperide and I drove off to Damanhur's local supermarket to have lunch at their organic café. As I worked my way through tofu, lentils and plenty of fresh vegetables, we were joined briefly by Mario 'Coyote' Cardo, who lectures on 'spiritual physics' at the University of Damanhur. The majority of scientists I have met while writing this book have stressed time and again the possibility that the higher realms can interact in our space-time reality and affect the results of scientific experiments; at Damanhur they take this concept to new heights with an academic discipline devoted to the subject.

The subject of time came up again and I shared with the group Professor Villoldo's comment that we are all capable of creating new timelines. 'Of course,' agreed Mario. To illustrate his point, he went into a great deal of technical science while sketching a thick line. Here is the greatly simplified version: 'On this straight line, which looks like a tree trunk, is your life going along day by day, formed by your choices, actions and thoughts on a regular basis. Branching off this main trunk are many, many smaller branches, which are possible future timelines in virtual reality – in potential. So, let's say a person has cancer and wants to shift his or her potential future timeline. As Villoldo says, this is not always easy, as the person may need to change virtually all his or her dietary habits, lifestyle and thoughts, which requires discipline and determination. All this person's day-to-day choices then assist in building a new "branch", and when sufficient "weight" is given to the creation of that branch, it starts to "set" and thus can become a new reality whilst the old reality, or timeline, dissolves.'

Mario's description reminded me of Bill Tiller's words back in Arizona – that our focused intentions and choices, if *sustained* over time, can eventually reach a plateau, 'couple' with the magnetic information wave level and thus manifest into this reality. As Gary Schwartz stated in chapter 11, manifestation of anything into this reality goes through a process – it moves from consciousness to information to energy to matter.

Listening to Mario, I finally began to more fully grasp how some coherent souls could have the ability to travel down timelines, either into the past or into our potential futures. The ability to do this is commonplace within Damanhur. At the beginning of this book, Dr Serena Roney-Dougal explained that in this physical space-time classroom, the future and the past are indeed linear – but once you start 'coupling' with other realities outside of space and time, then different rules apply. At last it was becoming clearer.

Before leaving Damanhur, I was keen to experience some of the healing technology, known as Selfica, which Falco says he has recreated from the intricate details in his visions. Sitting in an armchair between two large, complex machines made up of intricate copper spirals, a low hum in my ears, I felt as though I had entered the starship *Enterprise*! Falco agrees with Gary Schwartz that information can easily be programmed into material objects such as crystals, stone, metals and so on, and as he 'fired up' his devices, he told me they are structures that allow other intelligences to work within our space-time. His machines help to place 'correcting' energetic information into our field to encourage the body to heal itself.

As the humming intensified, I felt a tremendous energy surging in and around me. Falco invited me to direct the energies anywhere in my body that needed healing. Thanks to my long-term back problem, now and again I suffer pain in my gut due to the conventional painkillers I use from time to time; right now I was having an attack that had lasted two days. I was longing to direct the energy into my back – yet I could feel it strongly swirling around my solar plexus area.

During Lindsay's session, she later told me, she 'saw' a shape coming out of her body standing in front of her, yet she was not alarmed. 'It was as if my spirit self walked outside of me for a minute, then gently joined me again. When I stood up, I felt as though I had been realigned in every sense of the word.'

As always, there were many more questions to ask, realities to discuss – yet if I asked them all, this book would never end. It was time to return to our hotel, just a 15-minute drive from Damanhur, to pack our bags and return to the airport.

As we made our farewells and drove away, I tried to sum up how I felt about Damanhur. Before leaving the UK, I had searched for information on the place and found a joint statement issued in 2008 by Ruud Lubbers, former Prime Minister of the Netherlands and one of the founders of the Earth Charter, and Ashok Khosla, President of the International Union for Conservation of Nature. It read, in part:

Damanhur is harmony and it is beautiful. We were moved by this monument to the human spirit and the marvellous tribute it makes to the cosmos and to all the wonders of life. Our journey within the mountain took us within ourselves, to our inner sense and to our place in creation. Let our generation be a time remembered for the awakening of a new reverence for life, the firm resolve to achieve sustainability, the quickening of the struggle for justice and peace, and the joyful celebration of life.

For more information on Damanhur, go to www.damanhur.info, see Esperide Ananas's beautifully illustrated book *Damanhur: Temples of Humankind* or read Jeff Merrifield's *Damanhur: The Story of the Extraordinary Italian Artistic and Spiritual Community.*

Not everyone feels positive about Damanhur. After all, Italy is a predominantly Catholic country, and as in many nations and faiths, deep-rooted beliefs often based on fear still prevail. Hence why my next 'guest' is theologian Dr Miceal Ledwith, who offers riveting insights into the distortions and misinterpretations that great truths have been subjected to down the centuries. Considerable food for thought.

Always thinking of my stomach – it wasn't until Lindsay and I enjoyed our evening meal on our flight home that I realized my gut ache had completely disappeared!

Chapter Fourteen

The Theologian and the Scrolls

Jesus said ... you will do all the
works I did, and greater than these
will you do.

– John 14:12

God is a verb, not a noun.

– Dr Miceal Ledwith

May 2009 – Wells, Somerset

STANDING IN THE GROUNDS of Wells Cathedral in Somerset, a majestic edifice, parts of which date back to 1180, I wondered – like many people before me – how many have died over the centuries as a result of their beliefs?

I had travelled to the ancient city to spend an hour or two with Irish-born theologian Dr Miceal Ledwith. We had first met at the Orbs conference in Sedona in 2007, where I had realized that Ledwith was a man worth listening to. The breadth of his accumulated knowledge is astonishing.

Miceal chose a life in academia when, at the age of 17, he entered the Catholic Church as a student for the priesthood. He went on to become a professor of systematic theology in 1976 and for ten years was president of Maynooth College (then part of the National University of Ireland). Ledwith was also a member of the International Theological Commission, which helps advise the Holy See in Rome, and has had access to many of its ancient documents. In other words, this man knows what he is talking about.

These days he lives near Seattle on the West Coast of the US and is in great demand worldwide to lecture not only on theological subjects, of which he has an encyclopaedic knowledge, but also on his passion – as you have read in chapter 7 – for Orbs. His brilliant sense of humour shines through whether he is talking about ancient texts, how to make prayer work for you, higher-dimensional realities or – as I was about to discover – well-documented historical information implying that Jesus and others like him left a technology to help us attain coherence and thus become who we truly are.

As we meandered across the Cathedral Green, Miceal began by reminding me that there are currently in excess of 20,000 different churches and denominations around the world – and that history is littered with the corpses of people who dared to disagree with whoever was in power at any given time. As a particularly gruesome example he cited the case of Father Giordano Bruno, who in 1592 was imprisoned and tortured for seven years by the Inquisition in Rome before being roasted alive on the Pope's orders. And his 'crime' was to state in his book *On the Infinite Universe and Worlds* that 'innumerable suns exist, innumerable earths revolve around those suns, in a manner similar to the way in which the seven planets revolve around our sun ... '

'What a *dreadful* way to go,' I said. Yet such stories, I knew, are all too common in our history books.

'Indeed they are,' nodded my guest.

Miceal was keen for me to more fully appreciate just how much of the original teachings from the Koran, the Bible, the Torah and a host of other texts have been corrupted or reinterpreted down the centuries – even, at times, simply 'made up' – to suit the whims of political or religious dogma. How easily fiction can become fact and vice versa – and how dangerous the consequences.

'For instance,' Miceal said in his soft Irish lilt, 'let's take the word *hell*, which comes to us from the Old English and Norse languages, and which people today normally take as referring to a place of everlasting punishment for people who have died in serious sin.

'There is no mention in the original Greek New Testament of this sense of the word as we understand it today. The words that Jesus actually used, when speaking in metaphors about retribution after death for our deeds, were *Gehenna* and *Sheol*. Gehenna was the old rubbish dump situated in a valley outside Jerusalem, where child sacrifices had taken place in the remote past, and "Sheol" meant a shallow grave. To have your dead body cast onto the smouldering fires of the old Jerusalem rubbish dump, or to be buried in a shallow grave where the corpse might be defiled by being dug up and eaten by wild animals, would have been regarded as the ultimate disgrace by the Jewish people at the time of Jesus.

'However, over the centuries "Gehenna" and "Sheol" were gradually transmogrified into the Christian notion of a "Hell" of everlasting torments – a *monumental* mistake if ever there was one. I remember once consulting modern translations of the New Testament into English to see which ones had correctly translated the words of Jesus as "Gehenna" and "Sheol" and which had mistranslated them using the word *Hell*. Of the fifty English versions I consulted, only two had made the translation correctly.'

'So, in what context,' I asked, 'did Jesus mention such places?'

'He taught that as we sow, so shall we reap, and that if we mete out negative or violent thoughts, words and deeds to others, at some point they will come back to us. And in these contexts he warned that one's fate could be similar to being cast on a rubbish dump or – even worse for fellow Jews – being buried in a shallow grave where animals could come and eat them! These days most people on a spiritual path, as Jesus was, will say, "What goes around comes around." He was talking about karma, not hell. It has never ceased to amaze me how many people have been condemned to hell and damnation in the afterlife, when no such place truly exists except in our minds.'

It was amazing to hear such a statement from a man who spent a good deal of his life within the Catholic Church!

'Now don't presume,' added Ledwith, 'that I'm against the Church – there are some wonderful people within it, but so many central ideas, words and phrases have been misinterpreted or misused.'

I asked if he could offer a couple more examples.

'Well, let's take the word *apocalypse,* which has for centuries been used to denote perpetually imminent "end of the world" scenarios, most recently the millennium and then 2012. Yet thankfully we are still here! In fact, it's derived from the Greek word *revelation.*

'And,' he went on, 'the earliest record of Christmas as a time of celebration in the West started in AD 350 when Pope Julius I declared it the birth date of Jesus. Yet from all the documented evidence, it's more likely Jesus was born around 2 BC, most probably in the autumn. There are *huge* amounts of misinformation, misinterpretation and downright rubbish out there, some of which has caused untold misery and cost millions of lives.'

We walked on silently into the Cathedral, where Miceal took his time studying various artefacts and tombs. He was wistful when he spoke again.

'Millions of people believe that Jesus was the one and only son of God, born of a virgin. Yet there was Osiris in Egypt, Dionysius in Greece, Attis in Asia Minor, Adonis in Syria, Bacchus in Persia and Mithra in Iran – all presumed mythical characters, yet I believe they were real, though the true facts are lost in the mists of antiquity. And all these "characters" shared a story similar to that of Jesus. They were all "gods" made flesh, their mothers were virgin humans, they were all born in caves or barns in front of shepherds, and so on. Within the Holy of Holies in the Great Temple at Karnak, the hieroglyphs tell of a birth in a stable with angels singing, shepherds visiting, and an ox and an ass – drawn seventeen hundred years before Jesus's birth. All such stories were coalesced over the centuries to make the stewpot version of what we now term Christianity.'

As we admired the stained-glass windows depicting Mary and Jesus, Miceal remained serious. 'From all my studies I have come to see that people's image of God actually reflects themselves. We have made God in *our* image, not the reverse. If you study the chronological formation of the Old Testament, which stretched over a thousand years, you can see how the sultans and potentates of the ancient Near East were used as the models to picture God. In the early parts of the Old Testament, such as the Book of Joshua, you have an immoral God who commits a host of atrocities. Yet in the later Old Testament, God is described as a being who respects right and wrong, which reflected the people's moral evolution.'

'So what or who is God to you?'

'Well, like you and a growing number of people, I believe that God is neither a him nor a her, which are categories of our physical universe. This is why I say *God is more like a verb than a noun,* which is an earth-shattering statement once people truly understand what it means. God is like an infinite mind that is everywhere and in everything – I refer to its core as a "zero point" – and everything that ever was or will be emanates from this zero point.'

Noticing my frown, he suggested, 'Think about it for a while.'

It didn't take me long. To my mind it makes sense to think of God as a verb, since the ultimate Isness that is God expands its energy – which is information – everywhere and is growing through every one of us via our experiences.

When I shared these thoughts with Miceal, he agreed, 'Yes, God is expanding through every one of us – but if *we* didn't exist, God would still exist.'

Before our discussion became too deeply philosophical, I steered my knowledgeable guest towards the Cathedral coffee shop. As we queued, I quickly asked Miceal his thoughts on the eighth chakra, which Alberto Villoldo had mentioned to me in London.

'Hazel,' he said, smiling indulgently, 'forty thousand children die every day from malnutrition, and at any given time, hundreds if not thousands of men, women and children are being raped, tortured and murdered for a host of reasons. Therefore, my advice to anyone on a spiritual path would be, "Don't get bogged down in the details." When we have healed ourselves and our planet totally by waking up to who we truly are, *and* realized our virtually limitless capabilties, maybe *then* we can concentrate on subjects like the eighth chakra. The ship is sinking – stop polishing the brass on the *Titanic!*'

Laughter erupted between us as I appreciated the inherent wisdom of his words – especially the part about waking up to who we truly are.

'After all,' I said, thinking out loud, 'anyone on a spiritual journey must surely have read Jesus's lines such as *I have said, ye are gods,* which he quotes from Psalm 82 in the Gospel of John; or *You will do all the works I did – and greater than these will you do,* from John 12:14; or from Mark 11:24, *When you pray for something, believe it is already yours and then it will be so.*'

'Absolutely,' agreed my guest. 'The point being that Jesus was inviting and teaching his followers to find the divine presence that resides within every one of us, but evidence of this teaching has been sadly lacking in Western religions for over two thousand years. We are evolving, but it's taking us a while to get it. In my youth, during the 1940s and 1950s, the whole focus was on how we should be grateful to Jesus for suffering on our behalf. Then in the '60s emphasis shifted more towards the Resurrection. Now I truly believe we are ready for the next shift – towards ascension.'

'But surely,' I argued, 'ascension means different things to different people and has been somewhat misused and misunderstood?'

'In New Age terms it has been misused, but to me it means a profound personal transmutation in which our frequency is raised so that we can access levels of reality that exist beyond our physical world. Then we are really getting to the heart of why Jesus and others like him incarnated on this physical plane.'

'Which was to invite us all to become totally coherent, totally self-realized, enlightened?'

'Of course, and when you can achieve such a state, which we all will eventually, you do not lose your individuality. All you have done is brought the infinite, the light, God – whatever you call it – fully into your being. It is not that the drop is being absorbed into the ocean, but, paradoxically, it is the ocean that has come into the drop. Jesus taught a process that helps us incarnate into who we are. That is the goal of us being here, and this was the heart of Jesus's message.'

Just as Professors Gary Schwartz and Bill Tiller had reminded me many times, the All is in the small and the small is in the All.

As we made ourselves comfortable and savoured the fresh coffee, it seemed logical to ask Miceal, as an authoritative theologian, his opinions on the virgin birth and Jesus rising from the dead.

He sat back, sighing, as if he had answered the same question a thousand times. 'Two of the brothers of Jesus, James and Thomas, were apostles. But in the letters of James in the New Testament, there is no mention of either a virgin birth or a resurrection. In the Gospel of Thomas there is also no mention of either. And in the writings of St Paul, who spent two weeks with Jesus's brother James, there is no mention of a virgin birth. If such a miraculous event had occurred in their household, wouldn't you think that James would have mentioned it to Paul and that Paul would have included it in his writings? In fact, it wasn't until around AD 70 that St Luke first introduced the concept of Mary having a virgin birth –an amazing achievement, wouldn't you say, for a woman who the New Testament states had six children?'

Hardly drawing breath, Miceal continued. 'And then we have the whole debate: "Did he or didn't he physically rise from the dead?" Was he actually crucified at all, or was there a substitute? And if it was he who was crucified, then was he taken down on that Jewish Sabbath whilst still alive? A few Eastern traditions state that Jesus lived a long life after his crucifixion, married Mary Magdalene and had children. There's little point even discussing all these theories, as there is no concrete evidence as to what truly happened. We don't even know what Jesus looked like, and if he wrote anything, nothing has survived.

'In fact, there were no direct witnesses to the Resurrection. There are six different accounts of it in the New Testament, dating from approximately twenty to seventy years after the event: one in each of the four Gospels, one in the book of Acts, and one in Paul's first Letter to the Corinthians. Paul's is the earliest written account of the Resurrection, recorded about twenty years after the Passion of Jesus, yet Paul says nothing at all about an empty tomb. The Gospel of Thomas, written by Jesus's brother, a very early verified document discovered in 1946 at Nag Hammadi in Egypt, does not mention the miracles of Jesus or appearances at the empty tomb and omits all mention of the Resurrection entirely. Given that Thomas regarded his writings as information of central importance about Jesus, this should give people much food for thought.'

Indeed it should, I agreed.

'To my mind,' he went on, 'it would be far more interesting to chat about what happened to Jesus from around the age of twelve to thirty, when he reappeared to be baptized by his cousin John. After all, he went from being a carpenter's son to being a man who could supposedly heal the sick and raise the dead. For sure, he was not taught how to effect such "miracles" in his father's carpentry shop, so where might he and others like him have learned to do such things?'

After a decade of interviewing scientists and enlightened men and women, I had presumed that Jesus, like most fully enlightened people, spent years on a spiritual journey learning from great teachers how to take control of his conscious ego mind, his superconscious mind, his physical body, subtle body, mental body and so on – either, as some books claim, in Egypt, or in India and Tibet.

'You may believe such stories,' Miceal said, 'but one needs more than conjecture if the religious establishments are eventually to "fess up" to what some people have long known – that Jesus travelled to all of these places and evolved to become the person we know from the New Testament. In fact Thomas, Jesus's brother, is on record in the Acts of Thomas as doing more "miracles" even than Jesus, including raising people from the dead. Even Sai Baba today in India has been documented by several doctors as effecting similar feats. Jesus wasn't in competition with us, he was openly encouraging people to become like him. But Christianity in its current form could *never* concede that Jesus owed any of his knowledge to Buddha, the Hindus or the Egyptian mystery schools.'

With his irrepressible Irish smile, Miceal asked, 'How long have you got today?'

'Long enough,' I smiled back, wondering what might be coming next.

'Let's go and get some lunch,' he said, 'and I'll tell you a story that has taken me five years to research and verify, which could help us all to understand the technology that Jesus and others left as their legacy.'

With mugs of tea, some water and fresh chicken-salad sandwiches to nourish our bodies and brains, I hurried back and made myself comfortable. Miceal began his tale ...

'This story hinges on a Russian aristocrat called Nicolas Notovich who published a book in French in 1894 called *The Unknown Life of Jesus*. Notovich had set out on a great journey at the end of the Russo-Turkish war around 1879 to explore Eastern Europe and the Middle and Far East. Notovich reached India, Nepal, Tibet and little Tibet, called Ladakh, in 1887. He was interested in studying the customs and the history of the people and the geography of the magnificent landscape in the Himalayas.

'During his journeys, Notovich heard that in Tibet there were scrolls in existence, not just one set but several sets, that spoke of the life of Jesus in India during his teenage years. Notovich eventually arrived at a monastery called Hemis, about 25 miles outside the city of Leh, the capital of Ladakh. Hemis is hidden away in a valley more than 11,000 feet above sea level. Its remote location has preserved it from the unwelcome attentions of conquering armies down the centuries. Notovich claimed that he was shown a copy at Hemis of an ancient Buddhist manuscript which described the life of Jesus from his teenage years up to the age of twenty-six, and that this section of his life had been lived in India and Tibet. The account in those scrolls was allegedly written down three to four years after the crucifixion of Jesus and was based on the testimony of merchants from India who had witnessed the event personally.

'When Notovich returned to Europe, he was counselled against publishing the account of what Jesus was said to have done in India, Tibet and Kashmir. Among those who so counselled him were the Archbishop of Kiev and a Cardinal in Rome, unfortunately unnamed, who was close to Pope Leo XIII. The Cardinal tried to dissuade Notovich from publishing the translation of the scrolls and offered to buy his notes from him if he was short of money. Notovich declined the offer. Even a Papal Nuncio in Paris, one Cardinal Rotelli, tried to dissuade Notovich from publishing his notes. These are hardly the actions of men who believed the scrolls were fakes. Notovich became ever more determined, and his notes were eventually published under the title *The Life of St Issa, Best of the Sons of Men.*'

'And have these facts been substantiated?' I interjected.

'Of course they have,' replied the theologian. 'I wouldn't even be sharing this tale with you if they hadn't!'

Sheepishly, I returned to my sandwich.

Miceal's fascinating story continued for almost an hour. He told of the furore caused by the publication of Notovich's book and of the concerted efforts that followed to discredit his story. The scrolls apparently offered a lengthy and detailed account of Jesus's missing years, stating that he read and understood the Vedas, the sacred text of the Hindus, learned the teachings of Buddha and studied with several enlightened masters. In the scrolls Jesus was known as Issa, the same name he is often given today in Ireland and in many communities in India.

Miceal asserted that a great deal of the information reported in the scrolls agreed with what was known from the New Testament about the life of Jesus in the Holy Land, but there were some major differences. 'All four Gospels of the New Testament blame the Jews for the death of Jesus, but the scrolls lay the blame fairly and squarely at the feet of the Roman governor Pontius Pilate alone. In fact, the scrolls credit the Jewish authorities for going out of their way to save Jesus.'

'Are you saying that the Jewish people had nothing to do with Jesus's crucifixion?'

'Well, after the total destruction of Jerusalem by the Roman general Titus in the year AD 70, the Jewish world in the Holy Land to all intents and purposes was no more. So at the time the Gospels were written, Christianity was no longer merely a Jewish phenomenon, it was spreading into the wider Roman world – and in *this* context it would be very unwise to lay blame for the death of Jesus on the Romans, so the Jews were made the scapegoats. Politics hasn't changed much in the last two thousand years, has it?'

I was fascinated to hear about the Notovich scrolls, having read similar accounts of other writings, including those found by Agnes and Margaret Smith, who around 1892 discovered second-century New Testament scrolls in the Sinai mountains that told of Joseph being Jesus's biological father. Yet the establishment within most religions have tried to dismiss such major historical finds and their contents as being nothing more than hearsay. And they would most certainly do the same with the Notovich story, especially since no Westerner has laid eyes on the scrolls since 1939.

Miceal agreed. 'Of course no-one should accept a single source for such potentially explosive material, but once you examine all the evidence and testimonies of several highly sceptical academics – including a United States Supreme Court Justice who travelled to Hemis and later publicly supported Notovich's claims – then you might reconsider. And even if you didn't, to my mind the most compelling evidence that Jesus became enlightened thanks to his years in India and Tibet are the one hundred and twelve parallels between the teachings of Jesus and the teachings of Buddha, who lived around five hundred years before Jesus was even born.'

'Such as?' I queried, instantly alert.

'The major parables of Jesus with which we are so familiar are *all* found in the teachings of Buddha,' Miceal began. 'Also, it's important to know that Jesus travelled with his parents to Egypt in his infancy to escape the persecution of King Herod and there have been suggestions that he returned as an adult. As a descendant of the line of King David, through his mother, Jesus along with his family would have been welcomed into the highest echelons of Egyptian society, including the temple rituals and mystery schools. Most probably Jesus, like many enlightened men and women, would have had an "inner knowing" from his early years of the work he came to do and would have obviously been fascinated with their schools and rituals.'

This statement resonated with me, as when I had had a private meeting with Sai Baba back in 2000, I was told that he left home at 13 to do the work he inherently knew he was born to do. The Dalai Lama began his spiritual education even earlier.

We returned to the subject of Egypt. 'Initiates, for example,' said Miceal, 'training to become free from man's ultimate fear – of death – were placed blindfolded in the sarcophagus within the Great Pyramid, not knowing what was happening. After three days and three nights entombed, they might have become transformed or they might have died. If they survived this initiation, it symbolized the death of the ego and a rebirth into nonduality. Even more importantly, the experience would have erased negative neural pathways in the brain, so that no situation they faced from that moment on would trigger an ancient or deepseated fear within them with which they would have had to battle.'

Miceal's words made me wistful. I recalled how I began to think of my life prior to my near-death experience as BE (Before Easter) and afterwards AE .... Many cultures talk of the 'dark night of the soul' during personal transformation. And there were times during my experience when I might have welcomed being shut in a darkened space – though not a sarcophagus – in order to find the silence I craved. Freedom from any fear at times left me in complete and utter bliss. Even if arguments raged around me, it was as if I were 'in neutral' – I simply observed without judging. Hoping this was how the Egyptian initiates felt too, I asked Miceal if there is any real evidence to show that Jesus was connected to the Egyptian mystery schools.

'No scrolls such as those found in Tibet have ever been unearthed in Egypt, but if you reflect that the seven sacraments of the Christian Church are, in fact, all based on initiation rites of the Egyptian schools, this is a very strong indication that Jesus did indeed attend these schools. A particularly good example is the sacred meal of the Eucharist, the last supper, which has its roots directly in the ancient mystery schools of Egypt. The wine symbolized the spirit, which came directly from the Creator; the bread symbolized the body of the physical incarnation; and the water which was added to the wine symbolized the soul, which was the recorder of the experience of the incarnations. Or, let's take the cross, an extremely ancient symbol that long predates Christianity, which in the West has become the symbol of an ago-nizing death. In fact it symbolized the harmonization of the vertical and the horizontal, when we have managed to balance the spiritual and the material within ourselves. It represents a key to how the entire universe works. It's no wonder that in mathemat-ics the cross became the symbols of addition or multiplication. In pagan and early Christian traditions, the cross signified evolution and life but never death.'

'And what about Buddha's teachings?' I prompted my guest.

'Ah, yes, we have digressed. In fact there are similarities not only with Buddha's recorded teachings, but also with ancient Hindu texts. The parable of the sower, found in Matthew, Mark and Luke, tells how a sower cast his seed and it fell on a range of different soils with different results. Buddha told this same story five hundred years earlier. In Luke's Gospel, Jesus talks about how easily we see the speck in our brother's eye and fail to see the beam in our own; Buddha made a similar statement. The New Testament claim that if you have faith you can move mountains comes from ancient Hindu traditions; there are dozens of modern documented cases in which monks whose minds are sufficiently advanced can indeed move objects, alter their body temperatures at will and so on.'

Miceal listed several other identical stories, including how Buddha advised his followers, as Jesus did, to 'love their enemies'. He concluded, 'Many of these parables are so closely replicated, it would be almost impossible to maintain that both versions were independently created.'

'You're preaching to the converted,' I told him. 'I have always believed that Jesus and others pointed the way for us all to follow.'

'Well, there's the rub – millions of others don't feel that way. We have already touched on how information has been altered, corrupted, added to and misunderstood – but if we are all to become like Jesus and others like him, then we need to practise more of the advice that they left us.'

'And how do you personally do that?'

'I am a member of the Ramtha School,' Miceal replied, 'where, on a humble scale, students are first taught how to read what is on playing cards from the back of the card. We don't do this as a parlour trick; we are opening up abilities to access dimensions above the physical. Such practices are repeatable and have been scientifically validated by the Institute for Noetic Sciences near San Francisco. There is also a maze, and we learn how to intuit our way into it – again blindfolded. We also practise archery blindfolded, attempting to hit a small target from 150 feet away. There are people who can do this time after time. But I often suggest that people try it first with their eyes open so that they can see how difficult it is even without wearing the blindfolds!'

Just as most spiritual teachers advise – try walking before you can run! If you want to learn the piano from scratch, you find a good teacher. Some people are born with a huge talent which they can expand to great heights; others just have to practise regularly. And if we are to align with the Ultimate Mind from which we all emanate, then we too need to be willing to practise more. It's back to the same question I asked way back in chapter 2: how badly do you want to 'go home'?

'Thankfully, we no longer need to be entombed to wake up, as the Egyptian initiates were,' Miceal went on. 'There are movements the world over that encourage us to realign the neural pathways within our brains and thus increase our potential capabilities. Can you imagine how different our world will become when we can intuit our way through our lives and gain total control of our conscious minds? Misfortunes, sickness, old age and death will become things of the past as we raise our frequencies to exist on higher levels, which, to those living on them, are as real as this world is to us. Numerous scientists have verified that our physical world can be modulated by thought. Mind is everything. We exist within a mind and in the years to come we can merge back into this mind.'

By the end of our day together, my mind was buzzing, and I'm sure you realize that Miceal has far more to impart than space allows here. If you want to hear or read more, you can find details of Miceal's book *Forbidden Truth*, his DVD *The Hidden Years of Jesus the Christ* and his lectures and newsletters on his website at www.hamburgeruniverse.com.

After chatting with Dr Ledwith I found several books on the Notovich Scrolls, as well as a film entitled *Jesus in India* made by American director and producer Paul Davids that tells the story of a onetime Christian fundamentalist keen to find out what happened to Jesus during his lost years. Details are at www.jesus-in-india-the-movie.com. The documentary follows the path of Notovich and lends considerable support to his claims. Even Elaine Pagels, professor of religion at Princeton University, goes on camera saying, 'It is possible, as some people say, for Jesus to have travelled to India.'

Along the Great Silk Road, in Jesus's time, many traders did indeed walk to India, a journey that took about a year. I'll leave you with some thought-provoking words from a sign that stands today at Bareilly Railway Station in Uttar Pradesh in northern India on that fabled route: *The Allah of Islam is the same as the God of Christians and the Iswar of Hindus.*

If humanity could accept this ultimate truth, think how many could yet be saved.

In the meantime, if you want to know how to measure your current level of coherence, turn the page.

Chapter Fifteen

Calibrating Coherence and Finding Your Frequency

Just being ordinary in itself is an expression of divinity; the truth of one's real self can be discovered through the pathway of everyday life. To live with care and kindness is all that is necessary.

– Dr David R Hawkins MD, PhD

Autumn 2009 – Henley-on-Thames

How coherent or 'decohered' do you think humanity is collectively right now? With over 6 billion people living on this planet, you may wonder how on earth you could possibly place a figure on such an abstract concept.

Thankfully, there are souls far wiser than I who can help us measure coherence at every level of being – from the food we put in our mouths to assessing our levels of intention, entraining our hearts and minds, and tapping the energy of sound to aid in our own unique countdown towards coherence.

In chapter 5, I explained how Professor Tiller has demonstrated that our acupuncture meridian channels work at a 'coupled' higher-dimensional level – in scientific terms, a higher electromagnetic gauge symmetry state – *all the time*. They act as a bridge between this reality and others. And the practice of kinesiology, a form of muscle testing, offers a method of measuring that connection to determine levels of coherence at all levels of being.

Back in 1964 a chiropractor named Dr George Goodheart from Kansas, where he practised until his death in 2008 at age 89, made the first correlation between muscles reacting in a weak or strong way when his patients came into contact with certain foods, nutrients or chemicals, regardless of the patients' age, gender or beliefs. For instance, if he asked a patient to hold a chemical-based sugar substitute in one hand, no matter how hard the patient tried to hold his or her other arm up at a right angle to the body, the muscles would go inexplicably weak. His discovery, which later became known as Applied Kinesiology, is used by many healing disciplines today as an invaluable diagnostic tool alongside conventional medical tests. Dr Goodheart realized that at some level, the body inherently knows what serves its needs and what doesn't. Science is finally beginning to understand how this is possible.

Enter one Benoit Mandelbrot – Sterling Professor of Mathematical Sciences (now emeritus) at Yale University – who spent decades researching seemingly separate entities, from the shapes of coastlines to plants, blood vessels, human pursuits, music, architecture, even stock markets and clustering of galaxies. His painstaking research eventually demonstrated through mathematical analysis that underlying *everything* in our universe, no matter how seemingly random or chaotic 'things', events or statistics appear, is an underlying order. Mandelbrot termed these underlying patterns 'fractals' and went on to write a book entitled *The Fractal Geometry of Nature*. The approach to nonlinear dynamics that he pioneered has verified that there really is no chaos in the universe; rather, the appearance of disorder is *merely a function of limits of perception.*

Beneath apparent chaos there is indeed order, or, as Professor Frederick Travis terms it, an underlying intelligence. And kinesiology, when practised with the right intentions and in the right way, gives you *access* to this intelligence – whether you acknowledge its existence or not. You may also be interested to know that the mathematics of fractals happens to be the same as the mathematics of the hologram!

Now turn the clock back to 1939, when Dr David R Hawkins, today a world-renowned psychiatrist and consciousness researcher – who, like Stanislav Grof, has done huge amounts of work on higher states induced by spiritual breakthroughs – was a mere paper boy in rural Wisconsin. Since the age of three, he had experienced fleeting moments of a complete understanding of the phrase 'I am' – which eventually led to a fear that 'he' was not real at all.

In his fascinating book *Power vs. Force,* Hawkins relates how one night he was caught in a blizzard miles from home when his bike slipped on ice, scattering his load to the biting winds. Frightened and alone, he burrowed into a snowbank to try and escape the weather. He writes, '... Soon, the shivering stopped, and there was a delicious warmth, and then a state of peace beyond all description.... I became oblivious of my physical body and surroundings as my awareness fused with this all-present illuminated state. My mind grew silent; all thought stopped.'

In such states, linear time as we know it also ceases – and Hawkins had no idea how long he remained in his burrow until he was 'brought back' into his physical body when his anxious father found him.

The young teenager kept this experience to himself. What his story has to do with kinesiology and calibrating your levels of coherence will become apparent shortly. I am sharing it with you so that you will understand the *integrity* of Hawkins's calculations, should you choose to accept them.

During World War II, in the Navy, he was assigned hazardous duties on a minesweeper, but his fear of death was gone. He later became an agnostic. Following the war he worked his way through medical school, specializing in psychiatry, but at only 38 he was diagnosed with a progressive fatal illness: '... I was in extremis, and knew I was about to die. I didn't care about the body, but my spirit was in a state of extreme anguish and despair. As the final moment approached, the thought flashed through my mind, "What if there is a God?" So I called out in prayer "If there is a God, I ask him to help me now."'

Hawkins surrendered and lost consciousness, and when he awoke, a transformation of such enormity had occurred that he was struck dumb with awe. He was experiencing a state of total brain functioning, a state of coherence, which has been demonstrated by scientists such as Professor Travis to be the scientific basis for sudden remissions or complete healing.

For nine months, Hawkins writes, the stillness persisted. He had no will of his own. Eloquently he writes, '... In that state, there was no need to think about anything. All truth was self-evident; no conceptualization was necessary or even possible. At the same time, my nervous system felt extremely overtaxed, as though it were carrying far more energy than its circuits had been designed for.' And to reduce his intense blissful states – just as I had back in '98 – Hawkins stopped meditating, otherwise he simply couldn't function at a physical level.

Sound familiar? It certainly does to me. Hawkins went through his own unique birthing into who he was and who all of us truly are.

With his newfound awareness and understanding, Hawkins eventually returned to his medical practice. Because he had 'coupled' with other levels of reality, he was now able to intuitively discover the root causes of his patients' problems, and he went on to form a highly successful practice with 50 therapists. In 1973, he co-authored *Orthomolecular Psychiatry* with Nobelist Linus Pauling. With his growing success came a growing frustration that he could not see more patients in a day, and he began looking for faster methods to help people. 'And when,' he recalls in *Power vs. Force*, 'I first encountered kinesiology, I was instantly amazed by its potential. It was as if I had found a "wormhole" between two universes – the physical world, and the world of mind and spirit.'

Indeed he had. Hawkins and many others had come upon a simple and effective method of accessing the innate knowledge that is within us all. An extension of George Goodheart's technique, this method – based on the premise that the muscles stay strong in the presence of truth and are weakened by untruth – involves making a statement to the subject and then testing his or her muscle response. With his colleagues, Hawkins began using kinesiology to test every conceivable variation of emotional states, beliefs, substances, nutrients and so on to help patients recover at all levels of being – mind, body and spirit.

It was universally observed – by other practitioners and researchers as well as Hawkins – that 'Test responses were completely independent of the test subjects' belief systems, intellectual opinions, reason or logic. It was also observed that a test response where the subject went weak was accompanied by a desynchronization of the cerebral hemispheres.' In other words, if patients were exposed to a scenario, substance or emotion that did not serve the higher or the physical self, then their brain function became *less coherent*.

Most importantly for the purpose of helping people quantify levels of coherence in mathematical terms, Hawkins and his colleagues developed a set of parameters for calibration, assigning numbers from 1 to 1,000 to various states of human consciousness. I found the idea of being able to calibrate our feelings especially useful: for instance, Hawkins calibrates shame at 20, guilt at 30, apathy at 50, grief 75, fear 100, desire 125, anger 150, pride 175, courage 200, acceptance 350, reason 400, unconditional love 500 and joy 540.

From this level upwards is the domain of saints and highly advanced spiritual students. 'And near-death experiences,' he writes, 'characteristically transformative in their effect, frequently have allowed some people to experience the energy level between 540 and 600.' The memories of it still make me sigh .... At a level of 600 or more, he says, ordinary thought would cease and omnipresence would be experienced. And it comes as no surprise to me that Einstein and Freud calibrated at 499.

Hawkins reports that their lengthy investigations of the higher-calibrated levels of consciousness matched the degree of enlightenment of the great spiritual teachers of human history, saying, 'We have found that no human has ever lived who calibrated at a consciousness level beyond 1,000 and those who did calibrate in very high numbers were accorded the status of great teachers, Avatars, Christ, Buddha, and Krishna.' Consciousness levels beyond 1,000 and upwards through the spiritual hierarchy, he believes, represent power beyond the capacity of human imagination. Archangels calibrate at 50,000 and above.

Sadly, but not surprisingly, organized religions do not fare particularly well in Hawkins's calculations. For example, he writes that the original Koran calibrates at 700, but the level of truth in much of today's fundamentalist teachings is only 125. The level of Jesus's original teachings Hawkins calibrates at 1,000, but over the centuries that too has fallen dramatically, thanks to the misinterpretations and misunderstandings offered by a host of 'teachers' – just as Miceal Ledwith had explained to me at Wells.

His findings really bring it home to me just how far most of humanity has decohered. According to Hawkins, only one person in every 10 million even desires true enlightenment, and approximately 85 per cent of the world's population calibrates below 200. On a more positive note, he also writes, '... The collective power of that fifteen per cent has the weight to counterbalance the negativity of the remaining eighty-five per cent of the world's population. Because the scale of power advances logarithmically, a single Avatar at a consciousness level of 1,000 can, in fact, totally counterbalance the collective negativity of all mankind....' Conversely, the extreme negativity of a few individuals can sway entire cultures and produce a global drag on general levels of consciousness. In fact, by testing abnormal polarities, Hawkins has calibrated that only 2.6 per cent of the human population account for 72 per cent of society's problems.

Now perhaps you understand the urgency of working on your individual spiritual growth . . . .

Hawkins states that an individual's calibration only increases, on the average, by about five points in a lifetime. But, crucially, if we can separate ourselves from our ego mind, then it is possible to jump many *more* points in this lifetime – which is basically what Gary Renard told me back in chapter 2. As Bill Tiller advised back in Arizona, place your ego in service for the greater good and just watch those numbers climb!

We may be saying it in different ways – but our conclusions are the same. Without doubt, we are individually and collectively, through our thoughts and actions, creating our future timelines – and if we want them to become 'set' in more positive form, we need to act *now*. As Dr Ledwith so eloquently put it, we need to stop polishing the brass and focus on keeping the *Titanic* afloat.

After reading Hawkins's books in 2008, I began seeing an osteopath, Tony Ryman, based in London's Harley Street, who also happens to be one of the best kinesiologists I have come across. I call him 'the wizard'. In early 2009 a neurologist who believed I might have a hairline fracture in my spine sent me for a radioisotope X-ray, which necessitates an injection of radioactive material. For days afterwards I felt well below par without knowing why. But Tony tested me for less than a minute before he said, 'Radiation is your problem. What have you been up to?' I was astonished at how quickly he had zeroed in on the cause of my problem – and after taking high doses of a type of sulphate called glucosamine sulphate, to help eliminate the effects of radiation on my tissues, within days I felt altogether healthier.

When I made another visit to talk with Tony about kinesiology as part of my inquiries into coherence, I asked if he would mind testing the level of integrity of this book. To my delight, he calibrated it at 870. And when I further asked him to calibrate the level of *truth* offered, he said that at this time it too calibrated at 870 – which certainly made my day!

I'm sure by now you would love to have a go for yourself at this simple yet profound method for measuring coherence. Here's how to go about it. Two people are required, one to act as the test subject by holding out one arm to the side, parallel to the ground. The second person does the testing by pressing down with two fingers on the wrist of the extended arm and saying, 'Resist.' The person being tested tries to resist any pressure just to check that he or she can. Now the questions can begin – in the form of statements that will be judged true or untrue – and if the response is negative, then the arm loses all strength and down it goes like a blade of grass. Obviously to obtain true readings requires practise and discernment, but it's fun!

Tony told me that it's important to formulate the statements properly. For instance, if you state, 'This is a good decision,' what defines *good*? For whom and in what framework? Your motives in questioning are important, and you must be prepared for results or answers that may not suit your desires. The tester must remain 'neutral' when posing questions so as not to affect the outcome. As when you swallow any medicine, orthodox or otherwise, your beliefs can affect the efficacy of the process, so watch your thoughts. Those people being tested may find it easier if they close their eyes to prevent being distracted by external stimuli. Also, kinesiology cannot be used to predict the future. And if you choose to try to calibrate an individual's coherence (or your own) on Hawkins's scale, simply phrase your statements accordingly: 'The subject calibrates at 200 or more.' Then adjust the figures based on the responses to narrow it down.

As in most diagnostic practices, conflicting results can happen. Hawkins and his colleagues found, for instance, that if the thymus gland (situated underneath your breast bone) is underfunctioning, then results can be unpredictable. This is because the thymus is the central controller for your body's acupuncture energy system. Applied-kinesiology pioneer Dr John Diamond developed a simple technique known as the 'thymus thump' to rectify such problems. Basically, you tap on your breast bone for a few seconds several times each day while thinking of someone you love, and on each thump you rhythmically chant 'Ha, ha, ha ... '

Might seem somewhat 'off the wall', but it works.

These days, Dr Hawkins no longer uses the term *kinesiology;* his process is now often called the Consciousness Calibration Research Technique. If you would like to find out more about his fascinating work, you can find a list of his books and lectures at www.veritaspub.com. General information on kinesiology is available through the International College of Applied Kinesiology at www.icak.com. Tony Ryman practises either at The Wholistic Medical Centre at 57 Harley Street, London (www.wholisticmedical.co.uk), or at the Manse Health Centre in Andover, Hampshire.

Another way to measure your levels of coherence is by measuring your heart-rate variability. Numerous validated studies carried out at the Institute of HeartMath in Boulder Creek, California, have demonstrated that once you learn how to entrain your heart and mind as one, then production of the anti-aging hormone DHEA is increased, whilst cortisol production linked to stress decreases. You can literally entrain your alpha brain activity, which is produced during relaxation, to synchronize with your heart rate. Your heart can influence your brain.

By attaching a small sensor to your fingertip, you can watch your heart rhythms in real time on your computer screen – and then experience how your thoughts can change its beating. Over time, this can help you more easily connect to the space between your thoughts at the vacuum level of reality and thus enhance your ability to affect your physical reality, whilst also enhancing your overall health at all levels.

During studies, when advanced meditators entrained their hearts and minds while *simultaneously* intending to influence the DNA molecules in water several feet from their bodies, they were able to either wind or unwind strands of DNA at will. And if you can have such a measurable effect on DNA outside your body, imagine what might happen to your DNA strands *within* your body through focused intention!

The Institute of HeartMath offers inexpensive software, devices and downloadable books that can help you develop heart/brain coherence. Find them at www.heartmath.org. Professor Bill Tiller and his team have also developed a small device that can measure your levels of intention, as I mentioned in chapter 6. Find details of the device and more information on the Tiller Foundation at www.tiller.org.

The muscle-testing method of kinesiology and the software from the Institute of HeartMath offer you simple yet profound methods to more fully understand how attaining coherent states can help you in everyday life. But sound is also important for increasing coherence at every level.

Several years ago I attended a workshop presented by Dr Deepak Chopra, which he opened by inviting the audience of more than 1,000 to chant the ancient Vedic word *Om*. After a few minutes, as the sound resonated throughout and around my body, I felt myself becoming lighter and lighter – to the point where I felt so 'light' that to 'ground' myself I had to leave the theatre for ten minutes to literally lie on the ground outside. I wondered why this ancient word had such a profound effect on me. In writing this book, I have finally found out.

I'm sure you have heard the question 'If a tree falls in the forest and no-one is around to hear it, does it make a sound?' Some people say no, whilst others disagree. When I posed this question to parapsychologist Dr Serena Roney-Dougal, she told me, 'Of *course* the tree falling makes a sound; the waves will be compressed within the air even though there are no eardrums in the vicinity to pick up the compressed waves. When people state there would be no sound – they mean no *mechanisms* to hear or record the sound.'

The mechanisms are, of course us and any other sentient life, such as animals. Several times in this book, I have pointed out that our seemingly solid bodies are at a core level made up of frequencies; we are transmitters and receivers of energy and information. And for centuries various disciplines have utilized frequencies in the resonant form of sound as a means to align with the intelligence that underlies all existence. Aborigines in Australia have long spoken of 'singing' broken bones back together, and such practices take place in many indigenous cultures to this day. Sound can harm and sound can heal.

Most people have heard of the Schumann resonance, which describes the earth's fundamental signature frequency of 7.83 Hz, discovered by physicist Winfried Schumann in 1954. As I have already stated, we also emit our own signature range of frequencies – which are constantly in a state of flux, depending on our diet, thoughts, emotions and so on. And there are huge ranges of frequencies that can help us increase our levels of coherence at every level. To find out more I spoke with Jill Purce, one of the world's leading authorities on sound, who has spent 40 years teaching people how to use sound and their voices, not only to improve their health and well-being, but also to accelerate their individual spiritual growth.

Jill, the wife of biologist Rupert Sheldrake, whom you met in chapter 11, has a brilliant knowledge of science and spirituality. She began, 'If you are in close proximity to anyone who has done a lot of intense spiritual practice, you will feel a sense of order transmitting itself from them to you, which can induce deep states of calm. This is because these people emit ordered frequencies that we cannot "hear" yet we can "feel". They resonate and interact with our fields in a harmonious way, so that we are also able to experience that order.'

Indeed, I have found this to be true, especially in the company of totally enlightened masters of the self. Conversely, if you feel distinctly uncomfortable in a person's presence for no specific reason, it may be because you are not on a similar wavelength! This is why certain healers are more effective on some patients and not on others – it's all down to compatibility of frequencies.

Jill continued, 'In the seventeenth century, the whole of Western music was retuned, because it had been impossible with instruments with fixed structures and bridges to play music in certain keys or to change key. The new tuning meant that intervals between each note in the octave were all made a little out of tune in a way that it was assumed people wouldn't notice. Bach was the first to demonstrate the benefit of this when he wrote the Preludes and Fugues for the Well-Tempered Klavier showing how you could now play in any key.'

'Which means what to the average person?' I asked.

'It means that when we listen to Western music – and increasingly to world music, as Western tonalities have now been exported all over the world – we ourselves become out of tune. When you listen to music or make music out of tune, your whole being tunes with it. So we have become less harmonious in every sense of the word. the word sound means to be "healthy" or "true", and you cannot be healthy if you are constantly being entrained by music and sounds that are slightly out of tune, however beautiful they may seem to be.'

'And how can the average person get back into tune?'

'There is an inner resonant structure or geometry to our universe,' Jill replied, 'which can be revealed sonorously by chanting overtones.'

Before I could ask what an overtone was, Jill 'sang' an extraordinary sound down the phone. It was quite 'otherworldly' and sounded like several notes at once.

We laughed as she told me, 'Believe it or not, that was one note. Using resonance, I allowed that one note to reveal all the other notes that the one note contains.'

Throughout this book, I have been made aware, time and time again, that there are worlds within worlds within worlds. And to align with the core of who we really are, we need to peel away layer after layer after layer until we can discover the truth. Recalling the texts I had discussed with Miceal Ledwith, I reflected, *In the beginning was the Word* – and what is a spoken word? A frequency – which carries information.

'For millennia in Tibet and places like Mongolia,' Jill went on, 'religious ceremonies have included overtone chanting, which is one of the most powerful sounds to increase coherence or resonance at all levels of being. Overtones act like a tuning fork to help us align with the harmonic field of intelligence which underlies all of life.'

I told Jill my story about Deepak Chopra and the *Om* – or *Aum*, as it is sometimes spelt – then read her a quote that appears on a CD recorded by the enlightened teacher Swami Rumi before he left his physical body in 1996: 'AUM is the eternal sound that expands the individual consciousness to Universal Consciousness. The aspirant who meditates on AUM and contemplates on its meaning understands the Absolute Truth.' I asked Jill if she could explain why the group chanting with Dr Chopra had had such a profound effect upon me.

'When we make vocal sounds,' she replied, 'we use consonants and vowels. Consonants are vocal sounds that are characterized by an interruption in the flow of air within the mouth, such as when you use the letters B, C, D, F, G, H, J, K, etcetera. Whereas vowels, A, E, I, O, and U, are a type of sound in which there is no interruption. When understood acoustically, vowel sounds are pure resonance, pure order – the geometric structure of the sound is ordered – whereas consonants are noise, chaotic vibrations; they are disordered. And if you chant the word *Om* properly, it is made up entirely of vowels, which encourage coherence. It ends with MMMM, which incorporates that order, or spirit, into matter, represented by the disorder of the consonant sound.'

I listening in fascinated silence as Jill then began chanting Om – it sounded like AAOOUUUUMMMM ...

'*Om* in ancient Vedic scripts,' she told me, 'translates into "That which sustains everything", which is order, and it pervades everything.'

I had learnt something new. Amazing. For several months, I had chanted every morning to a CD of monks singing the *Om* – now I understood why it made me feel so calm!

Before saying goodbye, Jill added, 'When you chant, not only are you becoming more resonant, you are also tuning into ancient lineages of that specific chant and all who have used it. You are adding to the attainment of the field which has accrued by using that sacred sound over thousands of years, and in turn you are benefiting from it. This is far more than simply an acoustic quality. And as you become more resonant and coherent, you are healed in mind and body.

'Also, the vocal technique required to make these sounds stimulates parts of the brain and the glands which produce the bliss-inducing chemicals in the brain. So you produce more endorphins, nature's painkilling chemicals, and more serotonin, the feel-good hormone. These sounds can also help release deeply embedded emotions that need to be brought to the surface and cleared. The overtones bring you into harmony at every level.'

After listening to Jill, I immediately ordered her CD *Overtone Chanting Meditation* and planned to go and learn from her how to use overtones for my own spiritual growth. If you would like to find out more, visit Jill's website, www.healingvoice.com.

Other researchers have also done great work on how sound can affect our health. Dr Masaru Emoto in Japan is not a scientist, but a doctor of alternative medicine who became fascinated with the fact that water has a memory – and considering that our bodies are made up mostly of water, he began researching how sound affects the structure of water. Over the years he examined thousands of water crystals that were exposed to a huge variety of sounds – from classical music to heavy metal to voices saying 'I love you,' 'I forgive you,' 'Thank you' and so forth whilst other crystals were exposed to angry statements such as 'I hate you.' According to Emoto, the water crystals exposed to the calm music and loving words formed beautiful, perfect, 'coherent' crystals, whereas those exposed to angry words and disjointed sounds were severely misshapen. Interestingly, he found that spoken words had a greater effect even than the music. Although there are no validated scientific trials to verify his pictures, one double-blind trial conducted in Tokyo, in which 2,000 people were asked to send positive intentions to a water sample inside a shielded chamber in California, found that the samples to which the positive thoughts were sent did indeed form more aesthetically pleasing crystals – thus lending support to Emoto's theories. You can see his stunning pictures at www.masaruemoto.com.

The water at Lourdes is thought to be relatively coherent; if you look at pictures of ice crystals at Lourdes, they have beautiful, blue-tinged, regular structures. And if people go there with a heartfelt intention to be healed, they literally emit frequencies of unconditional love into the area and into the water. Sacred places such as Lourdes have become what Bill Tiller terms conditioned spaces; these areas have an innate intelligence, as people's prayers and intentions have over time 'woken up', or as Fred Travis says, 'unfrozen', the field of pure intelligence, pure coherence, which underlies all of life. As I have reiterated several times, coherence is catching.

And if you were to examine the crystalline structure of a snowflake, you would see that no two are the same, even though they look the same to the naked eye, rather like us. We are similar, yet every one of us is unique. If you melt a snowflake and then allow it to refreeze under natural conditions, it reforms into a similar unique snowflake pattern. Water has a memory – just as every atom and cell in our bodies has a memory. Water can also transfer frequency patterns and wavelengths carrying information, and this is the basic theory of how homeopathy works.

And as I have explained throughout this book, there are numerous ways to increase coherence. When I discussed this point with Professor Travis at the Center for Brain, Consciousness, and Cognition in Iowa, he told me that their experiments on advanced spiritual students had demonstrated that certain tones do indeed increase brain coherence – but to transcend to a state of total brain functioning, the basis for true enlightenment, ultimately required complete silence.

David Hawkins writes movingly of this need in *Power vs. Force:* 'When time stops, all problems disappear; they are merely artefacts of a point of perception. When the mind grows silent, the thought "I am" also disappears, and Pure Awareness shines forth to illuminate what one is, was, and always will be, beyond all worlds and all universes, beyond time and therefore without beginning or end.'

Perhaps now you can begin to understand why certain great enlightened beings, such as the legendary Babaji, are said to reside or appear in the Himalayas, where their totally coherent energy fields are not disturbed so much by intruding 'ordinary' folk. They need seclusion and silence. Yogiraj Satgurunath Siddhanath, a living saint in his own right, once told me that these great beings of light and time straddle many realities. I wonder what they would calibrate at?

How I would love to see such beings, yet Gurunath told me that very few people have ever been in their presence, as their light is so blinding. Gurunath writes movingly of his experiences with such beings in his book *Wings to Freedom.*

And so it was time for me too to move on. Although it was not to the Himalayas, I was headed for several more aha moments in Avebury in Wiltshire to meet with my final, fascinating 'guest'.

Chapter Sixteen

The Cosmologist, Consciousness and Co-Creation

We have collectively come to the edge of a precipice of global breakdown – or breakthrough. The choice is ours.

– Dr Jude Currivan

December 2009 – Avebury, Wiltshire

SOME 90 MILES WEST OF LONDON and 20 miles north of Stonehenge stands the largest known stone ring in the world. Dated at 2600 BC, the standing stones of Avebury are older even than Stonehenge and are set among a vast network of Neolithic sacred sites along a 200-mile line stretching across southern England. And Avebury's history is shrouded in legend and mystery.

Back in the 1700s, Dr William Stukeley, an antiquarian, spent 30 years making measurements and drawings around the site – and discovered that the ancient temple of Avebury formed a representation of the body of a serpent passing through a circle, thus forming part of a traditional alchemical symbol representing life, death and rebirth. If you look at a medic alert bracelet, you will see two serpents coiled around a central column, forming a caduceus – the symbol of medicine. For thousands of years our metaphysical kundalini energy has symbolically been represented by a coiled serpent rising around a central column – denoting our spines. We now know, thanks to the work of scientists such as Dr Harry Oldfield, that the kundalini is not a myth, but a very real metaphysical channel that runs from the base of the spine to the top of the head – through which an unbelievably powerful energy flows. And if you look at pictures of coiled DNA spirals, I'm sure you will realize the resemblance between the two is no coincidence.

Some of our ancestors knew far more than most people can even begin to comprehend.

With such a history, Avebury is the perfect home environment for Dr Jude Currivan – a cosmologist with a master's degree in quantum physics and a PhD in archaeology studying ancient cosmologies. After reading her inspiring book *CosMos:*

A Co-creator's Guide to the Whole World, co-written with the legendary philosopher Dr Ervin Laszlo, I was so impressed by the breadth of Jude's knowledge, that I became determined to interview her.

Dr Currivan has visited, and is an acknowledged expert on, more sacred sites than I have had hot dinners. Well, almost – from the temples of Egypt to Easter Island, Rawak in western China, Lake Titicaca in Peru, Table Mountain in South Africa, Akutan Island in the Aleutian Island chain off Alaska, Maui, Ethiopia and Kata Tjuta in central Australia, to name but a few – where she has met and learned from legendary shamans and wisdom keepers of many traditions.

Not only is she well travelled, but Dr Currivan also began seeing and hearing the spirit world and other realities at a very young age, and she too has been through an intense spiritual awakening. Like Dr Hawkins and others, Dr Currivan has integrated many realities into this one; she truly walks her talk and is in great demand to lecture worldwide. Where do you begin with such a knowledgeable woman? Having also read her other books, *The 8th Chakra* and *The 13th Step,* I had questions that ran to several pages of notes. Thankfully, we had a few hours to chat, and I trusted that wherever our dialogue led us, it would be perfect.

With the winter solstice approaching, on a glorious December morning I drove through the beautiful Wiltshire downs and on to Dr Currivan's light-filled home. She welcomed me with true Christmas spirit, saying, 'Come in, the kettle's on – and please call me Jude.'

My kind of woman. As I stood in her homely kitchen enjoying a steaming mug of tea, we chatted about the numerous sites she has visited. As I finished quoting the lengthy list of sacred sites, Jude laughingly added, 'You have omitted Silbury Hill. It's near here and is the greatest monumental mound in Europe. Like all sacred sites, energetically this is a very important area and it's the epicentre of the crop-circle phenomenon in the UK.'

As we made our way to her airy study, I knew I was in for a fascinating day.

Months earlier, numerologist Tania Gabrielle (www.taniagabrielle.com) based in Sedona had prepared an overview of my character and life purpose based upon the numbers that each letter in my name represents, and her interpretations had been incredibly accurate. Therefore I began by asking Jude about sacred numbers. One such, I knew, was the number 33, which Pythagoras identified as the highest 'master number' in esoteric law, associated with selfless love, healing and altruistic service to humanity. More than 500 years after Pythagoras, Jesus was reportedly crucified at the age of 33 and said to have effected 33 miracles. And in Islam the people who dwell in Heaven always seem to be written about as if they remain 33 years of age.

Jude listened intently before adding, 'There is also the sacred number of twelve. Jesus had twelve disciples, there are the twelve days of Christmas, twelve solar months, yet thirteen lunar months. All numbers have different resonant energies – everything in our universe can be broken down into numbers, which are a cosmic language. Many sacred ceremonies are about the twelve becoming the thirteen; it's no coincidence that the Mayan calendar ends in 2012. Moving from a twelve to a thirteen denotes moving from one state to another. Thirteen is the number of unity consciousness. In the simplest terms our consciousness is slowly but surely returning to a harmonic state – by moving up an octave. Mayan timelines often refer to the number thirteen as being a time of great spiritual growth and transformation.

'In principle the thirteen is all about the three as one. Plato long ago realized that "two things cannot be rightly put together without a third; there must be some bond of union between them." Space and time formed the two – and spirit the third. In Christianity you have the Holy Trinity of the Father, Son and Holy Ghost. The Chinese I Ching says, "The One engenders the Two, the Two engenders the Three and the Three engenders all things." And of course the winter solstice is on December 21 – two plus one equals three!'

As we sat chatting about other threes in Nature, between us we came up with the sun, earth and moon and the three states of water – liquid, vapour and solid. Water itself is made up of two hydrogen atoms and one atom of oxygen. Our universe is based on protons, neutrons and electrons. Positive, negative and neutral. The divine feminine, masculine and child. And the three primary colours of light from our Sun – red, blue and green – from which the seven colours of the rainbow are formed. In equal parts these three colours produce white light. In the beginning was an 'explosion' of light!

'Throughout every tradition,' Jude continued, 'there are examples of the trinity. For eons the knowledge that we are all one who have become many has been right under our noses – but only a few wise beings have ever really understood this till now. Finally we are "waking up". Most crucially, in spiritual terms, many people are now wanting to activate their kundalini energy. When you see the two serpents spiralling up the staff in the caduceus, most people don't realize that the two serpents crisscross at specific points, over the chakra energy vortices. The staff represents our spine, as you have said, and again you have the three into the one, two serpents and the staff. This symbol was first drawn thousands of years ago. Its full activation symbolizes unity consciousness, what you term coherence.'

The concepts of vortices and spirals, I reflected, were coming up time and again. Jill Purce, who spoke about sound waves in chapter 15, had told me that a spiral is a circle through time, whilst Bill Tiller in chapter 5 theorized that the Core, or what many people term God, had begun to decohere in the form of a spiral. The kundalini energy is a spiral. DNA is a spiral.

Jude agreed. 'And infinite spirals, known as Fibonacci spirals after the thirteenth-century mathematician who discovered them, are found throughout Nature from nautilus shells and whirlpools and to awesome scales within galaxies.'

'Which means what to the man in the street?'

'That there is an underlying order to everything, everything is interconnected and everything is unfolding exactly as *we co-create it,* based upon our choices and actions, which have effects.'

Listening to Jude, it was brought home to me yet again how our thoughts contribute to our reality.

'You have already mentioned,' she went on, 'the science of Benoit Mandelbrot, who found, along with other scientists, that underlying *everything* in our universe – no matter how random or chaotic things, events or statistics appear – there is an underlying pattern or order. In the beginning, at the moment of the Big Bang, everything was in an incredibly high state of order, which you term coherence – and this state of order is commonly termed "low entropy", which also means very low information. And as we began to decohere from a state of low entropy (high order, low information) towards high entropy (disorder and high information), this enabled the evolution of ever more complexity; and more and more consciousness was able to be embodied within our space and time as the cycle of the universe unfolded. The Big Bang also gave rise to linear time, which can only flow in *one direction* in this reality.

'I would agree with Bill Tiller that there have been civilizations like Lemuria that have existed both as physical and nonphysical societies, highly coherent, highly evolved. Bill terms these stages an in-breathing and out-breathing of the All, but I think of the ebb and flow of waves on the shore – they form, they grow, they peak and fall away again.

'Our universe is unfolding in a perfectly ordered way, even though we may not appreciate this. It is exquisitely set up to go through a vast cycle that enables consciousness to explore itself at ever greater levels of complexity.'

'But you agree that we *are* heading back to coherence?'

'At a soul or consciousness level, yes, I do, which of course can and does affect us physically as we grow in coherence at all levels of being. Everything that you are writing about is not black and white – you have to be able to fly on the wings of paradox.'

Many scientists have used this phrase and it's true. For instance, we cannot state that we *are* like biological computers *or* like a hologram in Nature – as depending on your definition of biological computers and holograms, I would say we are both. Many people simply don't understand such a concept – yet!

Turning back to Jude, I asked, 'So you agree that there is a higher intelligence that underlies everything?'

'Of course!' she exclaimed. 'From the moment of the Big Bang, as theoretical physicist Lee Smolin and others at the Perimeter Institute for Theoretical Physics in Ontario have determined, had the primary forces and physical attributes of our universe varied by more than an unimaginably precise one part in 10^{27} – that's one part in a thousand trillion trillion – our complex universe of chemistry, galaxies and biological life could not have evolved. We are made of elements from our universe, we are star-seeded – iron, copper, magnesium and so on – all the co-creation of the consciousness of cosmic mind.'

As she spoke I thought about the vastness of our universe and wondered how the position of certain planets could possibly affect us in our individual lives. 'What about astrology?' I asked Jude. 'How does that work?'

'My understanding is that we are all a part of Divine Consciousness exploring itself. All reality is integral, so just as the earth emits its unique signature frequency – the Schumann resonance – which affects us, so all the planets in our solar system also emit their own signature frequencies, which carry information just as we and our planet transmit and receive information. We are all part of a Whole and are therefore affected by huge amounts of criss-crossing information. And when each one of us, as a unique spark of the Whole, enters an incarnation at a specific time and date that is unique to us, then from the alignments of planets at that time it's possible to build a picture of what resonant influences are or were at play. And because our solar system, which I consider to be a group soul, continues to move, the planets form a dynamic matrix of influences throughout our entire lives, both on a personal and a collective level.' Fascinating.

There was much to take in and much more to discuss. As I needed a few minutes to read some research before asking my next questions on the nature of time, somewhat cheekily I asked Jude for another cup of tea. While she went off to the kitchen, I scanned a report stating that some scientists believe it may be possible to travel back in time mentally and change the outcomes of past events, which could then have the potential to change events in the now. Preposterous though this had seemed at the time, with all I had learned about the nature of time since beginning this book, I needed to rethink my paradigms.

This research centred on the work of parapsychologist

Helmut Schmidt, who back in the '70s became fascinated by the possibility of mind affecting random events. He started to record the blips of radioactive particles, which decay in a haphazard, random fashion, straight onto a computer – meaning there was *no conscious measurement* involved, therefore no prior information about what was on the recording. In other words, no conscious being heard these blips as they were recorded. Then, at a later date, the researchers asked subjects to listen to this haphazard series of blips – but before the sounds were played to them, the listeners were asked to set a firm, sustained intention that they would hear a specific number of blips. Much to the researchers' astonishment, the blips played back exactly as the listeners had intended. The implications are stunning: these experiments and others like them seem to show that as long as no conscious recording device (such as a human) has registered the results, then *by intention alone* it's possible to change an outcome from the past, which can thus affect the now.

Other experiments that grew out of Schmidt's work further demonstrated the effect that mind can have on random events – especially when there is a considerable amount of emotion involved. At the now-famous Princeton Engineering Anomalies Research (PEAR) Lab at Princeton University, scientists such as Roger Nelson and Robert Jahn devised the Global Consciousness Project, in which random event generators that create random patterns of zeroes and ones were placed around the globe and left switched on 24/7, in the hope that when a large event took place that triggered some collective emotion, their electronic equipment would record any resulting deviations. Today, some 65 such REGs are in place, and scientists have found definite pattern changes – for instance, when Princess Diana died (as well as during her televised funeral broadcast to billions) and after the terrorist attacks of 9/11. Most fascinatingly, when the scientists reviewed data from that date, they also found that there had been measurable spikes in readings a few hours *before* the two aircraft crashed into the Twin Towers. Just as Gary Schwartz told me in chapter 11, the manifestation of anything into this reality goes through a process, moving from consciousness to information to energy to matter. During a storm we see the lightning first, then hear the thunder.

The scientists at Princeton have yet to state categorically that it is our consciousness creating such spikes, but it certainly looks that way. Therefore, when Jude returned with more tea, I was keen to hear her take on such conclusions. She thought for a few seconds before responding.

'Experiments such as these,' she began, 'demonstrate that until something is observed, its potentiality remains in the underlying cosmic plenum – space filled with matter – essentially in every possible state that it could be in. Once observed, then the wave function becomes coherent and manifests into a particular quantum state; in other words, it comes into our reality. This implies that our futures are definitely not "set".'

'So,' I asked, 'do you see time as a web, with the past, present and future running concurrently – or do you see it as time-lines that we create through our thoughts and actions as we go?'

'Definitely the latter. The cosmos and its total form is all that is, all that's ever been, all that ever will be – but it is still not fully realized, not fully manifested, not fully crystallized. As Falco told you in Damanhur, as we go along through our lives we start to build timelines, and as we repeat events over and over, our timeline becomes more set, more crystallized. And as you have repeatedly noted, if people want to change what they have created either personally or collectively, then they have to change what they do and think on an everyday basis. But again the reader needs to consider the paradox of multiple levels of reality. Our perception of the flow of time at this level is real, but it's also a mental construct – *because everything is ultimately the cosmic mind exploring itself through holographic processes.* It is as though what we call space and time is like a written DVD; time and space are the template, but we are still, from our choices in every moment, altering the DVD. We are literally writing it as we go.'

I shared with Jude the concept I had heard from Tiller, Sheldrake and other scientists that all sustained information attaches in geometric patterns to some kind of vast grid and that sensitives can retrieve information from that grid. Nodding in agreement, she added, 'The nearer the event, the more it is crystallizing into this reality. When great seers like Nostradamus attempt to see way ahead, they see odd bits and pieces, but events are much "fuzzier" the further ahead in time they attempt to view – just as if you tried to tune in an old-fashioned TV set, if you were not on the correct frequency, you would hear white noise and see lots of static, but the closer you got to the correct frequency or wavelength, the clearer the picture would become.'

Staying on the subject of time, I asked Jude if she believed that we might be able to travel though time in our physical bodies.

'Maybe, but there is no scientific evidence as yet that we can, only anecdotal. From what I have seen and heard from highly evolved shamans and masters of the self, I believe there are star gates that enable them to travel down timelines, to the past or into potential futures.' Just as the Hualapai shaman had told me ...

'But as you know,' she went on, 'there is plenty of scientific evidence to show that we can travel in time via our *minds* and bring back verifiable facts. I have done this myself many times.'

'So do you concede that it may be possible to alter past

events and thus affect the now?'

'Within our universe,' Jude reminded me, 'linear time flows in one direction. But if you help people to "relive" specific events that happened in this life or that they believe happened in another life, what they do by revisiting such events in the mind is to add information, entropy, to those past events – which in turn affects the information as it "flows" into the present. So we are not necessarily changing the past itself; we are changing the emotional charge or imprint, the information, surrounding that event. People can literally turn their lives around when they go back in their minds to add information and healing to past events, because this helps change the way they feel and behave in the now.'

This is true. I know several people who have held grudges and anger within their hearts for a long time. They become bitter – yet if they can change their perspective on the past events, the changes can be profound. And as if on cue, just after Jude and I talked in December 2009, the journal *Nature* published research from Dr Daniela Schiller at New York University demonstrating that painful memories indeed could be 'updated' with new information that altered the emotional response in the present.

Jude was keen to add, 'When you see the level of healing that can take place for one person, imagine how much greater the effect could be on our global human family. If collectively we can all, as Gary Renard and others suggest, practise true forgiveness and let go of guilt, this would change the imprint on the grid.

'If a terrible event occurs, this event has the potential to add a negative imprint on the grid, and if we all react to such an event by being fearful and negative, then our added thoughts could act as a catalyst for further negative events in the future. Therefore, instead of everyone thinking negatively or with fear, as much as possible at such moments we need to send positive, loving thoughts so that more negativity is not imprinted on the grid. And we now know, thanks to scientists like Schmidt, that by sending loving thoughts to negative events in the past, it's possible to change the emotional charge in the now. All such actions help to heal the Whole.'

As we enjoyed our tea, I tried to gather my thoughts about time in the hope that Jude could shed more light. 'A while ago you told me that our futures are not "set" as such,' I said. 'But do you agree that *certain* events might have been set in place on the grid long ago?'

'Possibly,' she replied. 'I think it's feasible to suggest that there are moments of divine intervention that are part of the unfoldment of some bigger plan. Also, we create karma as we go. Most people refer to this as cause and effect, but I prefer to call it choice and implication. Most of us are not really conscious enough to understand the whole picture as yet.'

I shared with Jude the ideas I had discussed with Serena Roney-Dougal in chapter 10 about the possibility of being able to reincarnate into any period in time. 'That's definitely feasible in physics,' she responded. 'I realize to many people it sounds completely crazy; after all, why would anyone want to reincarnate into a world without chocolate! But we are talking at a soul level here. Also, of course, all consciousness is everywhere, at all "times", so within you are unimaginable amounts of information and realities.'

The whole issue of time and all the varying opinions I had heard while researching this book were rattling around in my head. Therefore, I asked Jude to bear with me as I attempted to verbalize my concerns once and for all. Hesitantly I began, 'We are sitting here in your office in the now. Let's imagine for a moment that we are both going to "die" physically tomorrow.

We transform into spirits without physical bodies existing as a field of information outside time and space. And, at a soul level, it's decided that we should reincarnate into, say 1750. Okay?'

'Yes ... ' Jude replied slowly, wondering where my question was leading.

'So,' I continued, 'we then live a life in the eighteenth century. But – and this is the paradox that I'm sure many people will be wondering about – we have also lived in the early twenty-first century, in the "now". And we have existed in and experienced this life already, which surely implies that the future *is* set – and therefore a good psychic living in 1750 might be able to predict details of our twenty-first-century lives?'

Jude pondered for a few minutes before responding. 'The eighteenth century is in our past; therefore there is information embedded within the space-time of that period. The present we are experiencing now, whilst the future is not yet defined. In my opinion, the psychic of the eighteenth century would be able to see fragments of your twenty-first-century life – only fragments – because the information of that life is already embedded on the grid. However, a psychic today could not do the same thing for our future lives, as he or she can only "see" and predict probabilities.

'Right now in science we know that it's possible to travel into the past via our minds and into potential futures the same way. Certain events may indeed be set, but we also know that by returning to past events, including perhaps past-life events, we can change the information surrounding certain of those events – which means we can overlay information on what happens in the now. Wherever you are existing in time, you are in the now, and *all* experiences add information to the Whole.'

As I listened to Jude, more pieces of my jigsaw began to fall into place. I could certainly appreciate more fully Falco's words – that 'time is a space we can navigate' – and Gary Renard's experience of time travel with Arten and Pursah. He had said that they took him six months forward in time for a look – and that when he arrived at that exact moment in 'real time', he could not change a thing except his *attitude* towards it. The science behind all these views is still unfolding, and there is much more to come.

From my wriggling in my seat, Jude could see that my back was on limits, and she kindly suggested a stroll in her apple orchard. As we walked in the lengthening shadows by her trees, we spoke about how disconnected many people have become from Nature. The earth may be pulsing her own unique frequencies – but how often do we stop to listen to them? Our modern world is bombarded by man-made electrical pollution from mobile phones, TVs, computers, satellite receivers, transmitters and a host of electronic devices. The basic rule is that moving electric fields – that is, mobile phones or power lines – are harmful, whilst static magnetic fields like the earth are generally beneficial to health.

It's no wonder that electrical pollution is now a major contributing factor in a host of medical conditions, from cancers to migraines, depression to insomnia. The Great Pyramid was constructed in such a way that no waves of electromagnetic radiation could permeate its walls. It seems the ancients knew more about this problem than we do.

'Absolutely,' Jude agreed. 'Basically the Great Pyramid is like a Faraday cage, the copper cages that scientists like Gary Schwartz use when testing mediums' abilities, as these cages are completely protected from man-made electromagnetic radiation, thus enabling the mediums to more easily access the vacuum level of reality, as the veils that separate this reality from others are thinner in such chambers. Also, the earth's magnetic field is weakening and our magnetic poles are shifting at the rate of about 40 kilometres a year – which causes whales and birds to go off course. Satellites have been launched to more accurately predict when the magnetic north and south poles will switch, which they do from time to time; the last switch was approximately seven hundred and eighty thousand years ago. But most importantly, as our magnetic field reduces in intensity prior to this magnetic pole shift, the whole *planet* is becoming more like a Faraday cage. Therefore, if we can reduce our exposure to man-made electrical pollution, then for a time we will find it far easier to access other realities.'

As I stood in Jude's magical garden imagining how great it would be if we could all become more psychic, I was thinking so intensely that my head began to throb. Where intention flows, energy goes. If you want the universe, which is informed energy, to work for you – then you must work with it! To help disperse the build-up, I placed my hands by my sides, palms towards the earth, and allowed the energies within and around me to flow into the ground. This is a great way to transmute negativity, especially in the summer if you do it with bare feet – it really helps you to relax and let go. I took a few deep breaths, too. We may be holographic at one level of being, but at this level of reality we also need to take care of our 'bio-bodysuits'!

Returning to Jude's warm study, aware that our time together was coming to a close, I was keen to return to one more point she had made. 'You stated earlier that everything is part of a bigger plan that's unfolding in a perfect way – so do you really agree that there are no victims?'

'If you are an "unconscious co-creator", then you may think you are a victim,' she answered. 'But I work on the principle that everything *is* perfect – what's in question is just your awareness of whether it's perfect.'

Before saying goodbye, I asked what her advice would be for people on their spiritual path back towards coherence. She brightened. 'On a practical, everyday level, we need to turn consumers into custodians and conflict into co-creation,' she said. 'We desperately need to open our hearts more and to integrate our hearts and minds with the empowerment of our purpose in being here – which is to discover who we truly are. I know we have a long way to go, but the more that people open their hearts, the more we can begin harmonizing or aligning with our core selves. Moreover, as we return to coherence at all levels of being collectively, "God", or the zero point, will no longer be zero – *but zero plus one*. Our experiences are causing God to grow.'

An inspirational statement to end what had been a highly meaningful day.

As we hugged goodbye, Jude said, 'Hang on a minute, I almost forgot – I have something that you may find useful.' Back she went into her study and emerged holding a feature from *New Scientist* magazine dated January 2009. I took it and read: YOU ARE A HOLOGRAM.

Just as I thought my quest was about to conclude, the teacher had given me more homework!

As you gather, I could have chatted with Jude for several days and still not begun to scratch the surface of her knowledge. If you would like to know more, visit www.judecurrivan.com.

Chapter Seventeen

The Final Paradox

You are the temple of God.

– Corinthians 3:16

December 2009 – En route from London to Cape Town

THE GRANDEUR OF NATURE THAT IS AFRICA was 35,000 feet below me. I was on board a night flight to Cape Town, on my way to spending a few days enjoying the quiet splendour of the Drakensberg Mountains northeast of the city.

Other than the occasional cluster of lights in the far distance, I could see nothing. From such a height you cannot make out fine details – just as the majority of us at ground zero are so engrossed in the minutiae of our everyday lives that we have forgotten why we are here, what we came to learn, where we need to be going and why.

Listening to my fellow passengers in various stages of slumber as sleep eluded me, I mulled over events of the previous twenty-one months. I felt as though a lifetime had passed since I had met the therapist Claire, back in April 2008, who had set me on the course that led to this book.

And as this odyssey had unfolded, even I had been amazed at the 'intelligent designs', the synchronicities that occurred almost daily as I was led from one mind-expanding question and one paradigm-shifting answer to another. Again and again, I would think, 'I could use information on such and such . . . ' and shortly thereafter, a magazine, an e-mail or an introduction from a friend would lead me to whatever or whomever I was searching for. Such experiences had left me in no doubt that spiritual teachers like Gary Renard, with whom I started this journey, are correct. When you choose to actively align with pure coherence – God, the All That Is, the Guiding Organizing Designer, Allah or whatever name you prefer – with an intention of in some way making a positive difference, then, as the Buddha said, 'anything thought of with utmost sincerity shall come to pass'.

Recalling his words brought to mind a near-forgotten incident involving a living saint. His Holiness Sadguru Shree Shivkrupanandji Swami – Swamiji, as he is affectionately known to his devotees – heads an ashram in Navsari, in the state of Gujarat in India. Physically, he's a tiny, fragile figure, and on the surface he looks like any other Indian gentleman in a white outfit. Appearances can indeed be deceptive.

On one of his visits to the UK, the weather had turned unexpectedly cold and he needed a jacket, so we went along to a large London department store. As we entered the lift, several people entered with us, all eager to reach their required floors. Swami stood passively at the rear of the lift, hemmed in like a sardine as the lift doors duly closed – yet the lift would not budge. Several buttons were pressed, the doors opened and closed a couple of times, but no movement. After a few minutes, our fellow passengers alighted, complaining about the unserviceable lift. Yet Swami stood quietly as the doors closed again – and the lift rose to the exact floor we needed. As I gave him a look, his eyes sparkled. Even fully enlightened, fully coherent people need to have fun sometimes! After all, ultimately, what are we made of? Light.

Swamiji told me that if something became his pure wish, then it could happen. And I believe that his words, spoken without any hint of ego or trace of duality, are correct. If little you (at the electric atom/molecule level) is in alignment, or coupled, with Bigger You (at the magnetic wave information level), then miracles can happen – and do.

Ever since I boarded a plane to Stockholm to check out Gary Renard's contention that our universe was going to disappear, I have been rediscovering and remembering what it means for us to align in this way – what it can teach us about the nature of our world and what it can help us to become. In listening to and learning from so many knowledgeable souls whom I found to have integrity, I have done my utmost to share the facts and theories that I found fascinating and useful and hoped that you, the reader, would too. Scientists such as Gary Schwartz, Bill Tiller, Fred Travis, Bernard Carr, Jude Currivan and a host of others I have mentioned have demonstrated their results through verified, validated and independent scientific experiments. After being on this journey and going through my experience, my belief in an underlying intelligence that exists at all levels of reality, throughout time, across every dimension and within everything, remains stronger than ever. Physicist William Tiller convinced me that our universe had its beginnings in perfect coherence before spiralling into increasing disorder – and like millions of others on a spiritual path, I too now believe that an epoch has begun that will take us on the journey home to coherence.

In David Hawkins's brilliant book *The Eye of the I*, I had read a statement that at first glance seemed a paradox: '... Evolution and creation are one and the same. Creation is the very source and essence of evolution. Evolution is the process by which creation becomes manifest .... Basically, there is no conflict between evolution and creation, as one is merely an expression of the other in the visible domain.' But his words reiterated my long-held belief that science and metaphysics are reaching the same conclusions.

Most promising of all, I discovered that our journey is to a great extent in our hands – we are co-creators. As more and more of us grow in awareness, finally accepting that we are indeed spirit having a physical experience in our temporary 'bio-bodysuits' and that we emanate from and exist within an intelligent coherent 'mind', real changes will take place. Professor Travis says that on the surface everything will look the same but our inner quality of life will change as every act becomes more in tune with all other parts of life.

Remember that a part of you, your acupuncture meridian and chakra system, already functions at a coherent level all the time – and, most importantly of all, coherence is catching. The more you work on your own growth to bring other parts of your whole self into alignment, the more the underlying field of intelligence will be 'awakened' into your reality. Over time, as this awakening process gains momentum, we will access higher-dimensional realities and knowledge with ever greater ease.

Such perfect alignment does not come automatically. It demands determination, sustained practice and a measure of silence. It all comes back to the question I asked at the beginning of this book: How badly do you want to go home?

Since the publication of my first two spiritual books, I have received numerous e-mails from wonderful people, some of whom ask if I am now enlightened and can I help make their wishes come true.

Wouldn't that be great? But I'm afraid not.

I'm merely a person who has gone through an incredible experience. Though at some level I must have grown a fraction more in coherence, otherwise I would not be sitting here writing this book. I would be out shopping! Yes, I meditate regularly, I chant, I occasionally practise qi gong, I receive energy healing, I exercise, I give money to charities as and when I can, as much as possible I treat others as I would like to be treated myself – and sometimes I become angry too. I eat a pretty healthy diet – with added organic cake! But I don't see myself living in an ashram, praying all day or fasting, because I'm sure by now you have gathered my weakness is food. As much as possible I respect the environment;

I recycle and so on, but I'm not a die-hard 'green'. Everything comes down to finding a respectful balance in all things.

I'm sure you have heard the saying 'Render unto Caesar the things that are Caesar's.' In other words, pay your taxes, go about your lives – but also become aware that you are in this world but not necessarily of this world. Eat healthier foods as much as you can, think positive loving thoughts as much as you can, learn to forgive yourself and others. Most of us are a way off 'perfect', yet we can do what we can where we can to grow in coherence. And this should be a joyful process – you really don't need to experience a Spiritual Emergency as I and many others have done.

Having spent time with several totally enlightened men and women, I note they eat a near-perfect diet and if they choose to enjoy something that might be considered 'not perfect' they do so consciously, fully accepting responsibility for their actions. They also spend considerable amounts of time in complete silence, fasting and meditation to retain their levels of coherence. Though, as Professor Tiller pointed out, to remain in a state of *total* coherence all the time is akin to balancing on a pinhead, virtually impossible to maintain.

Enlightened men and women are not generally affected at a level of mind by external events; they remain in a neutral state of oneness, as I briefly experienced in 1998. They have become beings of love, and that is what you should experience in their presence, never coercion or fear. If their followers tell you that their specific guru is the one and only God on earth, you might respectfully remind them that we are all part of God and all parts make the Whole. After all, why would someone or something as obviously brilliant as 'God' put all his or her eggs in one basket? Even today's computer systems implement multiple redundancy to ensure that if one part fails, the whole continues.

One apparent paradox for many people is that enlightened men and women can become physically ill too. On this subject, Swamiji had again made me smile when he complained of liver pains after sharing with more than 20,000 devotees the ultimate field of coherent energy that he has become: 'Many people energetically surrender their aches, pains and problems in my presence,' he said, 'whilst also praying for specific wishes – which cumulatively makes my liver very hot.' Is it any wonder that it takes him a couple of days of fasting to give his overheated liver a much-needed rest?

A cynical editor of mine once asked, 'If these so-called miracle-makers are so good at giving miracles, why do they get sick? Surely they should be able to drink poison till the cows come home and still be fine?' Smiling through gritted teeth, thinking about forgiveness, I related to him an insight from Professor Travis: 'Once people become enlightened, they are still different, and each one becomes the Whole, which works through them in a way that is most appropriate for their physiology. Individuals who are enlightened know that they are a reflection of the Whole, yet they still have their individual personality, and they need a physical body in order to anchor and reflect pure coherence back to others in this reality. And that body can be affected by the weather, by people's thoughts and so on. Yes, anyone who truly believes that in drinking poison he or she will be absolutely one hundred per cent not be harmed – can survive. But if they kept on doing it, eventually their physical bodies would become overwhelmed. Medical research has verified this. But enlightened people are not circus acts – why would they want to drink poison?'

Why indeed. Bruce Lipton shares several such fascinating cases of mind over matter in his book *The Biology of Belief* – but *please,* don't try drinking poison at home to test this theory out!

Talking of mind over matter, I once watched a TV documentary in which an Indian doctor and his team of researchers locked a willing, enlightened swami in a comfortable room in a hospital in Mumbai for 14 days. The team monitored him in shifts while their cameras recorded every second of those 14 days, at the end of which it was agreed that the swami had not eaten or drunk anything. Yet he was perfectly fit, healthy and happy.

I do believe, like Professor Villoldo, that at some point on our journey we will evolve from being dependent on physical food to being nourished by divine 'food', which is information. Many souls will begin to look 'lighter', more transparent, as I did at times during 1998, as they become more coherent at all levels of being. And when Professor Gary Schwartz mentioned that one of his scientific colleagues had been 'living on light', before finishing this book I was keen to hear his comments on this concept.

I knew that what we term 'matter' is basically organized energy, which has pattern, form and frequency, and that what *organizes* that energy is mind and intention. Mind and intention form patterns, which form matter. The Professor reiterated that food is 'matter', water is 'matter', air contains atoms – which are the building blocks of everything, including food. Matter is nothing more than informed energy, and as we evolve into 'lighter' beings we will learn how to 'digest' this information in its nonphysical form.

But Gary wisely told me, 'Firstly, no-one should just think, "Oh, gee, I want to become more coherent, so I'll stop eating and live on light." Doesn't work that way. This is a *process*. For some evolved souls it's become a reality – for others it would be irresponsible and could prove fatal.'

I knew he was right. In July 2009 I had received an e-mail from a doctor begging me to call, saying it was a matter of life and death. His wife, a pharmacist, had become obsessed with enlightenment and had decided to pray and fast for days, without any preparation or true understanding. As he related what was going on, I realized that dehydration and lack of nutrients had affected her brain chemistry. A doctor friend who understands spiritual breakthroughs spent several hours trying to help the woman, but she refused to eat or drink. Eventually she was committed to hospital for her own safety.

Conversely, I know several people, highly disciplined practitioners, who have gone through a process, as Gary says, eating first lighter food, then raw food, followed by only juices and then, with friends supporting them at all times, 'living on air' – and they have been fine, some without food and others without food *or* drink for several days or more. I know it's possible, just as swamis have known for thousands of years. But please be responsible. We are evolving, but it takes time.

Some of the most encouraging ideas I have encountered on this journey are Dr David R Hawkins's remarks in his book *Power vs. Force* that our levels of coherence can be not only calibrated but also raised – and that if we can separate ourselves from our ego mind, then it is possible to raise them all the more quickly. Getting started on any new path can be hard, but as Gary Renard and others suggest, a great way to begin is to practise forgiveness at all times. It can be challenging, I know – I'm still working on it. Yet after speaking to soul researcher Robert Schwartz, I have become somewhat more tolerant, realizing that I do not know the whole picture. These days, when I think of Mr Mugabe, I send him love and wonder what might have moulded him into the cruel man I perceive through the media. Dr Hawkins calibrates unconditional love at 500, which surely helps you to understand that the more we practise heartfelt forgiveness, the more we can help raise the calibration of the Whole. And to help on a practical, physical level, when I can, I send money to a wonderful charity called ZANE, whose workers and volunteers endeavour to relieve some of the misery that Zimbabwe is experiencing – especially among the children.

All children, no matter where and in what circumstances they are born, come into this reality with inherent traits, through their genes, and are moulded by their family, environment, culture and lifestyle. There is an urgent need to teach children tolerance, loving discipline, integrity and honesty – and to allow them to grow and develop in a safe, nurturing environment. If a child is heading towards a hot stove, you might shout or pull him sharply back to warn him of the imminent danger he is facing; the intelligence that underlies our universe is doing the same. But are we listening? Some are, others are not. Everything comes down to finding a respectful balance in all things.

It's important to realize that even those who have knowingly harmed their fellow man can change. I have friends who are teaching inmates in prison how to meditate and practise yoga, with heart-warming results. Scientifically based studies have also demonstrated that when prisoners are given a healthy, balanced diet, their mood improves and their tendency towards violence diminishes. Ditto in the case of violent or hyperactive children. The meditation further helps this process. And where prisoners have been given dogs to care for, the transformations have been profound. Why? Because the animals love the prisoners unconditionally and that essence of pure love affects even the most hardened of men. Coherence is catching.

So how can you work toward greater coherence yourself? You've heard the saying 'When the pupil is ready, the master appears.' And who do you think the master is? Look again in the mirror – for part of you is always linked to what most people would term God, the pure intelligence which underlies all of life. At a certain level, you are already 'home' and always have been – you just need to know this.

If you are practising a spiritual discipline regularly – whether this is meditating, chanting, yoga, breathwork, qi gong or simple forgiveness – and using your intuition more, then by now I hope you have started to notice more synchronicities coming into your life. It's a good idea to start keeping a spiritual diary so that if ideas pop into your head, you can write them down. You will be amazed at how the underlying intelligence wants to assist you!

And because our world is in such a state of flux on so many levels, make sure that you protect your own energy field every day. One way to do this is to visualize yourself inside a golden egg, totally cocooned in light. Imagine that any negative thoughts being directed your way simply bounce off the brilliant reflective egg, and ask for them to be sent into the light. It only takes a minute or two, and it's very effective.

Finally, remember that becoming coherent at all levels of mind, body and spirit is a process, not a race. Some will move toward the goal more quickly than others. Don't be envious, for their coherence will in turn help you, and all of us, towards the soul's ultimate goal of unity with the Core of who we really are.

In 1998, I felt that the Ultimate I to which I was connected came from the beginning of time. I am now realizing that this Ultimate I has been around *far* longer than our brief 14 billion years. And of course, outside our space-time there is no such thing as time! Even shaman-scientist Villoldo speaks of prophetical societies; Bill Tiller theorizes that we evolved from highly coherent, non-physical societies like Mu, Lemuria and Atlantis (note he says 'like', not stating categorically that they *were* these specific mythical societies) who 'intended' this universe into being long before the Big Bang. Robert Schwartz's description of time as a web and Falco's assertion that 'time is a space we can navigate' fired my imagination; to hear that as souls existing outside of space and time we might indeed be able to reincarnate into any period *in* time – and even make changes in the past that might affect the now – was mind-boggling. And when Professor Travis suggested that between sleeping and waking, as well as in the moments between sleeping and dreaming, we pass through the field of universal intelligence that administers all of life and contains all information, it really helped to explain how it's potentially possible for us to experience existences in other dimensions, astral travel and so on. Mind is everything, whereas our physical 'bio-bodysuits' are simply temporary vehicles enabling us to experience this physical reality. Incredible though such ideas may seem, I have seen and heard too much to dismiss them any longer.

Controversial author and speaker David Icke often says, 'If you want to manipulate every fish at the same time, you manipulate the sea.' In other words, by changing the collective consciousness, you can affect everyone.

The Global Consciousness Project demonstrates that our collective thoughts can be measured, and there are specialized computers in use that can not only read thoughts but also react to them, and Bill Tiller has shown through validated scientific experiments that our thoughts can and do affect this physical reality. Throughout this book, I have reminded you that your thoughts, which are 'things', count at every level; every time you send a negative thought it adds more 'negativity' to the whole sea of consciousness. Every time you think loving, positive thoughts, they too contribute to the Whole. And if we are all to go home to coherence, then the whole of the Whole needs to be healed. You are part of that Whole.

The Whole is eternal, which means you are eternal. Gary Schwartz and his team at the University of Arizona, as well as other independent research centres, have demonstrated in ever more complex and stringent experiments that consciousness does indeed survive physical death. And after my experience during the '90s, I am personally left in no doubt whatsoever that we all go on. The ever-increasing body of evidence on survival of consciousness – including Orbs, reincarnation, telepathy, prayer, hands-on healing and accessing other timelines via our minds – is so wide-ranging, extensive and authoritative that to my mind it's now completely up to the sceptics, as Gary Schwartz said, to show that such phenomena are not possible.

For every hundred leading-edge scientists who agree in varying degrees with the theories and findings I have shared, there will be another hundred who will offer perfectly cogent arguments as to why they are wrong. But I doubt that any of these people have themselves been through any kind of true spiritual awakening.

There is absolutely no substitute for *experience,* and the more you are aware of what to expect, the easier will be your unique countdown to coherence as the powers that lie within us all begin to manifest. Cosmologist Jude Currivan and others believe that more and more highly evolved souls will reincarnate to assist in this process that is coming to be called The Shift. She says that as we have collectively become more materialistic and limited our sense of reality to the physical realm, we have essentially dismembered our psyche – but that now, personally and collectively, we are waking up and expanding our awareness beyond the illusory limits of our human personas, to *re-member* who we really are: eternal beings of light and conscious co-creators.

As we do, she and I and a host of other seekers and scientists feel that our multidimensional relationships with each other, the earth and the wider cosmos will be transformed. Being psychic and telepathic in the years ahead will come to seem like child's play. Perhaps within the next century or so, we will also, to varying degrees, become adepts at manifesting. But, I reiterate, this process requires discipline, discernment and wisdom. The concepts at work are wide-ranging and some are highly controversial – yet one thing seems certain: scientists and the public alike are about to make a huge leap in our understanding of who we are.

As our countdown back to coherence unfolds, calls for peace will grow. A new spirit of conscious community will unfold. Damanhur is an amazing template for how our society could function in the future: their sense of community is strong and they have enormous respect for nature, each other and the higher dimensions. They are high-tech too – no need to go back to the Dark Ages or live in tents!

On the down side, Falco reminds us, 'We tend to confuse progress with evolution.' Jude Currivan was prescient when she shared with me this view from an eminent scientist: 'A system is measured by the amount of information it holds, and our system, our universe and the knowledge within it is increasing. Yet as information doubles, knowledge is halved and wisdom is quartered. An increase in information doesn't necessarily lead to a deepening of wisdom.' This is why discernment on one's journey is so important.

You only have to watch the news or read the papers to know that in some respects we are doing anything *but* evolving. From fighting in Iraq and Afghanistan to rape and torture in Darfur to an endless string of murders, child abuse, robberies and more. This world urgently needs a Good News Channel to help lift our spirits and generate more positive thoughts to attach to our grid. The clock has moved past midnight, and we all need to do what we can to improve our world. After all, as the great Irish philosopher and politician Edmund Burke said, 'All that is necessary for evil to triumph is for good men to do nothing.'

David Hawkins writes in *Power vs. Force,* 'Society needs visionaries of means, not dreamers of ends.' He is right – and it helps when the visionaries are people *with* means too. Thankfully, numerous wealthy and high-profile souls are stepping up to help their fellow man. CNN founder and media mogul Ted Turner has given a billion dollars to the United Nations; Bill and Melinda Gates have set up educational and health programmes in Africa and around the globe; the hugely wealthy investor Warren Buffett, a humble soul, gives millions of dollars to charity. Countless others from all walks of life do what they can where they can. It's our time to stand up and be counted.

———— ✖ ————

And so, as our aircraft headed across the deserts of Angola, a glorious turquoise dawn broke outside the windows. Was it really possible, I wondered, that all this beauty was an illusion – part of a computer simulation, as Nick Bostrum of Oxford argued, or an image no more real than a projection on a screen?

One of the most controversial contentions in this book has been Gary Renard's idea that we are nothing more than a hologram being projected from an ego mind that 'thinks' it is separated from God. Professor Tiller, Dr Serena Roney-Dougal and others have reiterated that *current* physics assumes that we are real; the level at which we move to the holographic reality is not the level of our everyday senses, through which I was seeing the dawn break, but the level of *mind*. Even the great physicist

David Bohm once said, 'At its *deeper* level, reality is a sort of a super hologram in which the past, present and future all exist simultaneously.' I believe he is right.

I rummaged through the pile of notes I had packed to read on my long journey and read once again the article that Dr Currivan had given me from *New Scientist* magazine, reporting on studies being carried out by one of the world's foremost research companies, Fermilab, who employ hundreds of physicists globally. They are one of the leading research companies into dark matter and energy, which are causing our universe to expand. And for several years at a huge facility south of Hanover they have been searching for gravitational waves – ripples in space-time, thrown off by super-dense astronomical objects such as neutron stars, to help them more fully understand black holes and the Big Bang. Their ongoing experiment is known as the GEO600.

They were looking for waves – but what they found was *noise* – and the detail within that noise suggests that our universe *could be* a projection of a two-dimensional hologram. According to physicist Craig Hogan at Fermilab, 'The GEO600 has stumbled upon the fundamental limit of space-time, the point at which space-time stops behaving like a smooth continuum and instead dissolves into a sea of "pixels".'

Another synchronicity. Before leaving for Africa, my daughter had given me an edited film of my grandson to play on my phone – and as each 30-second sequence shifted from one scene to another, the picture dissolved into hundreds of pixels, like so many grains of sand, before taking shape again with the next part of their film sequence. Ten years earlier as I sat with an enlightened teacher in London, I had watched in complete awe as he had transformed into a blur of golden light. His consciousness – who He truly was and is and ever will be – was still there, but I could no longer see little physical 'him' with my physical eyes. He had disappeared – the same way we will as we evolve, operating on higher and higher frequencies until we eventually reach 'home' and merge back into true and complete coherence.

As you read these words, I wonder what you think.

As I've said numerous times over the course of this book, there are many possible realities and many perspectives to consider. Bernard Carr, professor of mathematics and astronomy at Queen Mary University of London, summed it up for me thus: 'In a sense, the picture of the world which is provided by physicists is just a mathematical model. The picture of reality which we have in physics has really got very little connection with the everyday mundane reality. Many of the things which we take for granted as common-sense reality are shown ultimately to be illusions in physics. We know that the solidity of tables and things was removed by atomic theory; it is mainly empty space. We know our common-sense notion of space and time was demolished by special relativity; we know that the ultimate theory of physics may involve all these extra dimensions. So perhaps *our ordinary world of three spatial dimensions and time is just some pale imitation of some deeper reality*. In some sense what we call reality may just be a lower dimensional projection of a higher-dimensional reality.'

The final paradox is that we are every thing and no thing.

As I sat quietly praying for some inspiration to close this book, I considered again the need to reiterate that you should take what information resonates with you – and discard what doesn't: find your own truth. Then I picked up the copy of the *Daily Mail* which I had bought at the airport and, by yet another coincidence, turned to astrologer Jonathan Cainer's column. He had written:

'If you seem to be in a situation that's charged with tension – simply focus like a laser on the most practical thing you can do today to help things improve. Don't be distracted by other people's complaints or your own doubts. Resolve to be an island of purpose in an ocean of uncertainty. Slowly but steadily you *are* making progress in the right direction. All that matters is that you trust your vision and carry on.'

Thank you, Jonathan. I could not have said it better myself.

Finally, I felt as though I could let go and surrender to sleep. We still had three hours to run to Cape Town, and I had done my best.

With my whole heart I pray that this book helps you in some small way, and please, enjoy your own unique countdown to coherence.

Hazel Courteney

Bibliography

Ananas, Esperide, *Damanhur: Temples of Humankind,* CoSM Press, New York, 2006

Brown, Dan, *The Lost Symbol,* Doubleday, New York, 2009

Carr, Bernard, ed., *Universe or Multiverse?,* Cambridge University Press, Cambridge, 2009

Clarke, Isabel, *Madness, Mystery and the Survival of God,* O Books, Ropley, Hampshire, 2008

Currivan, Jude, *The 13th Step: A Global Journey in Search of Our Cosmic Destiny,* Hay House, London, 2007

Currivan, Jude, *The 8th Chakra: What It Is and How It Can Transform Your Life,* Hay House, London, 2006

Essene, Virginia, and Tom Kenyon, *The Hathor Material: Messages from an Ascended Civilization,* S.E.E. Pub. Co., 1997

Grof, Christina, and Stanislav Grof, *The Stormy Search for the Self: A Guide to Personal Growth Through Transformational Crisis,* Jeremy P. Tarcher, New York, 1997

Hawkins, David R, *Power vs. Force: The Hidden Determinants of Human Behavior,* Veritas Publishing, West Sedona, AZ, 1995

Hawkins, David R, *The Eye of the I: From Which Nothing Is Hidden,* Veritas Publishing, West Sedona, AZ, 2001

Heinemann, Klaus, *Orbs, Their Mission and Messages of Hope,* Hay House, London, 2010

Heinemann, Klaus, and Miceal Ledwith, *The Orb Project,* Atria Books/Beyond Words, New York/Hillsboro, OR, 2007

Joyce, Linda, *The Day You Were Born: A Journey to Wholeness Through Astrology and Numerology,* Citadel, New York, 2003

Kaku, Michio, *Parallel Worlds: The Science of Alternative Universes and Our Future in the Cosmos,* Penguin, London, 2006

Laszlo, Ervin, and Jude Currivan, *CosMos: A Co-creator's Guide to the Whole World,* Hay House, London, 2008

Ledwith, Miceal, *The Hidden Years: How Jesus Became a Christ,* DVD, www.hamburgeruniverse.com

Lipton, Bruce, *The Biology of Belief: Unleashing the Power of Consciousness, Matter and Miracles,* Hay House, London, 2008

Mandelbrot, Benoit, *The Fractal Geometry of Nature,* W H Freeman, New York, 1983

Merrifield, Jeff, *Damanhur: The Story of the Extraordinary Italian Artistic and Spiritual Community,* Hanford Mead, Santa Cruz, CA, 2006

Newton, Michael, *Journey of Souls: Case Studies of Life Between Lives,* Llewellyn, St Paul, MN, 1994

Newton, Michael, *Life Between Lives: Hypnotherapy for Spiritual Regression,* Llewellyn, St Paul, MN, 2004

Renard, Gary, *The Disappearance of the Universe: Straight Talk about Illusions, Past Lives, Religion, Sex, Politics, and the Miracles of Forgiveness,* Hay House, London, 2004

Roney-Dougal, Serena, *Where Science and Magic Meet: Exploring Our Psychic Birthright,* Vega, London, 2002

Schwartz, Gary E, *The Afterlife Experiments: Breakthrough Scientific Evidence of Life after Death,* Atria Books, New York, 2002

Schwartz, Gary E, *The G.O.D Experiments: How Science Is Discovering God in Everything, Including Us,* Atria Books, New York, 2007

Schwartz, Gary E, *The Energy Healing Experiments: Science Reveals Our Natural Power to Heal*, Atria Books, New York, 2008

Schwartz, Gary E, *The Sacred Promise, Beyond Words*, Atria Books, New York, 2010

Schwartz, Robert, *Your Soul's Plan: Discovering the Real Meaning of the Life You Planned Before You Were Born*, Frog Books/North Atlantic Books, Berkeley, 2009

Tiller, William A, *Conscious Acts of Creation: The Emergence of a New Physics*, Pavior Publishing, Walnut Creek, CA, 2001

Tiller, William A, *Psychoenergetic Science: A Second Copernican-Scale Revolution*, DVD, 2007, www.tillerfoundation.com

Villoldo, Alberto, *Courageous Dreaming: How Shamans Dream the World into Being*, Hay House, London, 2008

Index